151481467 5

FRENCH CAESARISM FROM NAPOLEON I TO CHARLES DE GAUL

Also by Philip Thody

ALBERT CAMUS
FAUX AMIS AND KEY WORDS (*with Howard Evans*)
JEAN ANOUILH
JEAN-PAUL SARTRE
MARCEL PROUST
ROLAND BARTHES: A Conservative Estimate
DOG DAYS IN BABEL (*a novel*)
A TRUE LIFE READER FOR CHILDREN AND PARENTS
CHODERLOS DE LACLOS: LES LIAISONS DANGEREUSES
ALDOUS HUXLEY

French Caesarism from Napoleon I to Charles de Gaulle

Philip Thody
Professor of French Literature, University of Leeds

Palgrave Macmillan

ISBN 978-1-349-20091-7   ISBN 978-1-349-20089-4 (eBook)
DOI 10.1007/978-1-349-20089-4

© Philip Thody 1989
Softcover reprint of the hardcover 1st edition 1989

All rights reserved. For information, write:
Scholarly and Reference Division,
St. Martin's Press, Inc., 175 Fifth Avenue, New York, NY 10010

First published in the United States of America in 1989

ISBN 978-0-312-02821-3

Library of Congress Cataloging-in-Publication Data

Thody, Philip Malcolm Waller, 1928–
French Caesarism from Napoleon I to Charles de Gaulle / Philip
Thody.
    p.   cm.
  Bibliography: p.
  Includes index.
  ISBN 978-0-312-02821-3 : $39.95 (est.)
  1. Civil-military relations – France – History.   2. Civil-military
relations.   3. Caesarism.   I. Title.
JN2610.C58T47   1989
321.9'0944 – dc19   88–31414
                                                                CIP

UNIVERSITY
OF BRISTOL
LIBRARY

To Françoise and Serge Warnier

Contents

Acknowledgements		viii
Introduction		1
1	Napoleon I: The Unifier	18
2	Napoleon III: The Imitator	48
3	Philippe Pétain: The Victim	75
4	Charles de Gaulle: The Winner	100
5	Conclusion	150
Notes		160
Appendix A		174
Appendix B		183
Appendix C		190
Appendix D		194
Appendix E		199
Further Reading		210
Index		213
Afterthoughts		223

Acknowledgements

A book of this kind cannot be written alone. It is the product of conversations, none of which have been more useful than the talks I have had over many years with my friend, colleague and co-author, Howard Evans, Senior Lecturer in the French Department of the University of Leeds. It was in the preparation of our book *Faux Amis and Key Words* that the idea of writing about Caesarism first occurred to me.

Annette Torode typed the many versions of my manuscript with exemplary care and good humour. Gwilym Rees made his accustomed and invaluable contribution to the accuracy and readability of what I had written. Any mistakes are entirely my own.

Introduction

I

This book tries to analyse a paradox and to examine the political careers of four men.

On 26 August 1789 the newly constituted French National Assembly resolved to 'set out in a Solemn Declaration, the natural, inalienable and sacred rights of man'. The document followed the example of the American Declaration of Independence in proclaiming truths which now seem to be so self-evident as to barely need stating. It asserted that all men were born equal, that governments existed only for the benefit of the governed and as a device for protecting human rights. It defined freedom as the ability to 'do anything which does not harm another person'. Articles v, vii and viii set out what the modern reader immediately recognises as the concept of the rule of law: nobody can be imprisoned except by reference to a law already approved; the law must be the same for everyone; punishments must be proportionate to the offence. Article ix stated that anyone accused of a crime is innocent until proved guilty. *La Déclaration des droits de l'homme et du citoyen* also proclaimed the principle of freedom of expression, and of equal and fair taxation. By insisting that the rulers were responsible to those they ruled, it embodied the whole eighteenth-century concept of the contract theory of government.

La Déclaration des droits de l'homme et du citoyen did not, it is true, talk about secret ballots, universal suffrage, and the right of political parties as well as private individuals to oppose the government by peaceful means without being accused of treason. Neither is Article vi, which sets out the basic principle of parliamentary control over public expenditure, very clear as to the exact mechanism whereby this is to be brought about. Its recognition of the right of property as 'natural, inalienable, sacred and inviolable' also gives the Declaration of the Rights of Man an eighteenth-century air rather than a twentieth-century one. It makes no bones about endorsing social distinctions based on merit. It was nevertheless the first coherent statement made on the Continent of Europe of the basic principles underlying what the English now call parliamentary democracy and the Americans the democratic society. In form and

1

2 *French Caesarism*

language it also looks forward to the infinitely more ambitious Universal Declaration of Human Rights endorsed by the General Assembly of the United Nations in December 1948.

Just over ten years later, on 9 November 1799, *le coup d'état du 18 Brumaire* gave virtually supreme power to a 30-year-old Corsican general, Napoleon Bonaparte. Initially, his title was First Consul, and he was to hold office for ten years. The two other consuls were, to begin with, one of the authors of *La Déclaration des droits de l'homme et du citoyen* Emmanuel-Joseph Sieyès, and Pierre-Roger Ducos, an ex-nobleman who had something of a knack for changing sides at the right moment. They were subsequently replaced by a 46-year-old lawyer, Jean-Jacques Cambacérès and a 60-year-old land inspector, Charles-François Lebrun. On 10 May 1802 the decision to make Bonaparte First Consul for life was ratified by a plebiscite in which 3,568,185 Frenchmen voted 'Yes' and only 9,704 'No'. On 18 May 1804 a comparable majority of 3,321,615 votes to 599 gave him the title of Emperor of the French, with the right to transmit the title to his children.[1] From November 1799 to his first abdication, on 4 April 1814, Napoleon exercised virtually unlimited power. There was no question of Article xii of *La Déclaration des droits de l'homme et du citoyen*, stating that 'la force publique' (the armed services of the state) had been instituted 'to the advantage of all, and not for the particular utility of those to whom it is entrusted', ever applying to him. He used the army of the Revolution to conquer Austria, Belgium, Holland, Italy and Prussia. In 1812 his '*Grande Armée*' took Moscow, albeit only to see it go up in flames. He reorganised France, giving it the structure which still provides its basic administrative framework. The Napoleonic Code gave permanence and reality to the central demand of the revolutionaries of 1789 for a legal system which would be rational, uniform and common to all citizens. Napoleon himself claimed to be the incarnation of the Revolution, and there is a sense in which his idea of 'la carrière ouverte aux talents' does represent its ambition to establish what is now called a meritocracy. But by no stretch of the imagination could he be seen as even trying to implement the central constitutional ambition of *La Déclaration des droits de l'homme et du citoyen*: that of making the government responsible to the governed.

A French proverb says that it is the good swimmers who drown. Napoleon I, in Charles de Gaulle's view the greatest commander in Western European history,[2] fell from power through military defeat. In 1814, the victorious allies in the coalition which finally overthrew

Introduction

him gave the French crown back to Louis XVIII, brother to the Louis XVI executed by the revolutionaries on 21 January 1793. Louis XVIII reigned as peacefully as he could, disturbed mainly by the attempts of his supporters to undo the revolution completely, until his death in 1824. He, too, was succeeded by his brother, Charles X, a monarch whom it is occasionally tempting for French as well as English historians to compare to James II.[3] Like James, Charles X believed in the divine right of kings; and like James he lost his throne. 'Les trois glorieuses', the three days of revolution which overthrew him in late July 1830, were more bloodstained than their name implies. Some 1,800 civilians were killed, as against 200 soldiers. Constitutional change was not cheap in nineteenth-century France. Neither did the July revolution give France the republic which many of the insurgents wanted. Louis-Philippe, son of the Duc d'Orléans, Philippe Egalité, who had voted in 1793 for the death of his cousin Louis XVI, was invited to become 'Roi des Français'. He accepted, and the apparent parallel with the events that brought William of Orange to the English throne in 1688 gave some hope to the idea that France, too, in Tennyson's words, might be in the process of developing a political system which by 'slowly broadening down from precedent to precedent' would enable it to forsake 'the blood-red fury of the Seine'.

But although Lamartine, like others, regarded the July Monarchy as 'la meilleure des républiques', it did not fulfil this particular promise. The French upper middle class, which had brought Louis-Philippe to power, was not keen to make further reforms. Agitation for a widening of the franchise, coupled with the poverty and urban discontent of the early industrial revolution, led to the revolution of 1848. On 24 February Louis-Philippe abdicated in favour of his grandson, the Comte de Paris. The Parisians, unimpressed by the Comte de Paris, proclaimed on 25 February 1848 that France was once again a Republic. Louis-Philippe himself fled to England, arriving at the Bridge Inn, Newhaven, under the name of Mr William Smith.

The First Republic had lasted, officially, either from its proclamation on 21 September 1792 to the coronation of Napoleon I on 2 December 1804, or to the point in 1808 when the words 'République Française' came to be replaced on the coins by 'Empire Français'. The Second Republic was shorter. Like the members of the 1789 National Assembly, its organisers and supporters had high hopes. On 25 February 1848 France became the first country to proclaim that all

4 *French Caesarism*

of its citizens had the right to work. On 9 April 1848 it held the first elections in Europe in which every man aged over 25 years had the right to vote. It abolished the death penalty for political crimes, did away with slavery in the colonies, and re-established the right to freedom of speech and assembly. In what became known as the 'springtime of the peoples', its example inspired comparable popular uprisings in Germany, Austria, Italy, Hungary and Poland.

On 2 December 1851, three short years later, the Parisians woke up to find their city under martial law. Louis Napoleon, nephew to Napoleon I, had followed his uncle's example and carried out a military coup d'état. He would, he informed the Parisians, now be President for ten years, not just for four. As though to emphasise his right to do so by family precedent, he chose a date which was a double anniversary: that of the coronation of Napoleon as Emperor of the French on 2 December 1804; that of the battle of Austerlitz on 2 December 1805, the engagement whereby the army of the first Emperor won his most brilliant victory over the combined forces of Austria and Prussia. The comparison was driven even further home by the way in which Louis Napoleon both legitimised his assumption of power and extended it. On 20 December 1851 a plebiscite provided an official majority of 7,499,916 in favour of his coup d'état and 646,737 against, with a million-and-a-half abstentions. But Louis Napoleon was not happy just to be President, albeit with a guaranteed ten years in office. He had to follow his uncle's example further and be Emperor as well. So on 20 November 1852 he organised yet another plebiscite: 7,839,532 votes were cast in favour of the re-establishment of the Empire. There were 253,145 against – this time with over two million abstentions. Although Napoleon I's son by Marie-Louise of Austria had never reigned in France, he was still considered by the Bonapartist party as having been the legitimate ruler of France from the moment of his father's abdication to his death in 1832. Louis Napoleon consequently took the title not of Napoleon II but of Napoleon III.

The official justification for what Karl Marx later called 'Le 18 Brumaire de Louis Napoléon' was that it saved France from chaos. Few historians have found it a convincing explanation for the way Louis Napoleon deliberately violated the Constitution of the Second Republic. On 10 December 1848, he had been elected with a very convincing majority as President of the Republic. He obtained 5,434,000 votes, three million more than his nearest rival, General Cavaignac. The civilian contenders, the socialist Ledru-Rollin, and

Introduction 5

the more moderate republican candidate Raspail, like the poet Lamartine, came nowhere. Article 45 of the Constitution was nevertheless quite clear: after four years in office, the President had to go; and he was not eligible for re-election until another four-year period had elapsed.[4] Louis Napoleon failed to persuade the members of the National Assembly to provide the two-thirds majority needed to amend the Constitution so that he could hold office for longer. The coup d'état of 2 December 1851 was his reply.

The Second Empire lasted from 2 December 1852 to 4 September 1870. Like the First Empire, it was in many ways the precise opposite of the kind of régime which the revolutionaries who had provided the occasion for its establishment had wished to set up. In 1857, Napoleon III remarked that 'Liberty has never served as a basis for government. It crowns edifices consecrated by time.' Unlike the Empire of Napoleon I, the Second Empire did become more liberal as the years went by. In 1869 a plebiscite of 7,336,000 to 1,560,000 supported the continued existence of an Empire in which the elected chamber was to exercise some control over the executive. But the Second Empire, again like the First, fell as a result of a military defeat. On 19 July 1870, in an unwise attempt to strengthen his régime, Napoleon III's government declared war on Prussia. Less than six weeks later, the French army had been totally outmanœuvred, outgunned and overwhelmed. The news that Napoleon III had surrendered to the Prussians after losing the battle of Sedan on 2 September 1870 led to an uprising in Paris and to the proclamation of a republican government of National Defence. In January 1875, this officially became the Third Republic, a régime which survived until 10 July 1940. Napoleon III, like Louis-Philippe before him, fled to England In 1873, he died at Chislehurst.

In 1953, General de Gaulle pointed out to Raymond Aron that the French carried out reforms only after a revolution had taken place. ('Les Français ne font de réformes qu'à l'occasion d'une révolution.')[5] Just as the First Empire had enabled the principal administrative reforms of the first French revolution to take permanent shape, so the Second Empire provided a framework within which France accelerated its transformation into a modern industrialised country. In particular, it saw the further development of an extensive railway network, with Paris as its centre, which had already begun under the July Monarchy; as well as the transformation of Paris itself into the 'Ville Lumière', the embodiment of the nineteenth-century concept of the well-ordered and glamorous middle-class city, where the

6 *French Caesarism*

poorer and more dangerous elements of the population had been exiled to the suburbs. The achievements of the Third Republic, following on the uprising which put an end to the Second Empire, were even more solid. In the seventy years of its existence France became a country in which parliamentary government was the norm and in which a reasonably determined effort was made to create a more egalitarian society. The Third Republic established, from 1881 onwards, a system of universal, compulsory, free and secular primary education. The law of 29 July 1881, familiar to most Parisians as well as to foreign visitors primarily as forbidding posters on certain walls, was in fact more important as the basis for a considerable extension of the freedom of the press. In future, it was the jury and not the stipendiary magistrate who decided on cases of libel. In 1882 the legalisation of trade unions marked the beginnings of a possible reconciliation between the working class and the capitalist system.

In 1905 the separation of Church and State fulfilled the ambition of the revolutionaries of the 1790s and of 1848 to establish a political and administrative system in which the Church played no part and over which it had no influence. From being what Thiers described in 1850 as 'the régime which divided Frenchmen least',[6] the Third Republic embarked on the 1914–1918 war in an atmosphere of 'Union Sacrée', and became the first régime since 1797 successfully to expel an invader from the soil of France. Great though its internal divisions were, it still seemed, at the time of the Popular Front of 1936, to be capable of fulfilling even more of the ideals of 1789 and 1848. By limiting the working week to 40 hours, by introducing paid holidays for all workers, by strengthening the power of the trade unions, by nationalising the French railways and by establishing greater public control of the banks, the Popular Front promised to shift the balance of power decisively in favour of the less privileged members of society. It may not have been the 'Bliss was it in that dawn to be alive / But to be young was very heaven' of Wordsworth's recollections of the first French revolution, but the promised social revolution of 1936 was still a considerable improvement on anything else available anywhere in Europe.

On 10 May 1940 the German armies invaded the Low Countries and on 13 May broke through into France. In less than a month, the French and British armies had been totally routed. On 18 May Paul Reynaud had asked Philippe Pétain, then aged 84, to take office as Deputy Prime Minister. On 16 June the French government decided to ask for an armistice. On 17 June, at 12.30 pm, Pétain ordered

Introduction 7

French troops to stop fighting. An official armistice was signed on 22 June, and on 10 July, on a motion proposed by the government itself, the same French National Assembly which had earlier introduced the reforms of the Popular Front voted to give power to a military man. It is true that 252 of its 932 members were absent, and that there were 17 abstentions. But it was nevertheless by 569 votes against 80 that it decided to give

> full powers to the government of the Republic, under the authority of Marshal Pétain, in order to promulgate by one or several acts a new Constitution of the French State. This Constitution should guarantee the rights of Work, of the Family, and of the Fatherland (les droits du Travail, de la Famille et de la Patrie).

Although this constitution was never officially promulgated, the vote of 10 July 1940 put an end to the Third Republic. It was replaced by what was officially known as *L'Etat Français*. The republican motto of *Liberté, Egalité, Fraternité* disappeared, and the new slogan of *Travail, Famille, Patrie* took its place. As late as 1959, coins with these words on the side and *L'Etat Français* on the other were still circulating in France.

It would have been difficult, in the disorder following the German invasion, to organise the kind of plebiscite which had enabled Napoleon I and Napoleon III to obtain official popular support for their seizure of power. Had one been held in the early summer of 1940, it would nevertheless almost certainly have given Philippe Pétain as overwhelming a popular majority in the country as a whole as he had already received from the National Assembly. When Henri Amouroux later called the second volume of his monumental *La Grande Histoire des Français sous l'Occupation* 'Quarante millions de pétainistes', there were few criticisms of his choice of title. In a crisis more serious than either of those which had provided the two Napoleons with their opportunity to seize power, the French had turned for a third time to a man who owed his prestige to his own or to other people's military victories; and unlike Napoleon III, Pétain could claim that they were very much his own. For in 1916 he had commanded the armies which won the battle of Verdun. In 1917 he had restored the morale of the French army after the failure of the Nivelle offensive, and introduced tactics capable of enabling the French to win local engagements against the Germans. With the death of Foch in 1929 and of Joffre in 1931, he was the sole survivor of the French victories of the First World War. His popularity was

8 *French Caesarism*

already considerable. In 1935 a book by Gustave Hervé was published with the title *C'est Pétain qu'il nous faut*. From 10 July 1940 to 20 August 1944, he remained – theoretically – the head of the French state.

In 1940, as in 1799 and 1851, no civilian politician came forward to take charge of events. There was no parliamentarian to challenge the victor of Verdun. On 18 June 1940 it was another military man, Charles de Gaulle, who broadcast on the BBC to urge his fellow countrymen to continue the fight. At first, few replied. By September 1940, fewer than 7,000 had joined de Gaulle's forces. Out of 2,000 wounded French servicemen evacuated through Dunkirk, only 200 chose not to be repatriated to France. No major political or military figure came over to him. The French Ambassador in London decided to take his retirement and live in South America. De Gaulle's one serious rival for the leadership of the Free French appeared only a year later, in the form of another general, Henri Giraud. In 1943 Giraud agreed to withdraw from the competition, and to concentrate on leading a French army of liberation in Tunisia and Corsica. There was then no alternative to de Gaulle, and on 23 October 1944 he was finally recognised by the Americans as well as by everybody else as the head of the government of liberated France.

Neither was this the last occasion on which the most cultured, inventive and sophisticated country in Western Europe found itself accepting a soldier as the one person capable of solving a political crisis. In November 1945 de Gaulle was unanimously elected President of the provisional government of the French Republic. He did not, however, agree with the way that the political parties were designing another constitution which gave overall power to the elected National Assembly. On 21 January 1946 he resigned, obviously with the hope of being invited back on his own terms and with his own constitution. But the Fourth Republic, which like its three predecessors had begun in a mood of revolutionary enthusiasm, showed itself tougher than he expected. Just as the Third Republic had been able, in the 1890s, to brush off the challenge of General Boulanger, so the politicians of the Fourth Republic had little difficulty in preventing de Gaulle from coming back to power through his *Rassemblement du Peuple Français*. In the absence of a serious crisis, or a major interruption in the normal process of government, the French political system has generally shown itself sufficiently robust to keep power in civilian hands. But in May 1958 the obvious inability of the Fourth Republic to solve the Algerian problem gave

Introduction 9

de Gaulle his opportunity. He did not, he is later reported to have said, come to power through a coup d'état. There was no state to overthrow. He did not seize power. He picked it up from where it was lying around.

Like his three predecessors, he nevertheless acted fairly quickly. On 13 May 1958 the French army and European settlers in Algeria had set up a Committee of Public Safety. They had, since 1 November 1954, been fighting a civil war to prevent the Arab and Kabylian *Front de Libération Nationale* from taking over the country. In their fear that the government in Paris might sell out to the rebels, the army and settlers organised their own movement to prevent this happening. General Salan, urged on by Léon Delbecque, shouted 'Vive de Gaulle'. On 15 May, de Gaulle announced that he was 'ready to assume the powers of the Republic'. He repeated the offer in a press conference on 19 May. On 29 May President Coty invited him to take over the government, and on 1 June 1958 de Gaulle received from the French parliament, by a less impressive vote than Philippe Pétain had received in 1940 (329 for, 224 against, 32 abstentions), full powers for six months and special powers in Algeria. On 28 September a new Constitution for what was to become the Fifth Republic was approved in a referendum by 31,067,000 votes to 5,420,000. On 21 December 1958 de Gaulle was elected as its first President, and remained in office until 27 April 1969.

II

The aim of this rapid and selective account of what happened in France between 1789 and 1969 is to bring out the paradox mentioned in the first sentence of this Introduction. Perhaps wrongly, because of the patronising attitude which such a view implies, one is not unduly surprised when a country in Africa or South America is taken over by a military junta or an ambitious general. Neither, however sorry one may feel, is it altogether amazing when a Franco assumes power in Spain or a Jaruzelski in Poland. Even the rule of Greece by a clique of colonels between 1967 and 1974 was an object of disapproval rather than of surprise – Athens had long since ceased being the city of Periclean democracy. But France is the country of Voltaire, Montesquieu and Diderot, of Alexis de Tocqueville, Emile Zola and Ernest Renan. It is the home of the symbolist movement in poetry, of

10 *French Caesarism*

impressionism in painting, of surrealism, existentialism and structuralism. It is the land of Proust, Gide and Camus, the country which has won 13 Nobel Prizes for literature as against 8 each for Germany, the United Kingdom and the United States. In its high level of cultural and intellectual tradition, it has nothing in common with the 19 African states listed in Ruth First's *The Barrel of a Gun* (Penguin, 1972) as having undergone a military coup d'état between 1952 and 1969. In Chinese thought, the natural order is deeply disturbed when military assumes predominance over civilian rule. General de Gaulle himself, undoubtedly the most successful of the French Caesars, argued throughout his very first book, *La Discorde chez l'Ennemi*, in 1924, how essential it was to maintain the subordination of military force to civilian authority. What is it about France that causes this natural balance to be so fragile, and what is it that makes the most sophisticated country in the world so vulnerable to the rule of military men?

One possible reason for the vulnerability of French democracy may lie in the pattern which emerges from the rapid survey which began this Introduction. An optimistic, forward-looking revolution tries to do too much. It adds to its country's problems rather than solving them; an element of chaos supervenes; and what *The Times* once called 'the smack of firm government' is needed to help the system pull itself together again. In *L'Ancien Régime et la Révolution*, de Tocqueville quotes an old French proverb: 'Par requierre de trop grande franchise et libertés chet-on en trop grand serviage' – by demanding too much liberty, men fall into great slavery.[7] But this explanation by recurring patterns of avenging conservative destiny does not stand up to analysis. Although the France of 1799 was threatened by anarchy, this was less obviously the case in 1851. Without the defeat of 1940, neither Pétain nor de Gaulle would have had a political career. The argument that the Popular Front of 1936 led to the collapse of France in 1940 has been abandoned even by the French right wing itself. The Fourth French Republic had been quite successful in putting France back on its feet after the Second World War. Its failure to decolonise had nothing to do with an excessive enthusiasm for left-wing experiments; and without the Algerian crisis, it is more than doubtful whether Charles de Gaulle would ever have come back to power in 1958.

French democracy nevertheless does seem to be vulnerable in a way that democracy in Anglo-Saxon or in Scandinavian countries is not. In 1962, in a book entitled *The Man on Horseback*, S. E. Finer

Introduction

categorised France as a step lower down than countries like the United Kingdom, the United States, Denmark, Norway or Sweden, Canada, Australia or New Zealand. For these countries have what Finer calls a 'mature political culture', defined as one where public sanction for a military take-over would be unobtainable.[8] A distinction has indeed to be made between an ex-soldier such as General Eisenhower, who is elected President in a normal election as the chosen candidate of an established political party, and figures like General de Gaulle and Marshal Pétain. For neither of them would have had the opportunity of even standing for office if a national crisis had not provided them with an excuse to use their prestige, and to do so in a contest which had not been scheduled as part of the normal democratic time-table. The Duke of Wellington was, it is true, made Prime Minister by George IV because of the prestige he had acquired by defeating Napoleon. But his power rested on a majority in two Houses of Parliament whose members had taken their seats in a normal way for the times and who had no fear of military intervention to make them vote for the government. Neither Austria nor Germany nor Italy has an unimpeachable record for democratic government. But in none of them has a figure owing his prestige to military achievements come to power because of the apparent collapse of the state and the absence of a viable civilian alternative. Hitler and Mussolini were non-commissioned officers who overthrew a democratic state through mass violence and intimidation. What is remarkable about the two Napoleons, as also about Pétain and de Gaulle, is the contrast between the lack of widespread popular support for them before they took power and their success in having their seizure of power endorsed by public or parliamentary opinion as soon as it had taken place.

In French, the word which is most frequently applied to all four men is the one which gives its title to this book. The major French dictionaries are more informative about the term *Césarisme* than either the *Oxford English Dictionary* or *Webster's*. The latter's entry restricts itself to the gynaecological peculiarity of the first Caesar's birth. Admittedly, the *OED* gives a useful idea of how the Victorians saw the two Napoleons. In 1958, the *Westminster Review* wrote of 'clumsy eulogies of Caesarism, as incarnate in the dynasty of Buonaparte', and quoted the *Pall Mall Gazette* of 1869 as commenting that 'In Napoleon's Caesarism there has been no flaw'. A more anecdotal awareness of the fate to overtake Napoleon III comes through in the description of the person who is 'not a Caesarist, because she says

12   *French Caesarism*

that the lady of Chislehurst has no ribbons'. But the *OED* offers little
by way of political analysis. To find this, you have to turn to the
French dictionaries, and note how the *Larousse du Vingtième Siècle*
links the exercise of absolute authority by one man to the almost
ostentatiously democratic origin of such power. The three French
Caesars who took power at a time when it was possible to hold
nationwide elections – Napoleon I, Napoleon III, Charles de Gaulle –
organised between them a total of six plebiscites and five referenda.[9]
When, in April 1969, de Gaulle failed to win a majority in the
referendum on decentralisation and the reform of the Senate, he
immediately resigned. No government in parliamentary history has
come to power with a larger majority in an elected Assembly than
Philippe Pétain did in June 1940. Caesarism, in France at any rate, is
inseparable from populist as well as popular democracy. Caesarism,
adds the *Larousse du Vingtième Siècle*, should be contrasted with
régimes like that of Louis XIV, based on the idea of divine right, as
well as those which try to limit the power of government by
establishing a clear separation between the legislative, executive and
judicial branches.

Once you let this particular remark sink in, however, doubts about
the applicability of the term begin to appear. A constant theme in de
Gaulle's own political thinking, certainly from the *Discours de
Bayeux* in 1946 onwards, is precisely the need for the separation of
powers. He wanted to give France a régime which would save it from
what he saw as the excesses of parliamentary democracy. He did not
want to abolish democracy itself. If, in 1960, at the end of his *Secrets
d'Etat*, the journalist J.-R. Tournoux noted that the controversy was
bound to grow as to whether the Fifth Republic 'was born of a
Caesarian', its whole progress since then has been to disprove Eric
Nordlinger's view that 'both the evidence and the underlying reason-
ing clearly suggest that the most common aftermath of military
government is more military government'.[10] The historical incident
which gave rise to the term 'Caesarism' can be used to emphasise an
important aspect of how the two Napoleons came to power. On 17
December 50 BC, Julius Caesar was acting illegally when he crossed
the Rubicon at the head of his army without receiving permission to
do so from the Senate. There is no doubt about the illegality of the
coups d'état of 9 November 1799 and of 2 December 1851, and
Napoleon III went so far as actually to call the preparations for his
seizure of power 'Opération Rubicon'. General de Gaulle may or
may not have known what was happening in Algiers in the run-up to

Introduction

13 May 1958. The question will be discussed in Chapter 4. There is nevertheless some interest in quoting what he wrote in 1932 in *Le Fil de l'Epée*: 'evangelical perfection does not lead to empire. The man of action cannot be imagined without a strong dose of egoism, pride, toughness and cunning' (*la perfection évangélique ne conduit pas à l'empire. L'homme d'action ne se conçoit guère sans une forte dose d'égoïsme, d'orgueil, de dureté, de ruse*).[11] Yet once the appeal to him had gone out, de Gaulle acted throughout the Summer and Autumn of 1958 with almost ostentatious legality. As his apologists maintain, there is also an important sense in which Pétain came to power quite legally and constitutionally. This question, too, will be discussed later on, and an account given of the tenaciously held view that the Vichy régime was in no way the legal government of France. But the apparent regard which Pétain and de Gaulle had for constitutional niceties as well as for popular endorsement is not the only feature of their behaviour which makes them very different from the soldiers who take power in other countries. Both of them, like the two Napoleons, ruled through civilians. There has, so far, been no equivalent in France to Cromwell's Major Generals. Albert Camus may have been right to say that it was because France is a military nation that Communism had a chance of coming to power.[12] But at no point in its history has the army wielded the same power in France as it did in nineteenth-century Prussia, in early twentieth-century Germany, or in the Argentina of General Galtieri.

It is, of course, not unusual for patterns to appear more clearly from a distance than at close range. The ideal distance to look at a portrait is four or five feet, not four or five inches. A more detailed examination of what happened in France under the two Napoleons, and under Pétain and de Gaulle, will emphasise the differences separating the periods during which France was governed by a sword which had been taken, albeit briefly, from the scabbard. There are nevertheless three general features of French society which stand out when it is looked at in the context of its apparent tendency to bring in a military man to solve its problems.

The first, which I have already mentioned, is the relative absence of civilian politicians able to deal with a serious crisis. There have, it is true, been strong men in French politics. Neither Thiers, Clemenceau nor Poincaré was afraid of exercising power; Richelieu and Louis XIV were even less inhibited. But there has been no Churchill, no Roosevelt, no Adenauer, no civilian politician who dominated his period and held office continuously for a number of

14 *French Caesarism*

years. When, in the late 1790s, the politicians of the *Directoire* were looking for a way out of their problems, they turned to a general, Bonaparte being only their third choice after Joubert and Moreau. Louis Napoleon was not, strictly speaking, a military man. But he did rejoice in the name of Bonaparte, and had an inordinate fondness for appearing in uniform. The voting in the Presidential election of December 1848 is also a fairly clear indication that the only acceptable alternative would have been General Cavaignac, the man responsible for putting down the attempted rebellion of the June Days. In 1940, and to a lesser extent in 1958, the civilian politicians capable of assuming and exercising responsibility kept their heads down very low. When, in Shakespeare's *Julius Caesar*, Cassius is tempting Brutus, he observes that Caesar would not be a wolf if the Romans were not sheep. The first general feature of French society which emerges from the story of the Caesarist phenomenon is the relative scarcity of high-quality French civilian politicians.

The second, in contrast, is the permanence of the French civilian administration. For if it is French civilian politicians who, in one way or another, make military coups d'état possible, the soldiers they bring to power do not then impose a military style of government. The First Empire offered its soldiers wealth and glory. The Julien Sorel of Stendhal's *Le Rouge et le Noir* looked back nostalgically, in the late 1820s, to the time when young men were either dead or generals by the age of 30. But the France of the First Empire was run by lawyers, administrators and financiers. Napoleon III paid his generals very well, and gave them prominent positions in the *Sénat*. But power remained with the upper middle class, and it was a civilian politician, Emile Ollivier, and not a military man, who declared war on Prussia in July 1870 'd'un cœur léger'. For obvious reasons, the prestige of the French army was somewhat diminished when Philippe Pétain came to power, and Weygand's attempt to keep an eye on the civilian administrators by having 'a general at the head of each *département*, a colonel looking after each *arrondissement* and a major or captain in each *commune*' came to nothing. On his own admission, these soldiers came fairly rapidly into conflict with the civilian authorities, and lost. The technocrats who hoped to make France into a more efficient country were all civilians. As Robert Paxton observed, Vichy was 'a régime of double firsts'.[13] The dominant issue between 1959 and April 1961 was the contest between de Gaulle and the army, and de Gaulle won. The French army, he said in 1960, had taken every possible opportunity to be wrong. It had insisted in the

Introduction 15

1890s that the wholly innocent Captain Dreyfus was guilty. In 1914 it had refused to acknowledge that 'le feu tue' (bullets kill) and tried to win battles by mass charges at well-entrenched machine-gun posts. In the 1930s it had preferred the Maginot line to the tank and the dive bomber. It was now in favour of *L'Algérie Française*. It is not surprising that the first 11 years of the Fifth Republic marked the beginning of the golden age of the French civilian administrators trained at the *Ecole Nationale d'Administration*.

There is a third aspect of French society to which a study of the career of the two Napoleons, of Pétain and de Gaulle draws attention: the question of whether or not France is, by nature, a country suited to democratic forms of government. I have chosen to define Caesarism as the assumption of power at a moment of real or alleged national crisis by a figure owing his prestige to genuine or associated military achievements. Such a definition makes it a more general phenomenon than Bonapartism. Unlike Bonapartism, it does not suggest the idea that the power thus obtained can be inherited by members of the same family. Neither is it automatically discredited by the military defeats which ended the reigns of both Bonapartes. But precisely because it is a general phenomenon, it invites speculation about the possibility, occasionally put forward by the French themselves, that they are not really a democratic nation. France has not, it is true, produced the equivalent of a Hitler, a Stalin, a Mao Tse Tung or a Pol Pot. Robespierre, after all, ruled for less than two years. France is still a very lucky country. The two great theoreticians of state absolutism, Hegel and Marx, were both Germans. Joseph de Maistre and Charles Maurras had an endearing eccentricity which prevented them from being really dangerous, as well as a total lack of understanding of how the modern world worked. But in 1965 Jean-François Revel put his finger on an aspect of French national behaviour which does deserve further comment when he wrote:

divers Français et amis de la France sont enclins à s'imaginer que les régimes autoritaires, paternalistes, d'ordre moral, monarchistes, catholiques, impériaux, dictatoriaux, de redressement, de renouveau, d'union, de sursaut, de rassemblement, d'urgence et de résurgence qui jalonnent notre histoire depuis 1789 constituent des accidents le long d'une pure ligne démocratique et révolutionnaire. Or, bien au contraire, ces régimes sont la France normale, et ce sont les gouvernements inspirés par le peuple qui sont exception-

16 *French Caesarism*

nels: ceux-ci occupent, en tout et pour tout, quelques mois en 1848, un total de quatre années disséminées çà et là au cours de la troisième République, et deux ou trois mois après la Libération.

(Various Frenchmen and friends of France tend to think that régimes that are authoritarian, paternalistic, based on the notion of moral order, monarchist, Catholic, imperial, dictatorial, established for the purpose of recovery, renewal, union, revival, national unity, to cope with a crisis, through a resurgence of effort, and which punctuate French history since 1789, are accidents along a pure democratic and revolutionary path. And yet the exact opposite is true: these régimes are the norm in France, and the exceptions are the governments inspired by popular sentiment: in all, several months in 1848, a total of four years scattered here and there throughout the Third Republic, and two or three months after the Liberation.)[14]

It is the existence of generalisations of this kind which explains why this book is being written by a literary critic and not by a professional historian. The task of the professional historian is that of correcting or confirming established views by the critical analysis of new or rediscovered evidence. It is the privilege of the enthusiastic amateur to speculate on issues such as national characteristics, the role of great men, or the Marxist theory of history. The main events of French history since 1789 are sufficiently well established for there to be no serious disagreement about what actually happened. The literary critic turned amateur historian can therefore come into his own with speculation as to why.

The answers he suggests are akin to those put forward by the literary critic or the philosopher. Faced with a selected sequence of events, the amateur historian can suggest looking at it in this way rather than that, somewhat as the Wittgenstein of the *Philosophical Investigations* invites the reader to experience the intentionalist nature of perception by seeing the same diagram sometimes as a rabbit and sometimes as a duck. It is, essentially, an aesthetic experience; and like the different features of a work of art, the number of patterns into which a set of historical events falls into shape is quite large. *Hamlet* is not only a play about procrastination. It can also be seen – amongst other things – as the account of three young men in search of vengeance; as a satire of conventional revenge tragedies; as an exploration of madness; as an essay in Oedipal tensions; as a remake of the Orestes legend; as a play about

Introduction 17

retarded adolescence; as a denunciation of the dangers of elective kingship; as an unconscious depiction of the social crises of Shakespeare's own time; or as the tragedy of the sensitive intellectual compelled to act in the real world of political intrigue. The text itself does not change, any more than the events of the First and Second Empire, of the Vichy régime or of the first 11 years of the Fifth Republic change, as they are seen in Marxist terms as a series of successful conspiracies against the working class; as an illustration of how unwise it is to have as violent a revolution as the French did between 1789 and 1794; as a reminder of how much nearer democracy France came in the nineteenth and twentieth centuries than almost any other country in continental Europe; as an object lesson in how dangerous it used to be to have a common land frontier with Germany; or in a more old-fashioned, moralising and self-satisfied way as the demonstration of how hard it is to introduce democracy into countries where the Protestant Reformation has been defeated or has never taken place.

These events change even less if you decide, as H. A. L. Fisher did, that history is just one damn thing after another. There is no way in which anyone can refute the argument that the apparent pattern of progressive régimes being regularly followed by military take-overs is a result of sheer chance; and that any resemblance between Napoleon I, Napoleon III, Pétain and de Gaulle is purely fortuitous. A sceptic might even argue that it is only in the absence from their death of any element of violence that the four French Caesars really resemble one another, at the same time as they differ from the original Julius. Napoleon I died of cancer of the stomach, Napoleon III as a result of a painful operation on his bladder, Pétain of old age and de Gaulle of a heart attack during a game of patience while waiting for the seven o'clock news to begin on television. None of the 33 plots hatched between 1958 and 1969 to assassinate de Gaulle succeeded, any more than did the various infernal machines directed against the two Napoleons. French Caesars, in this respect, were very lucky to have lived in an age when it was so much easier than in Republican Rome for the police to keep an eye on potential conspirators.

1 Napoleon I: The Unifier

I

Napoleon I was exceptionally lucky in his date, place of birth, and talents.

When he was born, on 15 August 1769, Corsica had only recently become French. It was ceded to France by Genoa on 15 May 1768. Napoleon's father, Carlo-Maria de Buonaparte, began by joining the nationalist leader Paoli in his opposition to French sovereignty and struggle for independence. After Paoli's defeat, in May 1769, and more especially after the French King had recognised Carlo-Maria in 1779 as having been of noble stock for over two hundred years, he changed his mind. His status now enabled him to obtain a scholarship for his second son, Napoleone, to go to the *Collège d'Autun*, in Burgundy, in March 1779.

Initially, the future Emperor was not happy. What little French he knew was made difficult to understand by a strong Italian accent, and he was nicknamed 'la paille-au-nez' from the way he pronounced his name. But in October 1779 he transferred to the *Ecole militaire de Brienne*, in Champagne, and was commissioned six years later, on 28 October 1785, as second lieutenant in the regiment La Fère, in the royal artillery corps. The *ancien régime* had established, under the leadership of Gribeauval, an excellent artillery. Because one needed a certain amount of mathematical or technical knowledge, this corps was also one in which it was easier for young men of talent to obtain promotion than in the cavalry or infantry. There, future officers had to prove four quarters of genuinely French nobility. Napoleon's later insistence on 'la carrière ouverte aux talents' was well in keeping with the spirit of 1789. But it was also the result of his own early experience. As a young man, he had been very poor, and only the lucky chance of the first French revolution breaking out when it did enabled him to escape from what would almost certainly have been his fate in pre-Revolutionary France: that of a capable and conscientious officer who rose by slow degrees to the rank of major.

There are innumerable anecdotes to illustrate Napoleon's talents. He was an excellent mathematician, capable of finding rapid solutions to the complex problems of 'combining in space and time the operations of different formations'.[1] He needed little sleep, and

Napoleon I: The Unifier

could take what he did need at a moment's notice. He had immense powers of concentration and would compare his mind to a desk with wholly separate drawers. When he needed to think about something, he simply opened the relevant drawer, and found all his ideas in order. When he closed it, the matter disappeared completely from his mind until it needed to be reconsidered. He could easily work 16 hours a day, and would frequently get up in the middle of the night to solve an administrative or a legal problem. Distance was no obstacle. The organisation of the *Comédie Française* is still based upon a decree issued in Moscow on 15 October 1812.

Meat remained for a long time something of a luxury in poorer Mediterranean countries such as Corsica, and childhood eating habits die hard. Napoleon preferred eggs and cheese, and in the early part of his career rarely spent more than 12 minutes at dinner. Unlike de Gaulle, who was also a fast eater, he nevertheless did not insist on the plates being cleared away as soon as he had finished. He would rise from table, and leave the Empress to entertain his guests. He had an excellent memory, a capacity for decision fostered by the possession of considerable power, and an enviable ability to inspire loyalty. He kept the same personal valet, Constant Wainj, from 1801 to 1814, and the same chief of staff, Berthier, from 1796 to 1814. From a military point of view, he was a genius, especially in his ability to appreciate the strategic possibilities of a landscape and to be so far ahead with his preparations that he would attack the enemy before they had even realised that he was there. He also had the great good fortune of inheriting not only the excellent artillery of the *ancien régime* but also a plentiful supply of men provided by the revolutionary policy of the *levée en masse*, and its subsequent transformation into a systematic recruitment policy by Jourdan. From a purely military point of view, he was very much the son of the Revolution in that it gave him enough soldiers for him to put into practice his favourite strategy of carrying out a powerful attack on what he judged his enemy's weakest point. He won battles, he often said, by using his soldiers' legs; and it is significant that he did better in the mountainous country of Northern Italy, where surprise was relatively easy, than in the open plains of Eastern Europe or Russia, where it was not. The first of the French Caesars was nevertheless able to base his power very firmly on his ability to handle an up-to-date sword. He also had as much an eye for the political main chance as for the lie of the land on the battlefield.

This chance was not slow in coming. The authors of the *Déclaration*

20 *French Caesarism*

des droits de l'homme et du citoyen discovered that it is much easier to start a revolution than to stop one. The fall of the Bastille on 14 July 1789 was only the first in a series of events in which the ambition to establish a respectable form of parliamentary democracy gave way to the desires and terrors of the poorer sections of the population of France. On 20 June 1792 the crowd invaded the Tuileries and compelled Louis XVI, a plump, agreeable, indecisive man, to put on the red bonnet of liberty and drink a glass of wine with his former subjects. Buonaparte witnessed the scene, and described Louis XVI, in the Italian which still came more naturally to him than French, as a *coglione* (silly fool). Had the king possessed the political will – and the military means – to kill four or five hundred of them with cannon fire, Buonaparte observed, the rest of the mob would still be running. It was a policy that he was only too happy to put into practice three years later, on le 13 Vendémiaire An IV (5 October 1795), in the last days of the assembly known as the *Convention*. By that time, the king had been executed – on 21 January 1793 – and the Revolution had gone through its most violent phase. The fall of Robespierre, on 27 July 1794 – le 9 Thermidor An II – had been accompanied by that of Antoine de Saint-Just, who was almost exactly Buonaparte's age, and is said to be the one civilian politician who might have imposed his will on the army. Robespierre's death had also put an end to the attempt by the more extreme revolutionaries to impose social equality by strict revolutionary discipline, and power lay with men who, like the Vicomte de Barras, had made a great deal of money out of the Revolution and were determined not to lose it. Barras had first noticed Buonaparte at the siege of Toulon, in December 1793. By grouping his artillery on the Point de l'Eguilette, dominating the bay, Buonaparte had compelled the English fleet to withdraw. The entrance to the bay was narrow, and the English were justifiably reluctant to be fired on with red-hot shot by the French batteries. In 1795, Buonaparte was also reputed to have been something of a Jacobin, a sympathiser with the left. The *Convention*, after all, was being threatened by a royalist mob. In 1793, his pamphlet in dialogue form, *Le Souper de Beaucaire*, had taken the side of the Montagnards against that of the royalists and Girondins, and he was closely associated with Maximilien Robespierre's brother Augustin. After the fall of Robespierre in July 1794, he was briefly imprisoned under suspicion of having been one of Robespierre's supporters. Although Barras had played a major role in organising the fall of Robespierre, he nevertheless felt in 1795 that he was calling on the right man.

Napoleon I: The Unifier 21

Buonaparte duly dispersed the mob, shooting down its leaders on the steps of the Eglise Saint Roch. It was the legendary 'whiff of grapeshot' celebrated by Thomas Carlyle as marking the end of the French Revolution.[2]

Buonaparte nevertheless gave Barras fair warning: 'Once the sword is out of the scabbard, I shall not sheathe it again until I have restored order.' Barras took the hint and rewarded Buonaparte by giving him, at the age of 26, his own position as Commander in Chief of the Army of the Interior. He also arranged for Buonaparte to frequent the salon of Madame Tallien, where Joséphine de Beauharnais was one of the reigning beauties. The couple were married, in a civil ceremony, in March 1796, in the same month that Barras also arranged for Buonaparte to be given command of the *Armée d'Italie*. Between March 1796 and December 1797, in a series of lightning campaigns followed by some brutal acts of repression, Bonaparte – as he then began to call himself – proceeded to conquer the whole of Northern Italy. As early as June 1796 he was able to write to the *Directoire*, the régime which had followed the *Convention*, to say that some twenty millions in gold were on their way to Paris. The financial crisis which had first set off the Revolution was still not over, but Bonaparte had hit upon one way of solving it. In 1796, the Pope was required to pay 21 million francs in coin for the privilege of signing a peace treaty with Bonaparte, and the rest of 1796, like 1797, was taken up on a series of campaigns whose principal object seems to have been as much financial as military. When Venice signed a peace treaty on 15 May 1797, it cost her three millions cash and three millions in various items of naval equipment. An anecdote, possibly apocryphal, tells how Bonaparte once harangued an Italian mob and reproved them for their immorality. 'Tutti gli Italiani sono dei ladri' (All Italians are thieves), he said. A voice from the crowd replied: 'Non tutti. Ma buona parte.'[3]

It is something of a habit of French Caesars to withdraw from France itself before coming back to rule. Napoleon III was to do it by spending the period 1846 to 1848 in England. After Philippe Pétain had won glory in the First World War, he played a relatively minor part in politics in the 1930s, and came back from being French Ambassador in Spain to take over in June 1940. Charles de Gaulle had an eventful period outside France between 1940 and 1944 before returning as head of the Provisional Government. He also had a rather less impressive period of internal exile, characterised by the failure of the *Rassemblement du Peuple Français* in 1953, before May

22 *French Caesarism*

1958 gave him his chance. None of the other three, however, went away from France quite so dramatically as Napoleon Bonaparte, or made such an impact on the countries they visited. It was not enough for him to conquer Italy far more effectively than any French monarch had done even in the great period of the Italian wars in the sixteenth century. He also became the first Western European to conquer Egypt. Bonaparte's military achievements when he seized power in November 1799 may have been less dramatic than those of the first Caesar. In 55 BC, Julius had already conquered Gaul before crossing the Rubicon back into Italy. They were nevertheless unparalleled in the Europe of the eighteenth century.

On 17 October 1797, on signing the treaty of Campo-Formio, Bonaparte had told Talleyrand that the only way in which the revolutionary government in France could survive was by destroying England. By the treaty of Campo-Formio, the Austrian Netherlands passed under French control, and France was recognised – albeit temporarily – as the dominant power in the whole of the North of Italy. But in 1798, Napoleon advised against the invasion of England, and decided that only an indirect attack through the Middle East would enable France to defeat England by cutting off the land route to India. The *Directoire* was not unhappy to see him go, for reasons of political expediency as well as scientific interest. He was less frightening when away from Paris than when actually there, and there was, again, always the money. The levies raised in Egypt were less spectacular than in the North of Italy, but were no less real. Neither did the battle of Aboukir Bay, on 1 August 1798, by which Nelson effectively isolated the French army in Egypt, discourage Bonaparte from pursuing his conquest, and he did not seem unduly put out either by his failure in 1799 to take Saint-Jean-d'Acre or by the outbreak of plague at Jaffa. But while Bonaparte was also laying the foundations for the science of Egyptology – the Rosetta stone, whose simultaneous scripts of Greek, demotic, and Egyptian hieroglyphics enabled Egyptian writing to be read, was originally discovered by a French officer in 1799 – the political situation in France was changing rapidly. Having proved his military genius, and shown by his action in October 1795 what he could do in domestic politics if given a chance, Napoleon was ready to take hold of the Revolution and provide it with its definitive form.

Napoleon I: The Unifier

II

The régime which Napoleon overthrew by the coup d'état of 9 November 1799 (*Le 18 Brumaire*) was known as the *Directoire*. It had been in existence since 27 October 1795, and had confirmed the move to the right of the Revolution after the fall of Robespierre. *La Déclaration des droits de l'homme et du citoyen* was revised to make room for more emphasis on property rights and less on social equality, and power was entrusted to five *Directeurs*. They were appointed, at least in theory, by two elected bodies, the *Conseil des Cinq Cents* and the *Conseil des Anciens*, with one *Directeur* retiring from power every five years. In fact, they moved rather faster than this, and the immediate reason why Napoleon came to power in 1799 was that nobody in France was prepared to make the system work. When, for example, the elections of 1797 produced a monarchist majority in both the *Conseils*, there was talk of putting on trial the three *Directeurs* who had republican sympathies. But Barras, Reubell and La Révellière-Lépeaux decided to act first. Bonaparte, then on campaign in Italy, agreed to send General Augereau to carry out the *coup d'état du 18 Fructidor* (4 September 1797): 177 elected members sympathetic to monarchism were expelled from the *Conseils*, and the minority became the majority.

As S. E. Finer observes in *The Man on Horseback*, it was 'the first coup d'état which, being carried out by a civil faction with military support, and using electoral malpractices which have become a commonplace, has an authentically modern tang'.[4] Military force had already become a major factor in the French Revolution, which could be said to have begun neither with the storming of the Bastille on 14 July 1789 nor with the publication of *La Déclaration des droits de l'homme et du citoyen*, but with the refusal of the *gardes françaises* to obey orders on 12 July 1789, and their consequent replacement by the voluntarily constituted National Guard. The 'whiff of grapeshot' on 5 October 1795 was important in a general as well as a specifically French context. For the first time since Cromwell, power in a major European state lay clearly with the army. The innumerable coups d'état which have been so marked a feature of twentieth-century politics have a clearly French ancestry, and the conditions which still make them possible were all there in the France of the 1790s: the collapse of traditional authority; the break-down of a civilian political consensus; the emergence of the army as the one body which is both successful and – apparently – disinterested; the real or alleged need to

24 *French Caesarism*

prevent chaos; the fear that an even less representative civilian clique will seize power. The only difference, albeit an essential one, is that in France it is not the army itself which seizes power. It is an individual soldier, who relies on civilians rather than on his brother officers actually to run the country.

The *coup d'état du 18 Fructidor* was not slow to produce offspring. When the elections in the following year returned a strongly Jacobin majority, the *Directeurs* invoked the *loi du 30 Floréal* (11 May 1798) and annulled the 98 elections which the Jacobins had won. Just over a year later, on 18 June 1799, the *journée du 30 Prairial* reversed this decision. The *Directeurs* responsible for eliminating the Jacobins – Merlin de Douai and La Révellière-Lépeaux – were replaced by General Moulin and Roger Ducos, who later became Third Consul. Napoleon's seizure of power in November 1799, like the coming to power of Pétain in 1940 or of de Gaulle in 1958, was not only the result of his own desire to rule. It was a direct consequence of the fact that the domestic political system was not working. The *coup d'état du 18 Brumaire* was as much the product of civilian incompetence and intrigue as of military ambition. It could not have succeeded in a society whose social structures were still intact, and where civilian politicians were prepared to play the game according to the rules.

Significantly enough, in this respect, this coup d'état was the result of a conspiracy in which Napoleon did not originally play a major role. The key figure was Emmanuel-Joseph Sieyès, who had first become famous in 1789 for his pamphlet *Qu'est-ce que le Tiers Etat?* His reply was that it was nothing, but wanted to become something, and it is hard to find a more succinct summary of the view that the French Revolution was essentially an attempt to seize power by the bourgeoisie. During the Terror, as he himself put it, Sieyès survived, and came back into politics with the *Directoire*. In 1799 he needed, as Barras had done in 1795, 'a sword', and Napoleon was not in fact the first soldier that he and fellow conspirators turned to. Their initial choice was Barthélemy Joubert, who had risen from the ranks and won himself a reputation for financial as well as political honesty. But Joubert was killed in action on 15 August 1799 at Novi, and the other potential candidate, Bernadotte, was simply not interested. Sieyès's third choice, General Moreau, also declined. Bonaparte had fewer scruples, and on 8 October 1799 had arrived back from Egypt – leaving behind him an army subsequently repatriated by the English – precisely with such a plan in mind. Sieyès also had the support of Talleyrand, sometime Bishop of Autun, of Fouché, later to become

Napoleon I: The Unifier

Napoleon's minister of police, and of Roger Ducos. The money for the conspiracy was put up by two bankers, Le Coulteu de Couteleu and Perrégoux. Both went on to be key figures in the establishment in 1800 of the Banque de France.[5] Napoleon was quite clearly brought to power in 1799 by people who had done financially well out of the Revolution and wanted to protect themselves against royalist reaction as well as against Jacobin egalitarianism. He was, as he later said himself, 'ni talon rouge, ni bonnet rouge' (having neither the red heel which distinguished the aristocrats at Versailles nor the red bonnet of liberty won by the extreme *sans-culottes*). He was also to prove less amenable than they had hoped to the people who helped him to win power.

Bonaparte did not personally shine in the coup d'état which brought him to power. There had been a certain amount of Jacobin unrest in Paris, so the *Conseils* decided on 9 November – *le 18 Brumaire* – to move to Saint-Cloud, to the south-west of the city. There, theoretically at least, they were under Bonaparte's protection, since he had been given charge of the army in Paris. The three *Directeurs* who were in the plot, Sieyès, Roger Ducos and Barras, resigned, and their two remaining colleagues were arrested. But when, on 10 November 1799 (*le 19 Brumaire*) Bonaparte entered the Chamber where the *Cinq Cents* were sitting, he was greeted with cries of 'Down with the Tyrant', and threatened with being outlawed. This is what had happened to Robespierre on the night of the *9–10 Thermidor* (27–28 July 1794), and it was a procedure which corresponded in fact to the death sentence. It was only the presence of mind of his brother, Lucien, who convinced the troops waiting in the gardens outside that Napoleon was being threatened by spies in the pay of the English, that saved the day. The hostile members were driven out, and those who remained voted to entrust the executive authority of the state to three consuls. Initially, these were Sieyès himself, Roger Ducos and Bonaparte. When the constitution came into operation, Bonaparte himself became First Consul and thus the first French Caesar. The ex-regicide, Cambaceres, became Second Consul; and an ex-royalist, Le Brun, Third Consul. Bonaparte was already showing that eclectic approach to political ideologies which is one of the more attractive features of his personality. Theoretically, the three consuls were to rule for a day at a time, in alphabetical order. But it was not really because Bonaparte begins with a B that he proved so difficult to dislodge.

For it was he who issued, at eleven o'clock on the evening of 19

26 *French Caesarism*

Brumaire, the Proclamation explaining what had happened, and its wording struck what was to become a fairly familiar note. Although, as Bonaparte claimed, all parties had come to him to entrust him with their secrets and ask for his help, he had 'refused to be the man of a party'. The legitimacy which a Caesar enjoys is something which comes to him directly from the people. There must be no intermediary bodies to prevent him from intuiting, like Rousseau's ideal legislator, what the will of the people really is. Charles de Gaulle was to provide a fuller development of this vision but it is already there in Bonaparte. An American historian, Lynn Hunt, offered an additional way of looking at this aspect of Napoleon's contribution to politics when she wrote that he 'established the first secular police state to stand above parties'.[6] What enabled him to do this was the failure of the French Revolution to attain the objectives set out in *La Déclaration des droits de l'homme et du citoyen*. Why it failed, and how Napoleon succeeded in achieving some of these objectives in a way which the revolutionaries did not envisage, are questions best considered side by side. For it was the inability of French civilian politicians to put together again the society which had been destroyed between 1789 and 1794 that enabled Napoleon Bonaparte to become, with his self-coronation on 2 December 1804, simply Napoleon.

III

In a phrase which suggests that the chaos and horror of the 1790s might have been avoided, the English historian Alfred Cobban described the first French Revolution as a 'fall of snow on blossoming trees'.[7] It is a tempting theory, comparable to the one put forward by Wladimir Weidlé when he argued that the Russian Revolution of 1917 put an end to a 'silver age' which might have enabled Russia to move peacefully into a democratic, industrialised society.[8] Cobban's thesis is nevertheless difficult to sustain, largely because the snow proved so heavy and the blossom so fragile. One of de Gaulle's most striking images is that of the comparison between the German invasion of 1940 and a flash of lightning. All the defects of twentieth-century French society, and of French military organisation, stood out in total clarity against the disaster. The same is even truer of the France of the eighteenth century at the time the first French Revolution broke out. The violence and tumult had the effect of

Napoleon I: The Unifier

showing that it was not a country amenable to social or political change.

It is true that there had been attempts at reform. In 1787, the use of torture as a normal part of the judicial investigative system had been abolished. But it was only for a trial period, and the other horrors of breaking condemned criminals on the wheel, tearing out their tongues, or hanging, drawing and quartering, remained on the statute book. The image of the French Revolution is inseparable from that of the guillotine. But the good Dr Guillotin had some reason for presenting Dr Louis' invention as a humanitarian measure. All that the patient would suffer, he claimed, was a slight feeling of coolness in the neck. Although evidence for this is obviously lacking, the guillotine was certainly a democratic measure in that it extended the privilege of decapitation from the nobility to the rest of society. Its use, especially at the height of the Terror, when between April 1793 and July 1794, there were 2,639 heads severed in Paris alone, is a considerable factor in the transformation of the French Revolution into a Caesarian dictatorship. A large number of those executed were civilian politicians.[9] Like the purges in Stalin's Russia, the Terror was an instrument for discouraging social dissent. Its long-term effect was to make the apparent guarantee of order by a soldier almost infinitely attractive. Soldiers direct their aggression, theoretically at any rate, against outside enemies.

Another tentative blossom on the tree of non-violent reform in pre-Revolutionary France which was also to take more dramatic shape after 1789 lay in the area of religion. One of the aspects of French society most criticised by the thinkers of the eighteenth-century Enlightenment was the lack of official religious toleration. In 1685, in what Kingsley Martin described as 'an extravagant act of piety and intolerance',[10] Louis XIV had revoked the Edict of Nantes which had, in 1598, put an end to the French wars of religion and provided Protestants with the freedom to practise their faith. The Edict of Toleration which gave the Protestants back some of these rights in 1787 was a step towards a more open society, and one which might well, in a more stable political climate, have received support from the aristocracy as well as from the generally more enlightened middle class. The French aristocracy of the eighteenth century had, at least in appearance, lost a good deal of its confidence in its right to rule. In 1784, the courtiers at Versailles had turned out in force to watch a nobleman being made a fool of by his servant in Beaumarchais' *Le Mariage de Figaro*, and on the night of 4 August 1789 gave

28 *French Caesarism*

even more dramatic proof of its readiness to entertain new ideas. In an extraordinary display of egalitarian enthusiasm, the members of the Second Estate – the Clergy was the First, the middle and other classes the Third – voluntarily renounced those of their feudal rights which involved an element of personal servitude. They did, it is true, insist that other rights could be abolished only after due payment, but their readiness to envisage fairly radical change in society could well have led to the reversal of the *ancien régime*'s tendency to intellectual totalitarianism. But although this movement towards reform found specific expression in the behaviour of one of the most eminent representatives, Charles-Maurice de Talleyrand, it did so in a way that was to shrivel much of the blossom of reform dead on the tree.

Louis XVI's original motive in summoning the Estates General on 5 May 1789 had been to try to find a solution for France's financial problems. The French monarchy had bankrupted itself by supporting the rebellious colonies in the American War of Independence, and George III held the view that the Revolution of 1789 was God's judgement on Louis XVI for the way he had behaved. The taxation system of eighteenth-century France worked by farming out the right to collect taxes to private financiers who generally did rather better than the King. Since everybody in France, Church, nobility, and middle class alike, enjoyed various forms of exemption from taxation, there was little chance of financial salvation coming from within. Talleyrand's suggestion thus made an immediate appeal to vested interests, as well as being well in keeping with the generally sceptical and anti-clerical temper of the times. It was that the property of the Church should be 'placed at the disposal of the Nation', and on 2 November 1789 the proposal was approved in the newly constituted National Assembly by 568 votes to 386. The size of the majority is an indication of the extent to which the anti-clericalism of the Enlightenment had affected the attitudes of the educated classes. To the aristocratic as well as to the middle-class readers of the *Encyclopédie*, nothing could be more noisome and useless than a priest, unless it be a monk. To solve the financial problems of the kingdom by taking from the Church the land which she owned – some 6 per cent of the total area of France, but perhaps up to a fifth of the area which could actually be used[11] – seemed an excellent idea. Since the state also undertook, at least initially, to pay the salaries of the clergy, it thereby strengthened its hold over them while at the same time avoiding the charge that it was persecuting religion. However, as in the steps to a more humane treatment of criminals and social

Napoleon I: The Unifier

dissidents, the measure had important consequences which nobody foresaw at the time.

It led, in the first instance, to one of the great inflations of modern history. The land was used as security for the issue of paper currency known as *Assignats*. Since these were easy to print, and since the revolutionary government had no knowledge of Gresham's law, they were multiplied way beyond the original value of the land. By 1797 they were worth only 1 per cent of their original face value, and eventually became collectors' items with no real usefulness as currency. The inflation which they encouraged made the problem of governing France even worse, and Bonaparte was not the first French ruler in the 1790s to use foreign conquest to try to solve the nation's financial problem. Although the *Convention* declared, in 1792, that it was ready to give 'fraternal assistance' to any people 'wishing to recover its liberty', it too had adopted a more practical attitude. In Alsace and the Palatinate, as in Belgium, Church lands were placed under the protection of the Republic, and the *Assignat* imposed as legal tender. But Talleyrand's proposal was to have even more far-reaching consequences than the encouragement of inflation both in France itself and in the countries it had conquered. For it had the same effect as the dissolution of the monasteries and religious houses had had in England in 1536 and 1539: that of creating a class whose economic interests were indissolubly tied to those of the Revolution. Any return to the *ancien régime*, and any attempt to restore the Church to its previous eminence, would have meant the transference back to its original owners of some very valuable property. Once the nationalisation of Church lands was under way, France was virtually predestined to become a secular republic. The separation of Church and State in 1905 was the direct consequence of Talleyrand's proposal.

Whether this is quite the fruit that Alfred Cobban's 'blossoming trees' were supposed to bear is open to question. What is certain is that the nationalisation of Church lands began the split in French society between Catholicism and republicanism which was one of the main problems that Napoleon found confronting him when he came to power. For Napoleon rapidly found himself cast in the role of unifier, and another reason for the relative ease with which he imposed himself as supreme ruler of France from 1799 onwards was that the power which his military prestige enabled him to wield provided the unity which the majority of the nation regarded as necessary. For it would be a mistake to regard the attitude of

30 *French Caesarism*

Talleyrand in 1789 as typical of that of the French nobility as a whole. Equally characteristic was that of the nobles who began to emigrate immediately after 14 July 1789. This was typified by Louis XVIII's brother, the Comte d'Artois, who was later to come back to France in 1814 with exactly the same belief in absolute monarchy that he had had in 1789. The view that the Revolution was perpetually threatened by aristocratic reaction was not a myth. From 1790 onwards there was an army of exiles, stationed in Coblenz, for the aristocrats to join.

Neither was this opposition to change something provoked by the excesses of the revolutionaries themselves. The Revolution of 1789 had been preceded by the events known as 'la révolte nobiliaire', the attempt by the French nobility both to reinforce its position in the state and to resist any reforms which the King might try to introduce. In the area of taxation, the nobility was particularly and understandably reluctant to abandon its various privileges of exemption.[12] Although it had, since 1695, been required like other members of society to pay the *vingtième* – a tax of 5 per cent on income – it did not have to pay the *gabelle*, salt tax. Its members were also much more generously assessed for the *taille*, the tax on landed property, than were non-aristocrats; and, naturally, there was no question of their being subjected to *la corvée*, the obligatory labour on either the lord's land or the King's roads. The *noblesse de robe*, or legal nobility, had attained aristocratic rank by purchasing offices whose attraction lay as much in their fiscal advantages as in their income or social prestige. There was little incentive either for members of this class, or for those belonging to the *noblesse d'épée*, the traditional, warrior aristocracy, to give up the advantages they had enjoyed for generations, especially since both classes had considerably improved their position in the eighteenth century. In 1789 every bishop in the French Church was of noble birth. Even the legal nobility was insisting on recruiting into its ranks by purchase only those who already were members of an established noble family. The various attempts made by the King to reform the system all failed. The summoning of the Estates General on 5 May 1789 was forced upon him by the resistance to change of those who most benefited from the *ancien régime*.

The reluctance of the French upper nobility to accept change was also linked to the fact that they were not, as a class, integrated into the rest of the nation. Louis XIV had built Versailles for a very practical reason: he wanted his nobles close at hand so that he could keep an eye on them. After the events of the *Fronde* between 1648 and 1652 he did not trust them not to repeat their attempt to

Napoleon I: The Unifier

31

overthrow the throne. Rather than have them reinforce their natural power base by administering their local area, he preferred to keep them as courtiers and have the serious work of administration done by people whom he appointed and whom he could dismiss, the *Intendants de Justice, de Police et de Finances*. From 1639 onwards, it was these forerunners of the Napoleonic *préfets* who governed France. By 1789, it is true, most of them were noblemen. This too was part of the attempt by the aristocracy to win back power, and it introduced a further element of tension into French society. Although theoretically in alliance against the Third Estate, the King and his aristocrats could never combine in order to establish a form of constitutional monarchy which the nobility would be prepared to support. Such a monarchy existed in England, but it did so for a very specific reason: the revolution of 1688 had made it clear that only a King who was, in the last resort, acceptable to an aristocratic oligarchy would be allowed to rule. France had had no such revolution. Indeed, the whole of French history in the seventeenth century had gone in precisely the opposite direction, with the nobility being domesticated at Versailles and revolving round the Sun King like so many dependent satellites.

Seen in retrospect, and with the inevitable advantages of hindsight, the Revolution of 1789 was bound to fail because of the tension at the top as well as lower down in French society. The aristocracy was at one and the same time dependent on the King and hostile to him. It could not exist without him; but it was not prepared to sacrifice any of its advantages in order to enable him to rule more effectively. The *Tiers Etat*, so ably defended in print by Sieyès in 1789 and so effectively served by Sieyès' *protégé*, Napoleon Bonaparte, was by that date equally opposed to both monarchy and nobility. It wanted to limit the power of the first and abolish the privileges of the second. The wealthier members of the middle class may, in the past, have been inspired principally by the desire to buy their way into the nobility. But the nobility had closed ranks, and the events of 1789 – the elections to the Estates General, the preparation of the *cahiers de doléances*, the Tennis Court Oath and the storming of the Bastille – were to make the middle class increasingly conscious of what distinguished it from the other orders. By nationalising the Church lands, and by taking further steps to bring the Church under state control, the Revolution produced other, deeper divisions. It is hard to see how these could have been even temporarily resolved except by recourse to what Henri Calvet called 'the theory of Caesarism,

32 French Caesarism

according to which France is incarnated in a single man'.[13] The definition of Caesarism as the 'seizure of power, at a time of real or alleged national crisis, by a leader owing his prestige to real or associated military triumphs' needs only one change to fit Napoleon I like a glove: the omission of the words 'real or alleged'.

It is always tempting for an Englishman writing about French history to explain what went wrong by comparison with what seems to have gone right in the history of the English-speaking peoples. S. E. Finer's classification of societies, in *The Man on Horseback*, as mature, developed, low and minimal follows a number of dividing lines, of which one of the most important is the degree of industrialisation. But there is another particularly noticeable line separating the mature from the developed cultures, and that is religion. Mature countries tend to be Protestant; developed ones – France, Spain, Italy, in particular – tend to be Catholic. In this neo-Whig interpretation of history, it is the traditional virtues of Protestantism – self-reliance, the querying of authority – which explain why England and America became democratic countries relatively easily while France experienced so much more difficulty. One of the most important events in French history, from this point of view, is the fact that the Catholics won the religious wars of the sixteenth century. From the moment that Henri de Navarre, a Protestant, had to abjure his religion in order to obtain the throne of France in 1589 – 'Paris vaut bien une messe' – what Anglo-Saxons think of as democracy had a much harder row to hoe on the other side of the Channel.

The significant political contrast here is between the failure of the *Fronde* in the 1640s and 1650s and the triumph of the Parliamentarians in the English civil war at almost exactly the same period. The nobles taking part in the *Fronde* give the impression of being motivated principally by self-interest. They had no guiding ideology comparable to that of the Puritanism inspiring Cromwell and his New Model Army. The lawyers who took part in what was known as the *Fronde Parlementaire* did have some concept of the rôle which law should play in the state, and one which could have developed into something comparable to Pym's or Hampden's belief in the supremacy of parliament and the importance of the rule of law. But there was nothing comparable to the fervent belief in those concepts which inspired the Puritans who played so central and effective a rôle in the English revolution. If French society in the 1790s turned out to be so profoundly divided that only a soldier could impose unity on the nation, one possible reason may lie in the general difficulty which

Napoleon I: The Unifier

non-Protestant societies experience in developing political systems which combine a respect for authority with the recognition of the importance of dissent. The *philosophes* of the eighteenth century certainly believed in many of the ideas which are now regarded as essential to a democratic society. Their disciples set them out in *La Déclaration des droits de l'homme et du citoyen*. They were rather shorter on notions of how these ideas might be put into practice, and tended to rely upon the intervention of an enlightened despot. In a way they found him in Napoleon, who was quite happy to see himself in such a rôle.

Historical generalisations are always dangerous, and the example of Prussia is there to show that Protestantism is no guarantee of democracy. It is impossible to read an account of life in eighteenth-century England without wondering why a revolution did not take place there as well. Defeat in the American War of Independence, a mad king, violent agitation for parliamentary reform, gross inequalities, corruption in high places, anti-Catholic riots, are all factors which would have provided a more than adequate explanation for a revolution if one had taken place. The apparent contrast between a Protestant, Northern, democratic Europe, and a Catholic Europe more vulnerable to Napoleon's or Franco's Caesarism, or to Mussolini's populist dictatorship, may be an illusion. A safer thesis to argue in the presentation of Napoleon as the greatest unifier among the four French Caesars is to see him not as the French equivalent of Cromwell – always mentioned unfavourably by French revolutionaries – but as a characteristically eighteenth-century sceptic, a man whose lack of fundamental religious beliefs enabled him to find a solution to the great divide which opened up in the France of the 1790s on the question of religion.

For the nationalisation of the Church lands was not the only measure which profoundly alienated the Catholic church, and Catholic believers, from the revolution. There was also *La Constitution Civile du Clergé*, decided by the newly constituted National Assembly on 12 July 1790. Indeed, if there was one single event which made the blossom wither on the trees which might have brought a peaceful harvest to the French Revolution, it was this attempt to apply democratic ideas to Church organisation. Like the nationalisation of Church lands, it stemmed from an ideological attitude which had been fostered by the suspicion of organised religion which runs through the whole movement of ideas in eighteenth-century France. Napoleon's solution to the problem was closely linked to the fact that

34   *French Caesarism*

he had an eminently practical attitude towards religion. In Egypt, on his own admission, he became a Muslim. On another occasion he remarked that if he were governing a nation of Jews, he would happily rebuild Solomon's Temple. He represented, from this point of view, another side of eighteenth-century thinking, the one which genuinely believes that the affairs of God can be separated from those of Caesar, to the distinct advantage of the latter.

Although *La Constitution Civile du Clergé* was not intended deliberately to complement the nationalisation of the Church lands, it had the very similar effect of splitting France between Catholic monarchists and agnostic republicans. The revolutionaries of 1789 had decided, on 26 February 1790, to divide France into 83 *départements*. The aim was to move away from the excessive centralisation of the *ancien régime*, while at the same time to impose unity by reducing local and provincial customs. No part of the *département* was to be further from the *chef-lieu* (main town) than a man might travel in a day on horseback. Local government officers were to be elected, and *La Constitution Civile du Clergé* set out to apply the same principle to the Church. Each *département* was to have its duly elected bishop, each congregation was to elect its own priest. The Papacy was not consulted. Conflict became inevitable from the moment that both bishops and priests were required, on 27 November 1790, either to take an oath of allegiance to 'the Nation, the Law and the King', or to risk dismissal. Only seven bishops and fewer than half the priests agreed to sign. When the Pope condemned the new arrangements, in March 1791, the conflict grew worse. Louis XVI, a pious man, was required to receive communion from a priest who had taken the oath to the new régime. This contributed to his decision, on 21 June 1791, to try to escape from France. He was arrested near the frontier, at Varennes, and taken back to Paris. He had, since October 1790, been encouraging his brother-in-law, the Austrian Emperor, in the idea of intervening to restore him to his original rights. The further discovery of documents proving his complicity with the aristocratic plot to overthrow the Revolution led on 10 August 1792 to his deposition and eventual trial. On 21 January 1793, he was executed. The breach between the Revolution and the monarchy was now absolute. Without *La Constitution Civile du Clergé*, some compromise might perhaps have been reached. With it, and with the increasingly active campaign of dechristianisation which went on throughout the 1790s, the split between Catholic and republican France was absolute.

One of Napoleon's first priorities, on seizing power in 1799, was to

Napoleon I: The Unifier 35

stop this particular conflict. By the *Concordat* of 1801, Catholicism was recognised as 'la religion de la grande majorité des Français et particulièrement celle des Consuls' (the religion of the great majority of Frenchmen and especially of the Consuls). Bishops were appointed by the State, but consecrated by the Pope. In the later years of the Empire, this arrangement ran into difficulties, culminating in the arrest of Pope Pius VII in 1811 and his imprisonment at Fontainebleau. Napoleon also showed how he saw the relationship between Church and State by the title which he gave to his heir, the Duc de Reichstadt, born on 20 March 1811 of his marriage to Princess Marie-Louise of Austria. He called him *Le Roi de Rome*.

The permanence of Napoleon's contribution to France can be measured by the fact that the *Concordat* was the shortest-lived of the measures whereby he solved the conflicts and problems created by the Revolution. It lasted just over a hundred years, and ended only with the separation of Church and State in 1905, a measure which finally achieved the republican goal of a society in which organised religion played no official rôle. The revolutionaries had, in fact, taken away from the clergy the responsibility for registering births, marriages and deaths on 20 September 1792, and Napoleon had benefited from this by marrying Joséphine de Beauharnais in a civil ceremony on 19 March 1796. It was only on the eve of the ceremony whereby he crowned himself Emperor, on 2 December 1804, that he went through the form of a religious marriage, and then only to take advantage of the presence of the Pope. With some reluctance, Pius VII had come to Paris to be present at the coronation ceremony, and the official painting depicts him as having a somewhat sour expression.

Religion certainly created more difficulty for Napoleon than any other of the domestic problems which he found facing him when he took over in 1799. Although he aimed, with the creation of the Imperial University in 1808, to establish a state monopoly in education, he never succeeded in persuading the French middle class to prefer the *lycées* to the secondary schools run by the Church. In this particular context, he was very unlike the three other French Caesars who took power, each of whom formed a successful alliance with the Catholic church on educational matters. He was certainly prepared to use religion to discourage dissent. In 1806, a majority of bishops approved a new catechism which went: Question: 'What should we think of those who would fail in their duties to the Emperor?' Answer: 'According to the Apostle St Paul, they would resist the

36 *French Caesarism*

order established by God himself, and make themselves deserving of eternal damnation.'[14] But although 29 cardinals had agreed by 1810 to accept the salaries offered to them by Napoleon, there remained a solid core of recalcitrants, 13 in all, who refused to comply. Had the Pope not also been a temporal sovereign in the Vatican states, fewer problems would probably have arisen, and a purely Gallican church could have resisted Napoleon with much less energy. Yet in spite of his constant bickering with the official authorities, the majority of ordinary Catholics remained faithful to Napoleon. While the Revolution had been obliged to fight a fierce civil war in the *Vendée*, in the West of France, there was little opposition to Napoleon after the signature of the peace agreement of December 1799 and of the *Concordat* in 1801. As in many other areas of internal policy, he succeeded considerably better than the Revolution had done, and this improvement is even more marked where financial policy is concerned.

He solved France's financial problems as well as anyone could whose foreign policy involved endless wars of conquest, not all of which were as profitable as the Italian campaigns of 1797 and 1798. Unlike the military men who take over in countries of low political culture, Napoleon did not have to rely upon his brother officers to run the civilian administration. There were only six generals among the fifty members of the most influential body, the Council of State, and it may well have been Napoleon's reliance on capable civilian administrators which enabled him to stay in power. A general without his gift for recognising and using civilian talent might well have been swept aside or compelled to play the role of a General Monck and bring back the Bourbon dynasty. He made it quite clear that no tests of belief or social origin would be imposed on those prepared to serve the state. Martin Gaudin, for example, who gave France the efficient tax-collecting system whose absence had contributed to the downfall of the *ancien régime*, had worked for Louis XVI, for the *Trésorerie* established by the Constituent Assembly in 1791 and for the *Directoire* of 1795 before becoming one of Napoleon's most able administrators. Nobles who wanted to have their names removed from the *liste des émigrés* were able to do so without much difficulty. Talleyrand, for example, who had served the Legislative Assembly before seeking refuge in England, and subsequently in America, came back to France in 1796 and served as Foreign Minister from 1799. Joseph Fouché, who had also been in holy orders before becoming one of the most brutal of revolutionary leaders, became

Napoleon I: The Unifier

Napoleon's Chief of Police in the same year. Like Talleyrand, he was later dismissed by Napoleon for intriguing against him at the time of his marriage to Princess Marie-Louise of Austria, in 1810. Both men thus showed how right Napoleon was not to have real trust in anyone. Talleyrand also negotiated with the allied armies in 1814, letting them know that they could safely advance on Paris. But the fact that they were so closely identified with the régime for so long is an indication of how eclectic Napoleon was in his choice of ministers.

The same is true of the people whom he appointed to less prestigious roles. Napoleon's Caesarism is, in this respect, markedly different from the kind of military régime to which we have become accustomed in the twentieth century. Not only had he been brought to power by civilian politicians, and had the expenses of his coup d'état paid for by bankers. He also ruled through the middle class, and used middle-class civilians to run the affairs of state. The unity he imposed on France was not that of a military coup, but of a well-ordered middle-class society, in which careers were open to talents for civilians as well as for military men. This is as true of the institutions which he set up as it is of the people to whom he entrusted the running of them. Two of the prestigious *Grands Corps de l'Etat, Le Conseil d'Etat* and *La Cour des Comptes*, although having their origins in the *ancien régime*, still exist today very much in the form which Napoleon gave them. The former acts as a final court of appeal in cases involving administrative law and as the body responsible for examining the wording of government and private members' bills before they go before the legislative chamber. The *Constitution de l'an VIII*, inaugurated after the coup d'état which brought Napoleon to power, entrusted the *Conseil d'Etat* with both functions; Stendhal described it as bringing together 'fifty of the least stupid Frenchmen'. Napoleon himself was present at 36 of the 84 sessions in which it drew up the Napoleonic Code, and used it as a training ground for bringing on his most able young administrators. The *Cour des Comptes*, which has the task of checking the accounts of all bodies responsible for spending public money, received its present form from Napoleon in 1808. Both bodies perform functions considered in British constitutional practice to be the prerogative of parliamentary committees rather than courts of law; and thus illustrate the greater rôle played by courts and lawyers in French public administration. Both attract the most gifted and ambitious members of the middle class, and are not scorned by the aristocracy either. Both provide a channel of social advancement for those anxious to rise in society. Both thus

38 *French Caesarism*

enable the French élite to maintain itself in power by the constant absorption of new blood. In this respect, they show that typically Napoleonic concern for combining administrative efficiency with 'la carrière ouverte aux talents' which makes France at one and the same time a paradise for civil servants and the country in which the rule of the established middle class is hardest to break. Had Napoleon known where to stop in his policy of military conquest, he might well have succeeded in his ambition to rule until his death and bequeath this model of efficient administration to a successor of his own blood.

For Napoleon did more than settle the religious disputes arising from the Revolution, and leave France with a legal system which represented the original drive of the Revolution for universality, rationality and formal equality. He also used the work of the revolutionaries of 1789 as a starting point for a centralised reorganisation of the French administrative machinery which only the most determined efforts of the socialist government of the 1980s have begun to alter. The Napoleonic *préfet* may, in 1982, have had his name changed to *commissaire de la République*, and work not in the *Préfecture* but in the *Hôtel du Département*. But he is still there as the representative of the state in each of the 98 *départements* into which France is now divided; and has now started officially to be called a *préfet* again. He no longer has the right to veto any financial measures proposed by the locally elected bodies. He nevertheless still has sight of the official documents coming to the local authority from Paris and is still very much on hand to counsel and to warn. Even nowadays, the paradox of the revolutionaries' attempt to reform French local government still remains basically unaltered. They had thought, by creating the *départements*, to give people a greater opportunity to organise their local affairs independently. In practice, by making the *départements* as small as they did, they prevented them from becoming viable self-governing units. They also, by destroying the original identity of the provinces, made the *départements* unable to combine in order to resist the all-pervasive authority of the *préfet*.

Napoleon's greatest achievement, nevertheless, remains in the legal system which he established. This was published on 21 March 1804 as *Le Code Civil des Français* and became, in 1807, officially known as *Le Code Napoléon*. It gave body to Article 6 of *La Déclaration des droits de l'homme et du citoyen* which stated that 'la loi doit être la même pour tous, soit qu'elle protège, soit qu'elle punisse' (the law must be the same for everyone, whether it protects or punishes). In the *ancien régime*, this had very definitely not been

Napoleon I: The Unifier 39

the case. Nobles were judged in different courts from commoners, members of the clergy in different courts again. Nobles also had the right to judge certain offences in their own, private courts, whose verdicts were binding upon their tenants. These courts disappeared with the abolition of the feudal system on 4 August 1789, and the Napoleonic Code gave force to the statement of the *Assemblée Constituante* on 2 September 1791 that 'A legal code will be made which is common to the whole Kingdom'. It did not do so in terms which would have pleased the more extreme revolutionaries who had come temporarily to power between 1792 and 1794. By insisting upon property rights, especially as far as the lands seized after the nationalisation of *les biens de l'Eglise* in 1790 were concerned, it provided historians who see the French Revolution as a central episode in the triumph of the middle class with one of their most convincing pieces of evidence. For it also placed the working class in a very subordinate position, with Article 1781 stating very clearly that whereas the employer's word was believed without question in any dispute about salaries, statements made by the employee had to be proved. It also confirmed the *loi le Chapelier* of 1791 in making illegal the formation of trade unions. Nor did women do very well out of the Napoleonic Code. Napoleon was very much a Mediterranean man, who infuriated Madame de Staël by simultaneously declining her advances and insisting that women were primarily for breeding. It was not until 1944, when de Gaulle gave women the vote, that this aspect of the Napoleonic inheritance began to disappear. When extreme left-wing political groups in France insist upon the idea that you cannot dissociate the women's movement from the wider struggle against middle-class. capitalist society, it is against this aspect of the Napoleonic legacy that their hostility is often directed.

IV

No military man apart from General de Gaulle has had so profound an impact as Napoleon on the politics or internal organisation of a European country. The tradition which he inaugurated is, in this respect, like a literary movement which begins with so undoubted a masterpiece that the books which ought to be seen as developing the tradition seem like rather pale imitations. Not even Napoleon's greatest admirers, however, could claim that this was all due to his own qualities. When he said that he did not usurp the crown but

40   *French Caesarism*

found it lying in the gutter, and that 'the people put it on my head', he was only partly exaggerating. In 1799, France was exactly at the point where it was ripe for a take-over, and Napoleon did not need to destroy the *ancien régime* before setting up his kind of society in its place. That had already been done for him, so that the military force which he controlled was essentially a bulwark against disorder, not a threat to established values. Here too he provided an example to be followed by at least two of his successors, Napoleon III and Philippe Pétain, and provided an illustration of the important difference between the rôle played by the army in countries of developed political culture and the one which it most frequently plays in societies of low or minimal culture. There, the army is responsible at one and the same time for destroying the old, colonial or neo-colonial régime – in Algeria, Egypt, Turkey – and for ruling in its place. It is generally better at the former than at the latter task. Napoleon's achievement as a unifier suggests that the word 'Caesarean' might, in a political context, profitably be used in an almost gynaecological sense.

J. R. Tournoux does this when he asks, in his *Secrets d'Etat*, whether the Fifth Republic might not be regarded as having been born 'of a Caesarean', and his account of the events of May 1958 shows that this is fair comment.[15] For in a Caesarean, the baby is already there. So, in 1799, was the form which Napoleon was to give France, and the degree of surgical force which he needed to use to enable France to give birth to this form was relatively slight – as, indeed, in the most successful Caesareans, it is. Napoleon nevertheless died a defeated man, an exile on the remote island of St Helena, with France retaining nothing of his immense military conquests. For every second he breathed, another human being died.[16] Although Napoleon is credited with the remark that you can do anything with bayonets except sit on them, he was quite unable to resist the temptation to misuse his own military power. He failed, in other words, to ride the tiger, and inaugurated one of the more unfortunate aspects of European history: the pattern whereby it is the leader who comes from just outside the country who proves the most enthusiastic nationalist. In the case of Disraeli, the results were not catastrophic. In those of Hitler, an Austrian, and of Stalin, a Georgian, they were. And they were none too glorious in the long run in Napoleon's case.

Napoleon did, it is true, inherit a situation in which France was at war with her neighbours. In 1792, almost every politician in France except Robespierre had wanted to go to war against Austria. Louis

Napoleon I: The Unifier

XVI thought that the revolutionary army would rapidly be defeated, and that he would be placed back on the throne. The Girondins hoped that a rapid victory would show what a new France could do to prove itself. They were justified in their hopes by the victories at Valmy on 20 September 1792 and at Fleurus on 25 June 1794, and Europe found itself facing a new kind of warfare. The stately manœuvrings of the eighteenth-century generals, whose concern was mainly to keep their armies intact, were replaced by a style of attack which reflected the aggressive nature of the new ideology. The age of the people's war had arrived, and Napoleon's military career combined enthusiasm for spreading the new ideas of the Revolution with an ambition which it is sometimes tempting to explain by psychological as much as by political or military considerations. For Napoleon was a second son, and Freud himself has argued that to 'eliminate Joseph (his elder brother), to become Joseph himself, must have been Napoleon's strongest emotion as a small child'.[17] Like that of other second sons, the aggression which he showed in trying to take his elder brother's place went far beyond any rational bounds, and eventually proved his total undoing.

A more down to earth view of Napoleon sees him as an Italian *condottiere*, a vulgar Corsican adventurer determined to get as much out of the situation as possible before it all disappeared. His mother, née Letizia Ramolino and officially known in the Imperial Court as 'Madame Mère', is credited with a simple reply when asked what she thought of her son's achievements: 'Pourvu que ça dourre ('dure' – she spoke with an even stronger Italian accent than her son). Mais ça ne dourrera pas' (So long as it lasts. But it won't). Not even his marriage on 1 April 1810 to the most eligible heiress in Europe, Archduchess Marie-Louise of Habsbourg-Lorraine, daughter of the Emperor Francis I of Austria and niece of the guillotined Marie-Antoinette, could give his régime the kind of legitimacy which he wanted. Marie-Louise did indeed give him a son, something which Josephine could not do, though both she and Napoleon were fertile with other partners. But when, in October 1812, the rumour ran that Napoleon was dead, nobody seriously thought of the Duc de Reichstadt as automatically succeeding to the throne. Napoleon's authority rested ultimately, in this reading of his career, on continued military triumphs. Once these ceased, his ability to rule France would disappear.

This is nevertheless not a very satisfactory way of looking at Napoleon's ultimate failure. He had no domestic need for an endless

42 *French Caesarism*

succession of victories. He had organised France so well that it is quite easy to imagine the gradual development of a policy of peaceful coexistence between him and the rest of Europe if he had been able to settle for half and stop his perpetual conquests. What prevented him from doing this was his attempt to defeat England by economic warfare, and there is a strange if superficial continuity in this respect between his behaviour and that of Charles de Gaulle. For de Gaulle succeeded, by his veto on 14 January 1963 of Great Britain's first application to join the Common Market, in keeping Europe, temporarily at any rate, under Franco–German domination. Harold Macmillan had no hesitation in comparing this veto to Napoleon's Continental System, and the pattern whereby the right-wing nature of French Caesarism tends to show itself in hostility to England was established very early on.[18] In the case of Napoleon, the decision to try to defeat England by economic warfare began after the battle of Trafalgar on 21 October 1805. From the moment that England confirmed her complete mastery of the sea, Napoleon had to give up any idea of an invasion. He was not able, in other words, to fulfil the promise that he made to Joséphine: 'I will take you to London, Madam. I intend the wife of a modern Caesar to be crowned at Westminster.'[19]

Bonaparte had already replied to the British blockade of France, begun in May 1803, by refusing to allow any ships trading with Britain to enter French ports. By the decrees of Berlin in November 1806 and of Milan in December 1807, he extended this ruling to all France's allies and occupied territories. This had the effect of compelling England to concentrate more on the American market, and there is again a parallel with one of the most famous exchanges between General de Gaulle and Winston Churchill. In May 1944, in one of their many quarrels about relationships with the United States, Churchill defined the inevitable British preference when he said, in the version given by de Gaulle, 'Chaque fois qu'il me faudra choisir entre vous et le grand large, je choisirai toujours le grand large (every time I have to choose between you and the open sea, I shall always choose the open sea).'[20] It was a remark which proclaimed a continuity of policy that both geography and the policies of Napoleon I made inevitable for England. The creation of the second British Empire, to replace the one lost with the American colonies, was an almost direct result of the struggle against Napoleonic Europe. Bonaparte, in contrast, showed how fixated he was upon Europe by cutting France's last links with the New World. On 30 April 1803, he

Napoleon I: The Unifier 43

sold Louisiana, together with what makes up modern Arkansas, the Dakotas, Iowa, Kansas, Missouri, Montana, Nebraska and Oklahoma to the United States for 15 million dollars.

The permanence of British hostility to Napoleon was in the well-established tradition of never allowing Europe to be dominated by a single power. This policy took the form, initially at any rate, not of direct military intervention on the continent but of subsidising a series of coalitions. The first such coalition had in fact begun before Napoleon came to power. In the Spring of 1793, Prussia, Spain, Austria, Russia, the Germanic states of the Holy Roman Empire, and indeed most of Europe, joined England in alliance against revolutionary France. This first coalition lasted until the dramatic victories of Napoleon I in Italy in 1797 forced Austria in 1801 to sign the treaty of Campo-Formio. The second coalition, aimed at the policy of the *Directoire*, also collapsed with the defeat of the Austrians at Marengo on 14 June 1800. It ended with the Peace of Amiens, in March 1802, which implicitly gave England the mastery of the seas and France that of the continent of Europe. It was a treaty which might have become a permanent settlement of the differences between the Revolution and the rest of Europe if Napoleon had not persisted on trying to obtain the domination of the Mediterranean by insisting that the English evacuate the island of Malta.

The third coalition, from May 1803 to December 1805, collapsed after Napoleon's most spectacular victory, when he defeated the Austrians under the command of the Holy Roman Emperor, Francis II, at Austerlitz on 2 December. This was, by a happy coincidence, the anniversary of his self-coronation as Emperor, and was later to provide a symbolic date for Napoleon III's coup d'état in 1851 and for his proclamation of the Second Empire in 1852. It was also a victory which enabled Napoleon to show that he still had the same eye for the financial main chance which had characterised his behaviour when he was still Buonaparte in Italy in the 1790s. He levied two million florins of Austrian gold upon his future father-in-law Francis II, who was shortly to have to term himself simply Francis I of Austria. For Napoleon then added insult to injury by deciding, in July 1806, to abolish the Holy Roman Empire of which Francis had had himself elected Emperor in 1792, and to replace it with the Confederation of the Rhine. Francis – the father of the Marie-Louise of Habsbourg-Lorraine whom Napoleon was to marry in 1810 – had to content himself with his earlier title of Francis I of Austria.

The fourth coalition ended with the battle of Friedland in January

44 *French Caesarism*

1807 and the treaty of Tilsit between France and Russia on 14 June 1807. Alexander I of Russia then agreed to take part in the Continental System, and Napoleon seemed well on the way to victory over England. But the classic British strategy of the long haul, of which these coalitions are perhaps the best example, was already beginning to produce results. The fifth coalition originated in the French invasion of Spain in May 1808, a result of the policy whereby Napoleon tried to close all continental ports to British goods. Although the coalition itself ended, like its predecessors, in a military victory for France – the battle of Wagram, on 6 July 1809 – Napoleon was already over-committed. The Spanish fought a different type of war, and one which could not be ended even by the most spectacularly successful Napoleonic battle. It gave us the word 'guerrilla', and meant that Napoleon was perpetually fighting on two fronts. Britain at last intervened militarily with the Peninsular Campaign of 1808 in support of Portugal. The sixth coalition followed the disaster of the invasion of Russia in 1812 and the retreat from Moscow in the same year. This invasion was, itself, made inevitable by the Continental System. Russia could not afford a continued trade war with England, and Napoleon's invasion was part of an attempt to make her persist in what was a totally self-defeating form of economic activity.

With the battle of Leipzig, in October 1813, Napoleon finally lost, and the sixth coalition won. It had indeed been a long haul for the British, and Napoleon's ability to keep defeating the Austrians and Prussians had very nearly prevented them from attaining their aim. But all his military genius could not prevent the invasion of France in 1814, and the return of the Bourbon dynasty in the portly form of Louis XVIII. France was back with the natural frontiers she had won before Napoleon came to power, and the episode known as the Hundred Days was to make her lose even those. On 26 February 1815, Napoleon escaped from the Island of Elba, came back to France, was triumphantly welcomed, and proved that plebiscitary Caesarism was not just a name. Without the seventh coalition, and the defeat of Napoleon at Waterloo on 18 June 1815, he might well have continued as ruler of France. But nobody in Europe trusted him, and his attempt at a come-back had unfortunate effects for France itself. She lost Savoy and the Saarland, was occupied for three years, and had to pay a heavy indemnity. The paradox whereby the greatest soldier that France has ever known ended his career by a military defeat was complete.

Napoleon's reorganisation of France remained, of course, and

Napoleon I: The Unifier

justifies his being seen as a twentieth-century figure rather than one whose example and achievements are limited to the late eighteenth or early nineteenth century. For it was not until the twentieth century that the idea of a military leader playing a major and independent role in national politics, and of the army intervening because of the failure of civilian politicians to run the state properly, became commonplace. For this to happen, other countries had to experience the equivalent of the French Revolution. Other countries, that is to say, had to witness the destruction of established, traditional author ity, and its replacement by the idea of popular sovereignty. Other countries had to discover that a revolution may be easy to begin, but is extraordinarily difficult to control. Caesarism is essentially part of the break-down of established order. It is the process which allows one man to become, temporarily, the incarnation of a particular moment in a nation's history. Few Caesars, from this point of view, have done better than Napoleon I in their domestic policy. Nasser is a possible rival, in his ability to unite a nation, give it self-confidence, and leave it with a system that eventually gives rise to civilian rule. But normally, the intervention of the army in politics is fairly disastrous. The seizure of power in Pakistan by Ayub Khan in 1970 led to the civil war in Bangladesh and to over a million deaths; the Nigerian civil war in 1967 was sparked off by a military take-over; few of the military men who have taken over in Central or South America have managed to make their countries more efficient.[21] By the standards of the people who followed him, Napoleon I was, in his domestic policy, the success story of all time.

This was as much a consequence of the class to which he unconsciously belonged as of his undoubted talents. In a book which is, involuntarily, one of the most amusing ever written about a political figure, a late-nineteenth-century French historian called Arthur-Lévy argued that Napoleon I was the incarnation of all the virtues which had made the middle class what it had become by 1893: the dominant class in Western Europe, and especially France. In his relationship with Joséphine, argued Arthur-Lévy in his *Napoléon Intime*, he was 'le bourgeois Prud'homme pour la compagne de ses jours' (the ideal middle-class husband for his life's companion).[22] He was devoted to his brothers, to his parents, and to his country. He managed his own affairs with prudence and sobriety. His concern was for the order without which a prosperous business cannot function. He had – according to Arthur-Lévy – no hankering after aristocratic glamour. He perfectly represented the class which the Revolution set out to advantage.

46   *French Caesarism*

None of this is very convincing. Although his normal wear was the uniform of a guards regiment, Napoleon adored dressing up in aristocratic garments. The whole symbolism of the Empire was based on Roman models. In no way did it foreshadow the drabness of nineteenth-century middle-class clothing. The *Légion d'Honneur* was originally an attempt to create a new nobility, not to provide civil servants and businessmen with the opportunity to wear a little rosette in their button-holes. It was only in response to objections from his republican supporters that in 1804 Napoleon made it simply a system of decorations. But in 1808 he did eventually create an Imperial nobility, and there were finally 31 Dukes, 500 Counts and 1,500 Barons. This officially replaced the old aristocracy, at least until the return of the Bourbons in 1815, and the First Empire sometimes resembles the Capetian monarchy in its desire to impose an entirely new political structure on France. But whatever Napoleon's own ideal self-image might have been, that of Hugues Capet, a new Charlemagne or a modern Augustus, the system he established reinforced a different tendency, and one that already existed in the society of the *ancien régime*. From the seventeenth century onwards, French society had tended to be dominated by lawyers and administrators. The care taken both in the *Concordat* and in the *Code Napoléon* to make sure that the lands taken from the Church and *émigré* aristocracy remained with their present owners meant that this administrative class acquired more independent property and succeeded in its long-term aim of ousting the old aristocracy. But it was not a particularly entrepreneurial class, and the slowness with which France began the industrial revolution reflects the traditional caution of middle-class landowners and lawyers. By another paradox, it needed the push towards state capitalism by Napoleon III and the Second Empire for France to follow the example of Germany and Great Britain in becoming an industrialised country.

In this respect, Napoleon I's domestic policy also anticipated one of the weaknesses shown by twentieth-century states other than France in which the military have taken over. Such states do not often show rapid economic growth. By putting the middle class firmly into power in France, Napoleon ensured that France remained, throughout the nineteenth century, one of the most socially stable countries. Politically, there were changes, often quite violent ones. But the same class remained in power, put there by the first soldier to take hold of a society at a moment of crisis and possible disintegration and compel it to take a form which seems, in retrospect, to have been

Napoleon I: The Unifier 47

inevitable. It is hard even nowadays to think of France without the Napoleonic Code, the centralisation, the cult of military glory, the formal egalitarianism and the continued rule of the middle class. Neither is it easy to avoid thinking of it as a country which turns to a soldier to solve its political problems because the civilian politicians can no longer manage; and in which the soldier, having successfully reorganised the domestic front, loses power because he has been defeated in battle.

2 Napoleon III: The Imitator

I

In many ways, Napoleon III is the odd man out among the four French Caesars who actually managed to take power. He was not a professional soldier. He liked the English. There is no doubt about the illegality of the coup d'état whereby he broke his oath of allegiance to the Second Republic on 2 December 1851 and thus laid the foundations of the Second Empire. He also remained in power for 22 years – a very long reign compared to his uncle's 15, Pétain's four, and the 11 years which elapsed between Charles de Gaulle's return to power in May 1958 and his resignation in April 1969.

For it could be argued that all the political rules had been so thoroughly broken in France by 1799 that Napoleon's *coup d'état du 18 Brumaire* was simply par for the course. Pétain was voted into power on 10 July 1940 by the enormous majority of 569 to 80, and all kinds of legal fictions have been put forward to present the establishment of the Fifth Republic by Charles de Gaulle in 1958 as a perfectly legitimate exercise. He was invited to form a government by President Coty, and insisted in his statement of 27 May that he had 'set in motion the normal procedure' (*entamé le processus régulier*) to do so. Only in the case of Napoleon III was there a violation of the Constitution which was so flagrant that no number of coats of whitewash could present it as anything but an act of usurpation.

The stumbling block to any legal attempt on Louis Napoleon's part to become permanent ruler of France was Article 45 of the Constitution of the Second Republic. This stated that the President should be elected for a four-year period, but was not re-eligible until after another four-year period had elapsed. It was a sensible precaution to take in the light of what had happened in 1802 and 1804, and Jules Grévy, who was to become one of the leading politicians under the Third Republic, argued strongly in favour of there being a 'Président du Conseil des Ministres' (Chairman of the Council of Ministers), elected by the National Assembly. This was the procedure adopted in the Third and Fourth Republics, and it had the mixed advantage of ensuring a weak executive. But the poet Lamartine, inspired by a

Napoleon III: The Imitator 49

typically nineteenth-century faith in the wisdom of the people, maintained that it would never be possible to make the whole of the electorate vote for a usurper, and argued in favour of the election of the President by direct suffrage. He also, somewhat surprisingly in the light of the actual election results, hoped to be elected President himself.

In fact, Lamartine scored just under 8,000 in the Presidential election of 10 December 1848. Louis Napoleon himself was the clear winner, with almost five-and-a-half million. His nearest rival, General Cavaignac, a military man with a considerable reputation for maintaining law and order, obtained 1,400,000. It was a tribute to the way Cavaignac had put the working class in their place in June 1848, while at the same time an indication of the stronger preference which the vast majority of French voters still had for the man who incarnated the Napoleonic legend. For the Second Republic had begun in a mood of even greater left-wing optimism than the First. Under pressure from the socialist elements which had, in February 1848, combined with the more moderate republicans to overthrow the July Monarchy, it proclaimed the duty of the government to provide work 'for all citizens'. But although it tried to fulfil this aim by setting up National Workshops (*ateliers nationaux*) in Paris, it rapidly discovered that these filled no useful purpose. Once they had replaced the paving stones torn up to make barricades at the time of the February revolution, and levelled the small hill on what is now the Boulevard Montparnasse, there was nothing further for the people employed by the *ateliers nationaux* to do. But they still had to be paid and the drain on the state's resources grew so great that on 22 June the government decided to close the workshops down. Any worker who had not already lived for six months in Paris was sent home. Those who remained in Paris were required either to take any work offered by private industry; or to join the army; or to go and work on the construction of the railway line between Paris and Lyons. When they rebelled, General Cavaignac was given the task of restoring order. He did so with vigour, using regular troops to reinforce the National Guard. The casualties ran into thousands. There were also 11,000 prisoners, of whom 4,000 were despatched to Algeria. Order reigned, but Cavaignac was still not elected. In an age of semi-illiteracy, you needed a name that everybody knew. 'Poléon' was the version most commonly recognised in the French countryside. The popularity of Bonapartism in the French provinces is, in this respect, an indication of ordinary, as well as political, illiteracy.

50 *French Caesarism*

It is easy to imagine a formalised system of family relationships which would make Louis Napoleon something more than simply the nephew of Napoleon I. For in addition to having Napoleon I's younger brother Louis as father, Louis Napoleon had as his mother Hortense de Beauharnais, the daughter whom Joséphine de Beauharnais, the great love of Napoleon's life, had had by her first husband. But in spite of the closeness of these biological and semi-adoptive links, Louis Napoleon had, in 1848, reached the age of 40 without any great achievement to his credit. In 1836, he had tried to organise an uprising in Strasbourg. In spite of the fact that he had brought with him a specially trained Swiss vulture to represent the Napoleonic eagle, this had failed. He had subsequently sought refuge in Switzerland, where he became an artillery officer in the federal army. Like his later service in 1848 in London as a special constable at the time of the anticipated Chartist uprising, it was not an outstanding military achievement, and he was not much better as a conspirator. In 1840 he organised another attempt at an uprising, this time at Boulogne; and again failed. He was imprisoned at the fortress of Ham, where he wrote his second book, *L'Extinction du Paupérisme*. This was published in 1844 and paralleled *Les Idées Napoléoniennes*, of 1839, in arguing in favour of more state intervention in the economy. Together, both books gave rise to the later description of Napoleon III by Sainte-Beuve as 'Saint-Simon on horseback'.[1] For Louis Napoleon was a very nineteenth-century man in his faith in the ability of science to solve society's problems, and shared with the followers of Saint-Simon the belief that the state should play a decisive and interventionist role in the running of the economy. When he eventually transformed the Second Republic into the Second Empire, in December 1852, he was able to put this belief into practice. Charles de Gaulle was to do much the same over a hundred years later. From 1959 onwards, 25 *Commissions de Modernisation* which made up the central *Conseil Economique et Social* made detailed plans for every section of the economy. It was a continuation, made more efficient by the greater authority at the disposal of the government of the Fifth Republic, of the economic planning introduced by Jean Monnet at the beginning of the Fourth in 1946.

Once he had been elected President on 10 December 1848, Louis Napoleon knew that he had only four years in office. He also knew that the Legislative Assembly, whose 755 members had been elected for a three-year period of office in May 1849, contained a majority of monarchists, so that there was something of a problem in obtaining

Napoleon III: The Imitator 51

the three-quarters majority needed to have the Constitution revised. He tried in July 1851 but secured a majority of only 446 to 278. The monarchists were hoping to bring back either the Duc de Chambord, the grandson of Charles X, or the Comte de Paris, the grandson of Louis-Philippe, to the throne, and were reluctant to commit themselves to a man whose ambitions went precisely in the opposite direction. He also failed in November 1851 by seven votes in having the law of 31 May 1849 changed so as to reintroduce a genuine version of universal suffrage. For this law, introduced as a result of the fear which the middle class had of a revival of the socialist agitation put down at the time of the June Days of 1848, had reduced the number of those eligible to vote from 9,600,000 to 6,800,000. It had achieved this by insisting on a residence qualification of three years, thus eliminating at a stroke the large number of agricultural and industrial workers who changed jobs with some frequency. Part of Napoleon III's populist appeal lay in his coupling of his own desire to change the President's term of office to the proposal to give the vote back to all men over the age of 25. He also adopted the more straightforwardly authoritarian practice of having himself followed around in the street by groups of tough men with walking sticks, who were caricatured by Daumier under the names of Ratapoil and Cazmajou. Realising how dependent he was going to be on the army, he carefully planned the removal of its commander-in-chief.

The French army, as a political force, has tended except for one or two occasions – as in the Algerian war of 1954–1962 – to try to keep out of politics.[2] The rule for serving officers in the nineteenth century was to do what the War Minister told them, and one of Napoleon III's crucial decisions was to appoint to this office, in November 1851, an obscure Brigadier-General called Saint-Arnaud. He was told about what Napoleon III rather appropriately called 'l'opération Rubicon', and rewarded for his help by a 'Bâton de Maréchal'. As part of his preparation for the *coup d'état du 2 décembre*, Napoleon also dismissed General Changarnier, whose earlier reproof to certain cavalry squadrons for expressing political support for the future Emperor had shown him to be on the side of the National Assembly. Changarnier was replaced by General Magnan, who had earlier served in Algeria and taken part in 1848 in the repression of a workers' uprising in Lyons which paralleled the Paris 'June Days' of 1848. He too received a Marshal's baton for his pains, as well as the Grand-Croix de la Légion d'Honneur. Napoleon III, in formal honours at any rate, paid cash. But one of the reasons for which he

52 *French Caesarism*

was keen to make sure that he did not have to leave office on 2 May 1852, the date at which he was due to cease being President of the Republic, was that he owed a great deal of money. He was heavily in debt, his creditors were pressing him, and the £320,000 said to have been given to him by his English mistress, Elizabeth Howard, was exhausted. Not even his annual salary of 1,200,000 francs, supplemented by a lump sum of 2,168,000 granted to him in May 1849, seemed able to make much of a hole in the millions which he owed. Like his uncle, who became fabulously rich in his own right as a result of his conquests, and like Philippe Pétain, whose financial situation improved quite dramatically when he became Head of State in 1940, Napoleon III was in politics at least partly for the money he could get out of it. Only de Gaulle, as will be seen in Chapter 4, died – as he had lived – a relatively poor man.[3]

In a modern coup d'état, the first aim is to seize the radio and television station. This prevents any opponents or rivals from advertising their existence or trying to obtain support. In 1851, it was essential for Napoleon III to make sure that he printed his own account of what had just happened, and of what was going to happen now. At the same time as a magnificent ball was being given at the Elysée palace, on the evening of 1 December, he was making sure that a special team of compositors was setting up his declaration, a document which had a direct and almost majestic simplicity to it.

Au nom du Peuple Français
Le Président de la République
Décrète

Article 1^e
L'Assemblée Nationale est dissoute

Article 2^e
Le Suffrage universel est rétabli. La loi du 31 mai est abrogée

Article 3^e
Le Peuple français est convoqué dans ses comices (electoral districts) à partir du 14 décembre jusqu'au 21 décembre suivant

Article 4^e
L'état de siège est décreté dans l'étendue de la 1e division militaire
(= Paris)

Article 5^e
Le Conseil d'Etat est dissous (the Council of State is dissolved)

Napoleon III: The Imitator

Article 6^e

Le Ministre de l'Intérieur est chargé de l'exécution du présent décret

When Parisians awoke on the morning of 2 December, they found the city occupied by troops and the declaration pasted up on every public building. There were brief attempts at resistance, during one of which the *député* Baudin responded to the challenge that the elected representatives of the people were not doing much to defend freedom by declaring: 'You are about to see how people die for 25 francs a day.' He mounted on the barricade and was immediately shot. Napoleon III's half-brother, the Duc de Morny, put down an attempt at armed resistance which took place on 4 December, one which caused 300 civilian casualties. There were also, surprisingly in the light of their subsequent reputation for conservatism, a number of uprisings in the provinces in support of the republic, and the *coup d'état du 2 décembre* turned out to be the most expensive in terms of human lives of all the acts of usurpation in favour of a military-style, right-wing ruler in France.

It was also followed by a fairly rigorous period of repression, in which there were about 30,000 arrests. Over 9,000 people were sent to Algeria, some 3,000 interned in France, others sent to French Guiana. Victor Hugo chose somewhat ostentatious exile in the Channel Islands, where he proceeded to denounce the man he called 'Napoléon le Petit'. In 1853 he wrote *Les Châtiments*, some of the best and most aggressive political poetry in French. Like his uncle, Napoleon III had little difficulty in obtaining massive popular support for his take-over. In a plebiscite held on 20 December 1851, 7,499,916 voted 'Yes' as against 646,737 'No', albeit in a contest in which electors openly announced which way they were voting. A million and a half of those entitled to vote abstained. Universal male suffrage had been restored for the occasion, and remained the rule for the whole of the Second Empire – as indeed for all future French elections, until General de Gaulle also gave women the vote in 1944. The transformation of the Second Republic into the Second Empire received comparably impressive support a year later: 7,839,532 votes for, 253,145 against, though with 2,062,798 abstentions. The Second Empire resembles the First very much by being essentially a plebiscitary democracy.

General elections were nevertheless also held, on a five-yearly basis, though with fairly vigorous support from the local *préfet* in

54 *French Caesarism*

favour of the official candidates. There was an official opposition, and from 1867 onwards it had the right to question the government on matters of specific policy. A step had already been taken towards a more liberal régime in social and economic matters by the relaxation in 1864 of the *loi le Chapelier*, forbidding workers to form trade unions. In 1868, the press was made answerable to the courts and not to the administrative authority vested in the *préfet*. In 1869, the Legislative Assembly acquired some degree of budgetary control, and had it not been for the disastrous defeat of France by Prussia in 1870, Napoleon III's régime could quite easily have moved into something very like the Third Republic. Napoleon III had an heir, Eugène Louis, born in 1856, who could well have become a fairly orthodox constitutional monarch. The success with which the Fifth Republic survived and prospered both before and after the resignation of de Gaulle in 1969 shows that it is possible for what was accused initially of being a Caesarian régime to become a much more conventional form of parliamentary democracy. If the Second Empire did not do so, it was because of Napoleon III's unfortunate insistence on trying to follow his uncle's example in foreign policy.

Initially, he was not wholly unsuccessful, albeit in a contest where there was little competition for prizes in military efficiency. In 1854 and 1855, French troops fought alongside British soldiers in the Crimean War. The fact that the treaty putting an end to this conflict was signed in 1856 in Paris marked the return of the French capital as the diplomatic centre of Europe, and was a sign that France was now fully forgiven for the excesses of the Revolution of 1789 and the horrors of the Napoleonic invasions. Theoretically at least, the French and English had won, and done so against a country widely seen as incarnating all the worst features of political tyranny and repression. In foreign policy, Napoleon III was very much a progressive in the terms of the mid-nineteenth century, and his support for the cause of Italian unification might have succeeded in placing him quite firmly on the side of the angels if he had not been led into quite so unfortunate a set of contradictions. For in 1849, French troops had been sent to Rome to help 'safeguard the liberal institutions' established by the revolution in February 1849. They nevertheless soon found themselves protecting the very reactionary-minded Pope Pius IX and ensuring that he retained his temporal power. It was an uncomfortable situation, and one which continued for a short time even after the fall of the Second Empire in 1870. It prevented Napoleon III from receiving the credit due to him for supporting the

Napoleon III: The Imitator

cause of Italian unification, a support which had led, in the battle of Solferino against the Austrians in 1859, to one of the few military engagements in which French troops were even moderately successful under the Second Empire. But Napoleon III, fairly characteristically, had also been unable to push home the advantage obtained by the defeat of the Austrian troops at Solferino. He got the price he asked for, in the shape of Nice and Savoy. But he thereby even further alienated the Italian nationalists whose cause he supported; and left potential allies such as England with the strong impression that he was pursuing a policy of self-interested expansionism. At a time when Bismarck's Prussia was doing this with so much more efficiency, it was an unfortunate by-product of what was in fact a fairly genuine attempt to serve the nineteenth-century idea of nationalism.

Napoleon III's Italian policy was nevertheless the height of success compared to what one of his chief ministers, Eugène Rouher, described as 'la grande pensée du régime': the attempt to counterbalance, by the creation in Mexico of a Latin or Catholic Empire, the influence in the North American continent of the growing power of the Protestant and English-speaking United States. It was a tragic anticipation of the slightly comic attempts made in 1964 by de Gaulle to increase French influence in Central and Southern America by an exhausting series of state visits, and marked the beginning of the decline of the Second Empire. De Gaulle's idea, carried to an even more curious conclusion in his visit to Quebec in July 1967, was to attack 'les Anglo-Saxons' – and more specifically the Americans – on what he was sorry to have to think of as their home ground. Rather than see themselves as obliged constantly to turn to America if they needed help from an economically more developed culture, countries such as Argentina, Bolivia, Brazil, Chile, Colombia and Paraguay should, in de Gaulle's vision of geopolitics, be encouraged to think of France as their first and most important foreign friend. It was not an outstandingly practical notion, except for French intellectuals anxious to benefit from the money suddenly made available for lecture tours in these exotic lands, but at least it did not cost anybody their life. Napoleon III's Mexican expedition, in contrast, caused what was by the standards of the time a fairly large number of casualties. It confirmed the tendency, dramatically inaugurated and abundantly illustrated by Napoleon I, for French Caesarist régimes to sacrifice by pointless foreign adventures the undoubted advantages acquired and bestowed by their domestic policies. Indeed, the impression often

56 *French Caesarism*

given by French nineteenth-century history, from Napoleon I onwards, is that there are some countries which would be better off if they could avoid having a foreign policy at all.

The immediate pretext for the French expedition to Mexico in 1861 was the money owed to England, France and Spain by the anti-clerical and liberal politician Benito Juarez. He had taken power in 1858, and decided to suspend the payment of all foreign debts. This refusal was of especial concern to the Duc de Morny, who was a close friend of the Swiss financier Jean-Baptiste Jecker. Jecker had taken out French citizenship in order to facilitate the reclaiming of the money owed to him by Juarez. There was consequently some rational, even though slightly sordid, reason for Napoleon III to follow his uncle's example in making sure that the foreign policy of France put money in the pockets both of his relatives and of his relatives' friends. The English and Spanish achieved their financial aims fairly quickly. Their fleets joined with the French in December 1861 in bombarding the port of Veracruz, and in February 1862 Juarez agreed to pay the money owing to their bankers. The French, however, were less easily satisfied. In 1845, at the request of Nicaragua, Louis Napoleon had worked out a rough draft for what was eventually to become the Panama Canal, and the opportunity of intervening further in this part of the world was too strong to be resisted. An expeditionary force of 6,000 men joined the French fleet under the command of Admiral Jurien de la Gravière,[4] and began what it was hoped would be a new conquest of Mexico.

In spite of some determined resistance by Juarez's guerrilla forces, and the even more devastating effects on European stomachs of the *vomito negro*, or Montezuma's revenge, French troops under the command of General Forey eventually took Mexico City in June 1863. But Forey was then replaced by Marshal Achille Bazaine, a man whose subsequent career may well have inspired the authors of the *Encyclopaedia Britannica* in their decision to analyse intelligence under the three discrete categories of animal, human and military. Like a number of other ambitious French officers, Bazaine had begun his career in Algeria, where he had won promotion in 1850 to the rank of colonel. He had married an Algerian wife, but she later committed suicide. Shortly after his arrival in Mexico, he fell in love with a young Mexican woman who urged him to intrigue against Maximilian of Austria, whom Napoleon III was trying to place upon the Mexican throne as a replacement for Juarez. Maximilian's reason for wishing to accept this offer was understandable. His brother

Napoleon III: The Imitator

Franz Joseph allowed him no part in the running of Austria, and Mexico appeared at first to be an acceptable alternative. Napoleon III chose to support Maximilian partly because his Empress, Eugénie de Montijo, wanted him to do so. She thought it was France's duty to spread European civilisation and culture to the New World, and shared the Emperor's erroneous view that since the Mexicans were Catholic, they would therefore also be monarchists.

In spite of the fact that the Mexicans themselves had not been consulted, Maximilian was quite happy to see himself as their king. He had accepted the Crown on April 1864, but had reckoned without the resistance of the Mexicans and the vagaries of French policy. The divisions between Bazaine and the Emperor led to a series of military defeats and Napoleon III was also faced with an increasingly hostile and vigorous United States. Originally, he had hoped to profit from the divisions and weaknesses brought about from 1861 onwards by the war between North and South. The North's victory in 1865 meant that the United States was able to put pressure on Napoleon III to withdraw his support for Maximilian; and in 1867 he agreed to do so. Bazaine left Mexico on 23 March, and in June 1867 Maximilian was compelled to surrender. In spite of the appeals by Maximilian's wife, Charlotte of Belgium, Napoleon refused to provide any more support. She went mad, and the news of Maximilian's own execution on 13 June 1867 reached Paris just in time to spoil the public relations effect of the great industrial exhibition.

Like his uncle, Napoleon III was more successful in his domestic than in his foreign policy; but here again there were ambiguities and uncertainties which prevented the Second Empire from being much more than an indifferent imitation of the First. The official ideology set out in the *Idées Napoléoniennes* was one of collaboration between the classes, and of a determined attempt to improve the living conditions of the working class. This is clearly in contradiction with what a Marxist would think of as the 'objective reality' of the régime, and figures can be quoted on either side. Those favourable to Napoleon III observe that the standard of living of the working class did improve as the Empire established itself, especially after the 1860 Free Trade treaty with England. But if it did so, the advantage still lay with the shareholders rather than with the workers themselves. Taking 1850 as a base-line of 100, profits had increased by 1870 to 386. Wages, in contrast, had risen to only 128. Differences in income remained quite extraordinary by modern standards. A railway worker earned 1,000 francs a year for a 12-hour day, and an

58 *French Caesarism*

elementary schoolteacher less than 800. The official salary of a *Conseiller d'Etat*, in contrast, was 25,000 francs a year, and that of a Senator 30,000. In the private sector, differences were even greater. The owner of the Schneider steel mills received 1,500,000 francs a year. The régime which began with what Zola called 'le guet-apens du 2 décembre' (the ambush of 2 December) and 'ended with the disaster of Sedan' remains to this day the one most vulnerable to a Marxist analysis.[5]

Indeed, Marx himself made one of his major contributions to historiography in his *Le 18 Brumaire de Louis Napoléon*, on 1852, analysing Napoleon's career in class terms and observing that *The Economist* itself had pointed out on 29 November 1851 that 'in all the Stock Exchanges in Europe, the President is recognised as the sentry of order'.[6] The view that Louis Napoleon's coup d'état was inspired by the desire to protect and favour the middle class in its struggle to keep down the new urban proletariat is also eloquently expressed by the progressively-minded contemporary French Catholic historian, Louis Guillemin. He quotes Louis Veuillot, a highly reactionary nineteenth-century Catholic writer, as saying that 'faced with the brutal and barbarous passions which once again threaten Christ's empire, the priest and soldier will join hands',[7] and it was at the time of Napoleon III that the French first began to use the phrase 'le sabre et le goupillon' (the sword and the censer) to talk about the natural alliance between Army and Church as the combination of the two forces most hostile to social progress. Napoleon III also won popularity with the Catholics in France itself by the support which he gave to the *loi Falloux* of March 1850. This broke the older Napoleonic idea of *L'Université Impériale*, or the state monopoly on education, and allowed the Church to open secondary schools. The state was not yet the sole examining authority and did not acquire 'le monopole des diplômes' until 1879. The position of the Church was thus considerably strengthened, since members of religious orders needed no further qualification to open a school. By 1870, there were almost as many pupils in Catholic secondary schools as there were in the state *lycées*, and the Church was the principal provider of primary education throughout the whole country. In French internal politics, the *loi Falloux* marks the beginning of a major difference between the ideology of the French right and the more left-wing, secular tradition in education later to be established by the Third Republic in 1881. It was not long after the setting up of the Fifth Republic that its first Prime Minister, Michel Debré, introduced in 1959 a law increasing

Napoleon III: The Imitator

state subsidies to the predominantly Catholic private schools; and there is an interesting anecdotal similarity between him and the Comte de Falloux: neither of them saw quite eye to eye with the Caesar of their time on a major issue of national policy. Falloux was a legitimist, anxious to bring about a return of the monarchy by a reconciliation between his preferred candidate for the throne of France, the Comte de Chambord, and Chambord's Orleanist rival, the Comte de Paris. He was consequently not an enthusiastic supporter of Napoleon III, especially after the Comte de Chambord had launched a manifesto, in 1853, urging the French not to confuse the genuine political stability offered by the monarchy with the apparent security associated with Caesarism, and its marked tendency towards adventurism. Although Michel Debré was one of those who worked most enthusiastically in the mid 1950s for a return to power of Charles de Gaulle, and became the first Prime Minister of the Fifth Republic, he was very much an *Algérie Française* man. He consequently had to accept, in the first four years of the Fifth Republic, a slow crucifixion which culminated in his removal from office by de Gaulle once the 1962 Evian agreement which gave Algeria its independence had been signed.

The alliance between the Army and the Church is indeed one of the major features of the Second Empire which makes it vulnerable to a Marxist analysis. So, too, was Napoleon III's habit of reviving his uncle's links with the major financial institutions of capitalism. Once he had violated the constitution and carried out the coup d'état of 2 December 1851, he gave every encouragement to the Péreire brothers, from the house of Rothschild, to set up their own bank, the *Crédit Mobilier*. This was one of the principal instruments of economic expansion in the Second Empire, and was closely linked with the most important economic development of the period, the construction of the French railway network. This grew from 1,931 kilometres in 1848 to 18,000 in 1870, at the same time as the number of telegraph stations rose from 17 in 1850 to 1,500 in 1870. The Duc de Morny launched what reads in late twentieth-century Britain like a very contemporary appeal to businessmen to take part in politics, and another of the major achievements of the Second Empire, the rebuilding of Paris under the direction of Baron Haussmann, also had marked political overtones. The rebellion of February 1848, which overthrew the July Monarchy, was the last occasion when a French régime collapsed as a result of internal pressure. The Second Empire itself fell because of the defeat of France by the Prussians, the Third

60 *French Caesarism*

Republic because of the defeat of 1940, and the Fourth because of an uprising in Algeria. The wide avenues and extensive boulevards of the new Paris made the erection of effective barricades virtually impossible. Proof was provided of this in the repression of the *Commune*, the uprising which followed the humiliating peace treaty which ended the Franco-Prussian war in 1871. The French government troops, watched by the Prussian soldiers who were still occupying France, had little difficulty in clearing the centre of the city. They encountered real opposition only in the older, working-class areas, which had been less effectively urbanised. In 1934, at the time of the anti-parliamentary riots sparked off by the Stavisky affair, as in the student riots of 1968, the government was able to remain in physical control of the capital. In a Paris which had retained the narrow streets swept away by the Haussmann rebuilding programme, this might have been a good deal more difficult.

The immediate cause of the war which brought down the Second Empire was the episode known as the Ems telegram, a document which Bismarck doctored in such a way as to make it appear as though the French Ambassador had been deliberately insulted by the King of Prussia. For the initial ambition of the French to prevent the unification under the same Crown of the Kingdoms of Prussia and Spain had already been granted by the withdrawal of the candidature of Leopold of Hohenzollern to the Spanish throne. But the nineteenth century was above all else the time of nationalism in Europe, and the French National Assembly was eager for a more startling triumph over Prussia. Napoleon III's earlier failure to intervene in 1866 in order to prevent Prussia from defeating Austria in the Seven Weeks' War had left a clear sense of national humiliation. The old fear of encirclement, going right back to the sixteenth century when Charles V combined the office of Holy Roman Emperor with that of King of Spain, inspired the French with an excessive ambition to make the Prussians do what they wanted them to do. They thus played straight into Bismarck's hands, and he was able so to insult the French as to make them declare war and thus present himself as the innocent party. When Albert Ollivier, the Prime Minister at the time of the declaration of war in July 1870, greeted the prospect of conflict 'd'un cœur léger' (with a light heart), he was showing that neither French Caesars nor French generals are the only people who can act foolishly.

Like the Mexican expedition of the 1860s, the Franco-Prussian war of 1870 was indeed an extraordinary display of political and military

Napoleon III: The Imitator 61

incompetence. To start with, Napoleon III had ensured that France would have no allies. By using French troops to delay the absorption of the Papal States into Italy, he had alienated the Italian government, which might perhaps otherwise have been expected to show some gratitude for his help in defeating the Austrians at Solferino and bringing about Italian reunification. He had forfeited any support which he might have received from Great Britain. In 1866, a certain amount of diplomatic manœuvering had accompanied the Seven Weeks' War in which Prussia won such a dramatic victoiy over Austria at Sadowa-on 3 July 1866. In the course of these manœuvres, Napoleon III had suggested to Bismarck the reward he expected for France's neutrality: the annexation of Luxembourg and the eventual handing over to France of the Belgium whose existence had been guaranteed by England in 1830. Bismarck had kept secret the document putting forward the proposal. He now communicated it to the British government. After its publication, Gladstone wrote to Queen Victoria: 'Your Majesty will, in common with the world, have been shocked and startled by it.'[8] French military preparations had been equally ineffective. In spite of Maréchal Lebœuf's assurance that the French troops were ready 'to the last button of their gaiters', soldiers turned up at their barracks to find no equipment waiting for them; while elsewhere, uniforms and rifles remained unclaimed until it was too late. Napoleon III himself had some very sensible ideas about weaponry. He had encouraged the adoption of the accurate, breech-loading, Chassepot rifle, and had written a manual about the use of artillery. But there were not enough modern rifles to go round, and the French high command had failed to appreciate the new potentialities of accurate artillery fire. At the same time, the generals in charge of the campaign were so confident of victory that the maps they issued gave details only of German territory.

The result was a foregone conclusion, and a remarkable anticipation of the defcat of 1940. The Prussian high command, inspired by the genius of Moltke, fought a war of rapid movement which kept the French continually off balance. The Prussians mobilised over a million men, and used the new railway system to bring them rapidly to the front line. The French, in contrast, were able to put only 400,000 men into the field; and tried to move them by forced marches. The French railway system, by which all lines led to Paris, was an adequate means for moving men west to east. It was less effective for moving them along the front from north to south, even if the French high command had had anything so sophisticated in mind.

62   *French Caesarism*

Zola's account in *La Débâcle* of what it was like to serve in so ill-commanded a force remains a very accurate one, and Napoleon III, who finally assumed responsibility for taking command of his army in the field, had an additional problem of a kind which his uncle had never had to face. The Empress Eugénie, who had already encouraged him to undertake the disastrous Mexican expedition, kept telling both him and his generals what to do in the field of battle. It is hard to imagine Joséphine de Beauharnais or Marie-Louise of Austria giving military or any other advice to Napoleon I. When General Mac-Mahon expressed the desire to withdraw from Châlons to place himself in a position from which he would be better able to defend Paris, she insisted that he move forward along the Vallée de la Meuse. Instead of enabling him to reach Metz, where Bazaine had already allowed himself to be surrounded with an army of 180,000 men, this move led him to be surrounded at Sedan. There, together with the Emperor, he was unable to move out of the range of the terrifying bombardment of the Prussian artillery. On 1 September, he was wounded and taken prisoner. On the same day, Napoleon III wrote a dignified letter of surrender to William I of Prussia.

Monsieur mon frère,
    N'ayant pas pu mourir au milieu de mes troupes, il ne me reste qu'à remettre mon épée entre les mains de Votre Majesté.
    Je suis, de votre Majesté, le bon frère

                                Napoléon.

On 3 September Comte Palikao announced to the National Assembly that the Emperor had surrendered. On 4 September the now traditional site of the Hôtel de Ville saw the proclamation of the Republic. Initially, this tried to follow the heroic example of the First Republic, which had defeated the Austrian and Prussian armies at Valmy on 20 September 1792, in a battle described by Goethe as beginning a new period in the history of the world. But on 27 October 1870 Bazaine surrendered to the Prussians, handing over to them not only 180,000 prisoners of war but also 1,500 cannon in full working order. Moltke was thus free to use his whole army to besiege Paris. During the Second Empire, the forts and boulevards protecting the city had been extended to the point where military and civilian authorities, Adolphe Thiers included, thought that Paris would be

Napoleon III: The Imitator 63

virtually impregnable. But like the preparations for the Franco-Prussian war itself, this calculation took no account of recent developments in the range and accuracy of heavy artillery. The steady Prussian bombardment of the city, coupled with a food shortage which led the price of a rat to rise to twice the daily living allowance of a member of the National Guard, placed the defenders in an increasingly impossible position. On 28 January 1871, the French government signed an armistice with the Prussians. This was eventually transformed into a peace treaty which required the French to hand Alsace and Lorraine over to Prussia. The French also had to pay an indemnity of 400 million francs – in gold – before the Prussians would agree to withdraw their armies from French territory. Originally, this had been 500 million, but Adolphe Thiers had obtained a reduction in return for the right of the Prussian armies to enjoy a triumphant parade down the Champs Elysées. The resentment felt by Parisians when they learnt of this clause was one of the contributory causes of the *Commune* of 1871. Marshal Bazaine, who had continued to add to French problems by refusing to join the French government at Versailles and by trying instead to negotiate secretly with the Prussians, was eventually arrested and court-martialled. The death sentence was commuted to one of twenty years' imprisonment, but he escaped and ended his days in Spain.

The Second Empire, like the first, thus fell as a result of a military defeat. For a Frenchman anxious to end a war on the winning side, it is clearly not a good idea to allow either a genuine military man like Napoleon I or a uniform-loving civilian like his nephew to take over the government. Indeed, if one's long-term objective is to pursue what used to be the central aim of French policy and weaken Germany, it is a much better idea to follow the example of Louis XIII and entrust the conduct of foreign affairs to a clergyman. Cardinal Richelieu's policy of prolonging the Thirty Years' War by encouraging both Gustavus Adolphus of Sweden and the German Protestant princes in their fight against the House of Hapsburg was certainly one of the most cynical pieces of *realpolitik* ever to be pursued, even by a European statesman. It also contributed to one of the major demographic and cultural disasters in European history, the reduction between 1618 and 1648 of the population of Germany by roughly one-third. But at least it ensured that for well over a century after the Cardinal's death France would be faced with no serious military threat on her eastern frontier. The final outcome of the foreign policy pursued by both Napoleons was very different. By abolishing the

64 *French Caesarism*

Holy Roman Empire, and replacing it in 1806 by the Confederation of the Rhine, Napoleon I set the Germans on the path to unification. Where, before 1806, there had been 234 separate territories, there were then only forty. Between 1806 and 1811 the Confederation grew from 16 to 36 states, extending from Oldenburg in the north to Bavaria and the Tyrol in the south. It was placed under Napoleon's protection, and given the beginnings of an internal unity by the introduction of the reforming legislation of the French Revolution. At the same time, Napoleon's policy of perpetual conquest exacerbated the rise of Prussian nationalism. It thus set in motion the process which his nephew was to complete by allowing his country to be defeated by Prussia in 1870. German unification was finally achieved under Prussian leadership, and it was the foreign policy of the two Napoleons which helped to set Europe on the road to the abyss of 1914–1918 and 1939–1945.

Napoleon III thus completed one of the major paradoxes of nineteenth-century French Caesarism by leaving his country in a far worse international position than the one in which he had found it. At the time of his usurpation, in 1851, not even the disasters of the Napoleonic wars had prevented France from remaining the dominant power on the continent of Europe. Germany and Italy had still not been unified, and England was not really interested in what was happening across the Channel. She was still too busy exploiting the mastery of the sea which she had acquired during the Napoleonic wars and as a result of the battle of Trafalgar. One of the most unintended consequences of the policies pursued by Napoleon I had indeed been the opportunity these policies provided for Great Britain to replace the first, American empire lost in 1776 by the new second Empire which gave pride of place to India but which also included the West Indies, South Africa, Australia and New Zealand. Napoleon I's sale of the Louisiana territories to the United States of America had ensured that France would continue to remain excluded from the European empire of the West. The defeat of his nephew marked the beginning of her decline to the status of a power subordinate to Germany on the continent of Europe.

Like his uncle before him, Napoleon III did his best service to France in the field of domestic policy. While less effective and less dramatic than the reorganisation of France under the first Napoleon, the Second Empire of Napoleon III did provide France with the political stability essential for her to continue with the industrial revolution begun under the July monarchy. As the example of

Napoleon III: The Imitator   65

Charles de Gaulle was to show in the twentieth century, the best services rendered to France by her successive Caesars can be found more in the realm of domestic than of foreign affairs. It is perhaps a paradox, in that the association of Caesarism with strength might lead one to expect a successful as well as a dynamic foreign policy. This, certainly, was the contribution which both Julius and Augustus Caesar brought to Rome. A further paradox lies in the fact that the régime which followed the Second Empire, the Third Republic, though governed by civilians, was until its closing years to differ from the Caesarian régimes which had preceded it by being almost equally successful on both the domestic and the foreign fronts. It was, after all, the first régime for over a century to end a war on the winning side. Its victory over Germany in 1918 appeared at the time as convincing as any of Napoleon's more temporary triumphs over the same enemy. It nevertheless had to survive a remarkably large number of crises before it finally disappeared in June 1940. Several of these had Caesarist overtones in the sense that the threat came either directly from a military man or from a right-wing group with semi-military ambitions.

II

Although proclaimed on 4 September 1870, in an upsurge of indignation against the Second Empire set off by news of the French defeat by the Prussians at Sedan, the Third Republic did not officially come into existence until five years later. Even then the decision actually to call the régime a republic was taken by a majority of only one, with the passing of an apparently anodyne amendment presented on 30 January 1875 by a *député* called Henri Wallon. This stated that the President of the Republic was elected by both the *Chambre des Députés* and the Senate, that his period of office was seven years and that he was re-eligible for office.

Such a vote was not a particularly solid basis for a régime. Yet it is a sign of the attachment to parliamentary institutions which was to develop in France in the last quarter of the nineteenth century that the Third Republic weathered so many storms. This attachment was partly the result of a disillusionment with Bonapartism because of the military defeats with which it had now come to be associated; partly a product of the failure of the French monarchist movement to change with the times; and partly a consequence of the fact that the

66　French Caesarism

Republic, as Adolphe Thiers observed, was the régime which divided Frenchmen least. The first President of the Third Republic was nevertheless a military man, Marshal Mac-Mahon, one of the least successful even of the generals commanding the French armies in the Franco-Prussian war. After being surrounded, defeated and made prisoner by the Prussians at the battle of Sedan, he was freed by them in order to take command of the army which the official French government of 1871, then situated at Versailles, was preparing to use in order to repress the *Commune*. This was a predominantly working-class and lower-middle-class rebellion which had taken over in Paris in March 1871, partly in protest against the peace treaty with Prussia, partly for economic reasons, and partly – as was much argued in retrospect by left-wing idealists – to establish an advanced socialist government in France.

The head of the French government, Adolphe Thiers, anxious above all else to defeat the *Commune* and put the French working class back in its place, dismissed Mac-Mahon's justifiable hesitations with the bluff remark that everyone had been defeated at some time or another. Mac-Mahon then proceeded – on the orders of Thiers himself – to play something of the same part in the repression of the *Commune* that Cavaignac had played at the time of the June Days of 1848: 20,000 supposedly rebellious Parisians were summarily executed in the last week of May 1871. No régime dominated by a soldier ever came to power in France with quite so much blood on its hands as the one presided over by the strictly civilian Adolphe Thiers. Mac-Mahon was then elected as first President of the Third Republic, on 24 May 1873, and seen by the royalist-minded politicians who put him there as a stop-gap until the monarchy could be restored.

This proved more difficult than expected. The legitimist pretender, the Comte de Chambord, grandson of Charles X, refused to abandon the traditional white flag of the Bourbon monarchy. This refusal to accept the tricolour of the Revolution was an action which, as Mac-Mahon himself observed, would make the rifles go off by themselves in protest. The monarchists had consequently no choice but to keep Mac-Mahon as a kind of regent, and this arrangement worked quite well until 16 May 1877. Then, however, Mac-Mahon used his official powers as President to dismiss the republican and secular-minded Jules Simon and replace him with the more conservative Duc de Broglie. When de Broglie was then outvoted in the *Chambre des Députés*, Mac-Mahon used another of his constitutional powers. He dissolved the Chamber and caused elections to be fought

Napoleon III: The Imitator

on the issue of whether the President or the Assembly was to have the last word. The elections, held under the same system of *le scrutin uninominal à deux tours* (single member two ballots) later used in the Fifth Republic, produced a parliamentary majority of 321 to 208 against Mac-Mahon's reading of the Constitution. He nevertheless made one further attempt to assert presidential power by appointing as Prime Minister a former comrade-in-arms, General Rochebouët. But what is perhaps the central issue of parliamentary democracy then came to the fore when it became obvious that Rochebouët could govern only if the *députés* were prepared to vote in favour of his budget. When they refused, the monarchists in the Assembly advised Mac-Mahon to carry out a coup d'état. Faithful to his republican principles, he refused to do so, and in 1879 resigned from the Presidency.

He was replaced by a staunchly republican Jules Grévy, and the Presidency of the Third Republic took on its definitive form as an essentially honorific function. As popular wisdom – or perhaps de Gaulle – put it later, the President opened exhibitions of chrysanthemums. The Third Republic had avoided its first risk of a coup d'état partly because Mac-Mahon had no Caesarist ambitions, but also because the situation was not a particularly critical one. The repression of the *Commune* had removed any serious threat from the left, and the majority of voters were clearly in favour of the more moderate form of republicanism which the various administrations serving under Jules Grévy proceeded to introduce. The official designation in February 1879 of 14 July as the National Day and of *La Marseillaise* as the French national anthem; the establishment of a system of free, compulsory, universal and secular education in 1881; the widening of press freedom by the law of 29 July 1881; the greater responsibilities given to elected mayors of large as well as small towns; the amnesty in July 1880 for any surviving Communards still in France; the legalisation of trade unions in 1884, and of divorce in the same year; the preparation of the first major, scholarly editions of the works of Diderot, Rousseau and Voltaire, all marked a move towards what was then the political and intellectual left in France, and the gradual fading away of the danger of a successful military coup d'état. Late-nineteenth-century France remained a society in which military virtues were highly prized. After 1889, military conscription became genuinely universal, with everyone – priests included – serving for three years. Military training was an integral part of the syllabus for the older pupils in the *lycées*, and there was an obsession with *la*

68 *French Caesarism*

revanche, the next round of the conflict with Prussia, and the opportunity to recover Alsace and Lorraine. But the army itself, 'une des plus grandes choses du monde' when de Gaulle joined it in 1910, became an even more a-political body, referring to itself with some satisfaction as 'la grande muette' (the great but silent service).

This became apparent during the two major crises which threatened the Republic in the late nineteenth century: General Boulanger's attempt to seize power in the late 1880s, and the Dreyfus case of 1894–1906 in which a French officer of Jewish origins – his family had chosen to leave Alsace in 1871 rather than live under German rule – was falsely accused of selling military secrets to the Germans. In both of them, the running was made by civilian politicians rather than military men, with the army in the Dreyfus case being very much on the defensive. General Boulanger's ability to look well on horseback might nevertheless have made him a successful Caesar, especially in the form which the Caesarist phenomenon tended to take in France during the Third and Fourth Republics. For the kind of parliamentary democracy which established itself in France after 1877 was vulnerable to a number of criticisms. Because there was no single dominant party, most governments were made up of coalitions. This meant that they tended not to last very long, since it was enough for one of the parties involved in them to withdraw its support for there to be a ministerial crisis. The instability was more apparent than real. The same politicians tended to recur in only slightly different posts. It was also – as British parliamentary government was on occasion under Lloyd George – not exempt from certain forms of corruption.

Thus in 1887, Grévy's own son-in-law, Daniel Wilson, was involved in a scandal which revealed that decorations such as the *Légion d'Honneur* were being bought and sold. This led to what was later to become the rallying cry of the French right about the corruption inseparable from parliamentary régimes, and from which Boulanger derived a certain amount of his popularity. He was of relatively humble origin and owed his promotion solely to the efficiency he had shown as a serving officer in North Africa, Italy and Indochina. He was also strongly nationalistic, urging a swift response to any German provocation; anti-clerical, in that it was under his period as War Minister that priests were required to join the army ('Les curés, sac au dos'); and aimed his appeal deliberately at the working and lower-middle classes. In this respect, he foreshadowed the way the right was to move in Europe in the late nineteenth and

Napoleon III: The Imitator   69

first part of the twentieth century. Although his actual constitutional proposals were not well defined, he also launched the slogan of 'Dissolution, Constituante, Révision' (Dissolve the present National Assembly, and elect a Constituent Assembly capable of bringing in a new Constitution). In this, indeed, he resembled the two Napoleons, Pétain and de Gaulle, all of whom found it essential to change the system of government which had enabled them to come to power.

Boulanger's tactic for proving his popularity was to stand as candidate in as many by-elections as possible. He succceded in a number of constituencies and on 29 January 1889 was triumphantly elected in Paris, with 245,236 votes against 162,875 cast for the republican candidate Jacques. But Boulanger refused the opportunity which this apparently presented of marching on the presidential residence, and declined the suggestion which the nationalist poet Paul Déroulède claimed to have made to him that he turn up next day at the *Chambre des Députés*. There, Déroulède assured him, he would find a crowd of supporters to help him take over. But Boulanger again refused, arguing that all he needed to do was wait. It was, he argued, a failure to do this which had led Napoleon III to shed blood by his coup d'état. But he was proved wrong. There was no mass movement in support of him, and the government used purely legal means to prevent him reviving his campaign. It dissolved Déroulède's *Ligue des Patriotes*; and cut the ground away from under Boulanger's feet by changing the electoral law. It re-introduced *le scrutin uninominal d'arrondissement* (single member constituency voting); and forbade the same candidate from standing in more than one by-election at a time. Boulanger himself was threatened with arrest, and fled to Belgium. He was sentenced in his absence to life imprisonment, and spent some time in England. He then came back to Brussels and shot himself on the grave of his mistress, Marguerite de Bonnemain. An indication of his relative lack of the genuine thirst for power which characterises the successful Caesar can perhaps be found in the fact that he had earlier chosen to enjoy her favours on the very night of his election victory of 29 January.

It is again significant, in the light of the difficulty which Napoleon III had earlier experienced in finding a general to help him seize power, that Boulanger received no support from the French high command. When, in 1851, Changarnier and his brother officers refused to co-operate, Napoleon III had needed to bring the obscure General Magnan in from Algeria in order to carry out his coup d'état. Gabriel Monod may have been right to claim, as he did at the time in

70 *French Caesarism*

an article in *The Contemporary Review*, that the French had no genuine love for democratic government. 'The truth is', he wrote in April 1889,

> that the temperament of the majority of the nation – a temperament at once military and democratic – a levelling but not a liberal spirit – is a Caesarean temperament; and our administrative organisation, centralised to excess, is also favourable to Caesarean government.[9]

The fact nevertheless remains that there was no overwhelming ground swell in favour of so obviously potential a Caesar as Georges Boulanger; and no support for him in the army. French public opinion is normally willing to support the kind of bid for power made by a military man only if there seems no other way of resolving a serious political crisis, and the French army does not have a marked predisposition to interfere in the running of the country. In the one event in the nineteenth century in which it found itself in conflict with the civil powers, the Dreyfus case, it made no attempt to overthrow the government. Indeed, it is tempting rather to see the whole series of events from Dreyfus' arrest on 15 October 1894 right through to his rehabilitation on 22 July 1906 less as the prelude to an attempted military take-over than as a trap deliberately aimed at discrediting the army and showing its total incapacity to rule.

It is true that once the original mistake had been made, and Dreyfus sent to Devil's Island for allegedly having passed military secrets to the Germans, it was difficult for the army to go back. Although few people knew it at the time, the identification of the handwriting on the 'bordereau' (list of information available for sale) was made by only three of the five experts brought in. It was also suspected, and made public at the time of Zola's trial in 1898, that Dreyfus had been found guilty on the basis of documents not revealed to the defence. No group of officers wishing to seize power would behave in a way that made them so vulnerable, and the hostility which undoubtedly existed towards the Republic on the part of certain army officers had the ultimate effect of strengthening rather than weakening the régime. By resisting to the very end the demand that Dreyfus be given a retrial, the army made itself look quite extraordinarily stupid. At the same time, by finally accepting Dreyfus' innocence and organising an official ceremony on 22 July 1906 to re-integrate him into the army, it openly acknowledged the supremacy of civilian authority, and civilian law, over military

Napoleon III: The Imitator 71

jurisdiction. When the Third Republic decorated Dreyfus with the *Légion d'Honneur*, the army promoted him to the rank of major.

Given its traditional alliance with the Church, the behaviour of the French army at the time of the Dreyfus case could nevertheless be held responsible for one of the most important changes in French society, the separation of Church and State in 1905. This measure, accompanied by deliberate attempts to humiliate the Church by making a complete inventory of everything which each parish possessed, was part of the way in which the now victorious Dreyfusards triumphed over their erstwhile opponents. As though to rub in its subordination to the civilian authorities of which many of its officers continued to disapprove, the army was made to provide protection for the civil servants responsible for carrying out the inventories. It also found itself in the position, admittedly a highly illegal and irregular one, of having the suitability of its officers for promotion checked by the Freemasons. The separation of Church and State nevertheless had the effect of making the Church more influential by freeing it from state control. It also made the Republic more powerful than it was before. There was now no officially sponsored body in society to question its authority.

It is again significant that it was a civilian, Paul Déroulède, who tried to use the occasion of President Félix Faure's funeral, on 23 February 1899, in the very midst of the Dreyfus case, to encourage the troops to invade the presidential palace. He failed, as might have been expected, and the principal contribution which the Dreyfus case made to the general phenomenon of French Caesarism is the confirmation which it gave to the division of France into two hostile ideological groups. On the political left, there were the supporters of Dreyfus, who saw themselves as the heirs of the Revolution of 1789. They grouped themselves into the *Ligue des Droits de l'Homme* and were hostile to the army only in so far as they saw it as a force which could be used by other, non-military, clerical or monarchist factions against the Republic. On the right, there were authoritarian or antisemitic bodies such as *La Ligue des Patriotes* and *L'Action Française*, whose desire to overthrow the Republic did not necessarily involve bringing in the army at all. It is only in so far as the ideology developed by the French right also became that of Philippe Pétain that there is any kind of real connection between the Dreyfus case and French Caesarism.

One of the most remarkable features of French life in the late nineteenth and early twentieth century was the unifying effect which

72 French Caesarism

the experience of compulsory military service had on all classes. This reinforced the almost mystical belief which its supporters had in the virtues of the Republic, and accounts for the enthusiasm with which the French reacted to the outbreak of the First World War. The estimates which put the possible number of those refusing to join the colours as high as 10 per cent were proved quite wrong. Less than 1 per cent of those mobilised refused to obey the call, and it was only with the disastrous effects of the Nivelle offensive of 1917 that mutinies broke out in the French army and that Pétain increased his already high reputation by quelling them without excessive bloodshed. The experience of victory in 1918 again reinforced the 'sacred union' between the army and the nation. It was not until the Depression of the 1930s that the Republic was again threatened by right-wing, para-military groups. But it is again significant that none of these received open support from the regular army. *L'Action Française*, the most virulent of movements both in its antisemitism and in its opposition to the Republic, was an almost exclusively civilian organisation. It was only when France had been defeated in 1940 and Pétain brought to power that Charles Maurras, the principal ideologist of *L'Action Française*, was able to welcome the events as a 'divine surprise'.[10]

It was a movement grouping together the ex-servicemen of the First World War – and not one openly supported by serving officers – that made most of the running in the potentially fascist, para-military opposition to the Republic in the 1930s. The movement known as *Les Croix de Feu* was open to all ex-servicemen who had spent at least six months in the front line. It was led by an ex-officer, Colonel de la Rocque, and resembled the Boulangist movement as well as *L'Action Française* by the ferocity with which it denounced the supposed inefficiency and corruption of French parliamentary government. In 1933 the existence of this corruption showed itself in the Stavisky affair, a case in which a professional confidence man had obtained support and protection from certain *députés*. This scandal led in February 1934 to an enormous demonstration in which a right-wing crowd came down the Champs Elysées, filled the Place de la Concorde, and attempted to take the Palais Bourbon, the meeting place of the *Chambre des Députés*, by storm. On the night of 6 February it was prevented from doing so only by the readiness of the police to open fire. At least twenty people were killed, and a large number wounded. But *Les Croix de Feu* remained throughout a civilian affair. Although Weygand was unwise enough to accept the

Napoleon III: The Imitator 73

gift of one of the black berets which formed part of the unofficial uniform worn by members of right-wing leagues, no military man stepped out of line or promised his support. The government, in turn, was able to count sufficiently on the loyalty of the police not to feel obliged to call in the army, and what might in a politically under-developed country have become the prelude to a military dictatorship led in fact to the Popular Front government of 1936.

The Vichy régime is often seen in France itself as a kind of revenge of the French right both for its defeat in the Dreyfus case and for its failure to win power in the 1930s. The first of these episodes, however, was one in which the army was on the defensive, while in the case of Vichy itself it could play no significant part for the simple reason that it had been so heavily defeated. It was not the French army which ruled, in the way that armies rule in so many third world countries, by placing its officers in key positions. It was a single man, drawing his charismatic quality from the fact that he had been a highly successful soldier, but deriving his authority from a vote in a civilian assembly. There were, it is true, five high-ranking army officers in Pétain's cabinet, and Weygand wanted to put a staff officer in each *département* to keep an eye on the civilian administrators. But this proposal came to nothing, as Weygand himself acknowledged, and although Henri du Moulin de Laborthète wrote in his diary that there were 'des feuilles de chêne' (oak-leaves; the badge of rank for Generals) everywhere in Vichy,[11] they were there principally for decoration. The country was still run by civilian technocrats. The importance given to the army, especially in the immediate aftermath of the defeat of 1940, had little to do with internal politics. The French, like the Irish, are a people obsessed with events from the past, and do not limit themselves to what happened in their own country. After the defeat of Prussia by Napoleon I at the battle of Jena on 14 October 1806, the revival of Prussia and her eventual dominance in Europe were both based upon the efficient organisation of the small army allowed her by the second peace treaty of Tilsit. The French, mistakenly as it turned out, had hopes of doing the same after 1940.

Pétain, like de Gaulle after him, was consequently another military man who came to power with civilian help, did not rely on the army to reinforce or support his power, and ruled principally through civilians. This, again, if one excepts the example of Napoleon III, is what makes Caesarism a peculiarly French phenomenon and disting-uishes it from military governments in other countries. It is also, once

74 *French Caesarism*

Napoleon I had shown the way, a phenomenon in which it is reputation as much as actual achievement that enables the military man to come to power. This was certainly the case with Pétain. Had he not been the 'Victor of Verdun', nobody would have thought of appealing to him in 1940. Napoleon III would also have been nothing without his uncle's example, and the de Gaulle who came to power in 1958 did so because of the reputation he had created for himself between 1940 and 1946. He is undoubtedly the most successful of the French Caesars, and that for a variety of reasons. He has at least three achievements to his credit: as the man who enabled France to be clearly on the winning side in 1945; as the politician who solved the Algerian problem; and as the founder of the Fifth Republic. He is also, as far as one can judge at the moment, the man who at one and the same time applied the myth and reality of Caesarism with the greatest success and made any future Caesar superfluous. But before examining de Gaulle's career, we have to look at the other military man to come to power in twentieth-century France, Philippe Pétain.

3 Philippe Pétain: The Victim

At first sight, there is something paradoxical, if not actually perverse, in considering Philippe Pétain as a Caesar. For as the adoption of the word in Russian under the form of 'Czar' clearly indicates, one of its primary associations is that of strength. Caesars are in command of the situation. They do what they want and they exercise genuine power.

This, for a number of reasons, was something which Pétain could never do. He came to power in 1940 because France had been defeated, and he left – like his two predecessors – because France was being invaded. Indeed, one of his chief lieutenants, Pierre Laval, went so far as to regard the liberation of France in 1944 as an act of aggression; Pétain himself simply recommended an attitude of prudent neutrality.[1] Pétain may, in terms of the motion which made him titular Head of State on 10 July 1940, have enjoyed greater powers than any French ruler since Napoleon I. Although he could not declare war, he could take any decision whatsoever concerning the executive or legislative branches of government. The ministers of his administration, as he often insisted, were directly responsible to him. But as he said at his trial for high treason in 1945, he had to fight every day 'with a knife at his throat' in a despairing attempt to protect the French against the constantly increasing German demands. At one point, on 23 October 1941, at a time when the Germans were beginning their policy of executing hostages as part of the fight against the resistance movement, Pétain tried to present himself at the demarcation line separating the occupied from the unoccupied zone so as to be taken as the one single French hostage. His attempt came to nothing, but it was symbolic of the situation in which he found himself. Having, as he said in one of his most famous phrases, made a gift of his person to France to reduce her suffering – 'Je fais à la France le don de ma personne pour atténuer son malheur' – his rôle tended to become that of a sacrificial victim rather than that of a ruler.

It is, in this respect, understandable that his trial in 1945 should have ended with the death sentence. In him the French nation was to a great extent punishing itself; and was doing so in eminently

75

76 French Caesarism

ambiguous terms. A special High Court was established, consisting of a jury of 24 members and three presiding judges. There were 12 members of the jury chosen from the resistance movement, 12 from among the eighty parliamentarians who had voted against giving full powers to Pétain in July 1940. The judges – all of whom had taken an oath of allegiance to Pétain in 1941 – had the right to vote as well. There was a majority of 14 to 13 in favour of the death penalty, all three judges voting against. Immediately afterwards, a petition was circulated in favour of not carrying out the sentence. It secured a majority vote of 17. Somebody, not for the first time in the France of the 1940s, had changed sides. It is understandable, in the circumstances, that de Gaulle should have decided to commute the sentence to one of life imprisonment.[2]

Yet in spite of his inability to exercise real power, there is a case for including Pétain as a Caesar, and one which illustrates the definition of Caesarism put forward in this book: the taking of power at a time of real or alleged national crisis by a man owing his prestige to genuine or associated military achievements. For Pétain was the best-known general still surviving from the First World War, and the one who had, at Verdun in 1916, won what the French still see as the greatest battle ever fought. As though to provide in advance an illustration for S. E. Finer's 1962 study *The Man on Horseback*, he chose to have himself depicted, in the statue erected to him at Verdun in 1938, as mounted on a horse and holding out his hand to a soldier. But there was, in May 1940, no chance of repeating his earlier triumphs. When Paul Reynaud brought him back from Spain, on 16 May, it was obvious that France was heading for a disastrous military defeat. The German panzer divisions had crossed the Meuse, come through the allegedly impenetrable forest of the Ardennes, and were spreading out rapidly throughout France. The speed of the victory was not due solely to the fact that the French had fewer tanks. They had 2,946 as against the German 2,977, which is not hopelessly disproportionate. It was more a result of their inferiority in the air – they had only 680 aeroplanes with which to oppose a German airforce which had 3,328 – and of their decision to spread their tanks out over a thin defensive line in support of artillery and infantry rather than concentrate them in a single, powerful striking force.[3] But it was a very real victory for the Germans and perhaps the most serious crisis that France has ever had to face. For on the day that Pétain agreed to become Deputy Prime Minister (*Vice-président du Conseil des Ministres*), 18 May, Churchill was already considering withdrawing the

Philippe Pétain: The Victim 77

British Expeditionary Force. Within the month, by 18 June, the British army had been evacuated through Dunkirk. Pétain, who had taken over from Paul Reynaud on 17 June, was asking for an armistice and telling French troops to stop fighting. It was the swiftest and most comprehensive military defeat then on record. The French government withdrew to Bordeaux, and then to Vichy. On 10 July 1940, by a vote of 569 to 80, with 17 abstentions and in the absence of 252 of its members, the National Assembly agreed to give full powers to Marshal Philippe Pétain to promulgate a new Constitution, which should protect the rights of Work, Family and Fatherland (*du Travail, de la Famille, de la Patrie*). It was not a change of régime that the Germans had requested, or even suggested. It was an attempt, by the French themselves, to break with what they saw as the moral and political errors of the past. They chose, as a guide, the most prestigious military leader available.

Although Pétain seems, in retrospect, to have been the obvious and inevitable choice, there were other possibilities at the time, though none of them civilian politicians. This is one of the key issues in this study of French Caesarism, since it highlights a curious fact about political life in France in the nineteenth and the first part of the twentieth century: the scarcity of civilian politicians capable of taking command in a crisis. There were other military men, such as General Weygand. He had been supreme commander of the French armies, and became Minister of National Defence in Pétain's first cabinet. He had not, according to Paul Reynaud, greatly regretted the defeat of 1940. Since France was a republic, he thought that it totally lacked the right to defend itself which belonged to a kingdom such as Holland.[4] But although his own philosophy was thus very much that of the Vichy government, he might have been a much better choice than Pétain. In spite of his refusal to join de Gaulle and 'les dissidents de Londres', he did everything possible within the limits of the armistice to rebuild a viable French army, and made himself so unpopular with the Germans that in November 1942 they finally deported him. There was also Admiral Darlan. As the man whose political skills had enabled him to build up the strongest fleet in French history, he was in a very good position to make a bid for power there and then if he had wanted to do so. But because of the political system of the Third Republic, in which no politician could stay in power long enough to put a systematic policy into action over a continuous period of time, no civilian came forward to play the equivalent of the rôle of a Churchill. Léon Blum was discredited by

78   *French Caesarism*

the collapse of the Popular Front and by his insistence on remaining neutral during the Spanish Civil War. Although he personally voted against the motion giving full powers to Marshal Pétain, he made no effort to persuade the other members of his party to follow his example. As a result, 95 members representing the SFIO (*Section Française de l'Internationale Ouvrière*), the central driving force behind the Popular Front, voted in favour of establishing the Vichy government.

The French politician whom Churchill mentions with most enthusiasm, Georges Mandel, had been given the post of Minister of the Interior in Reynaud's cabinet reshuffle of 5 May, and might, with luck, have become a rallying point for a resistance based upon civilian leadership. But he had the disadvantage, in the France of the 1940s, of being a Jew; and was one of the politicians who left metropolitan France on the *Massilia* on 23 June 1940. On his arrival in Algiers, he was prevented from landing by General Noguès and arrested. On being returned to France, he was sent to Buchenwald with Léon Blum, and then back to La Santé prison in Paris, where he was murdered by the Vichy militia in 1944. Paul Reynaud, the cleverest politician of the time, was unable to gather support either for the idea of continuing the war from North Africa or for the union between France and England which Churchill was recommending. He had also been under the influence of his mistress, Hélène de Portes, who was firmly opposed to the war. He finally had to resign, on 16 June, and was involved in a car crash, in which Madame de Portes was killed and he himself seriously injured. Since Edouard Daladier was also unable to muster support for a more vigorous policy, it would clearly be unfair to lay all the blame on individual politicians. The French political system prevented any one of them from having the support of a large and coherent party, so that they were compelled to act as individuals. Paradoxically, the only time the civilian politicians of the Third Republic acted with anything like unity was when they decided to hand the government of France over to Marshal Pétain.

Like the first Napoleon, Pétain was also given his chance by a civilian politician, Paul Reynaud. Without the invitation sent to him on 15 May, he might well have ended his days quite peacefully in Madrid, where he had been French Ambassador in the government which General Franco had established after the Civil War. There, he was performing the very useful function of ensuring that France did not have to face an enemy on her southern, Pyrenean border. Franco liked him, and made every effort to persuade him to stay, arguing

Philippe Pétain: The Victim

that he would be taking on the responsibility for a defeat in which he had played no part. But Pétain's reply was a simple and honourable one: my country needs me and it is my duty to go. Whatever the formal act of accusation at his trial in 1945 may have said, there is little evidence that Pétain had a deliberate, long-term plan to seize power, or that he envisaged in advance the possibility of collaborating with the Germans in order to do so.[5] There had indeed been a campaign organised by a journalist called Gustave Hervé, who in 1935 had gone so far as to publish a series of articles entitled *C'est Pétain qu'il nous faut*. But Pétain apparently asked him to put an end to the campaign, and this in spite of the fact that he did enjoy considerable popularity. Earlier in the same year, *Le Petit Journal* had published an opinion poll which presupposed that France could be saved only by a dictatorship, and asked who would be the best person to take charge. Pétain came top with 38,561 votes over Pierre Laval's 31,403 and Gaston Doumergue's 23,864, and had he attempted to seize power at that time, he might well have succeeded. But French politics went temporarily in the opposite direction with the triumph of the Popular Front in May 1936, and it was not until the defeat of 1940 that he came back into the public eye. When he did so, it was not as a politician who had openly pursued power, but as a stern as well as a reassuring father figure called in to save a desperate situation.

Everything about 'the Victor of Verdun' made him admirably suited to play such a role. For when he was made Head of State on 10 July 1940 he was 84 years old. He was born in the North of France, in the austere Artois region, on 24 April 1856, the son of a farmer. His mother died when he was just over a year old, his father remarried, and he was brought up principally by two of his uncles. One of them, a priest called Philippe-Michel Lefebvre, had been born in 1771, served as a young man in Napoleon's army in its Italian campaign of 1797, and did not die until 1867. To derive one's first vision of the world from a man who knew warfare at a time when cannon had a range of 800 yards, and to die as Pétain did, on 23 July 1951, six years after the explosion of the first atomic bomb, is an extraordinary if involuntary achievement. Had the First World War not broken out when it did, he would have retired with the rank of colonel in 1915. But he certainly understood the nature of warfare in the early part of the twentieth century, and the legendary association of old age with prudence was strongly reinforced for the French of 1940 by Pétain's very real achievements in the First World War.

80 *French Caesarism*

Like de Gaulle, he had begun by being a rebel against the French military establishment and against the conventional military wisdom of his time. This, in 1914, was still based upon the Napoleonic idea of winning battles by a combination of artillery preparation and the momentum of infantry and cavalry charges. What Pétain recognised, before anyone else on the French general staff was prepared to do so, was that 'le feu tue' (bullets kill); and that the advent of the machine gun and barbed wire, as well as more powerful artillery and accurate, rapid-firing rifles, had completely altered the art of war. His own victory at Verdun in 1916, the result of dogged persistence rather than of brilliant generalship, had been followed by the disastrous and spectacular failure of the Nivelle offensive in April 1917. This had adopted what was still, even after the battle of the Somme in the previous year, the conventional wisdom of a massive frontal attack, and had caused so many French casualties that it had had to be abandoned on the fourth day. Mutinies had followed in the French army, and on 15 May 1917 Pétain had been given the task of restoring both order and morale. This he had done with as much compassion as circumstances allowed – officially, there were only 54 executions for mutiny – and his naturally cautious personality had expressed itself in what were at the time the only tactics to hold out any hope of success: modest, well-prepared, but essentially limited operations. Together with a concern for the physical welfare of his men, this strategy had made him the most popular if not the most dramatically successful of all the French generals to exercise command between 1914 and 1918.

It was this memory of what he had done during the First World War which was the main source of his popularity in 1940. This was especially the case with the millions of men who had served in the victorious French armies between 1914 and 1918, and who had the immense moral advantage over their sons of having won the war in which they had taken part. Perhaps wisely, Pétain had not played a very active rôle in French politics between the wars, serving briefly as War Minister in Gaston Doumergue's government in 1934 but declining invitations to link his name with one of the vigorously right-wing, potentially fascist parties which tried to overthrow the Third Republic during the 1930s. He was certainly wise in this abstention. The experience of General Boulanger in 1889, like that of General de Gaulle between 1947 and 1953, is a clear indication that even an inefficient political system in France can stand up to internal agitation until a major crisis threatens it from the outside. This was what happened in 1940, and the first way in which Philippe Pétain can

Philippe Pétain: The Victim 81

be seen as a victim is in the circumstances in which he came to power. Whatever the official position created by the vote of 10 July, it was circumstances rather than Pétain that were in command. Jean Zay may well have been right to comment that this was the first time that a general had been given supreme power as a reward for defeat.[6] But he had been given it by a vote in a civilian political assembly, and as a result of a series of decisions taken by civilian politicians. Indeed, without Reynaud's invitation to return to France from Spain, and without the skill displayed by Pierre Laval in persuading the deputies and senators of the Third Republic to vote for him in such overwhelming numbers, Pétain would have had no chance of coming to power. The defeat itself was also less Pétain's own than that of a whole nation, and of a whole way of thinking about warfare.

For it is misleading to say, as Paul Johnson does in his *A History of the Modern World from 1917 to the 1980s*, that Pétain 'dominated French military policy' between 1920 and 1936.[7] He did, it is true, give an unfortunate hostage to fortune by the Preface which he wrote in 1936 to General Narcisse Chauvineau's *Une Invasion Est-elle Encore Possible?*; and to which the answer was a clear 'No'. Indeed, he showed how serious an error he realised that this Preface had been by ensuring, after coming to power in 1940, that all copies of the book were withdrawn from military libraries. But his insistence on the importance of defensive fire power was based on the experience of the First World War, and his own military thinking was not always as neolithic as his critics suggest. In 1935 he pointed out in a Preface to General Sikorski's book on *La Guerre Moderne* that the development of tanks and armoured vehicles had introduced a totally new factor into modern warfare. Where he differed from de Gaulle, and failed to anticipate the events of May 1940, was in his view that a combination of tank traps and artillery fire would hold up an advance long enough to enable a defence in depth to become effective. But the French economy could not afford the cost of making such a defence a practical possibility, any more than French industry could produce the aeroplanes which Pétain also considered essential in modern warfare. He did, it is true, fail to appreciate the devastating effect which the German use of dive bombers as a new form of mobile artillery was to have on the British and French armies in 1940. But he shared this failure of anticipation with de Gaulle himself, whose 1934 book *Vers l'Armée de Métier* (*Towards a Professional Army*) also gave air power a long-range, strategic role rather than a short-range, tactical one. Neither could Pétain be held personally responsible for

82 *French Caesarism*

the decision to base the defence of France on the Maginot line, or for the failure to extend this line along the Belgian frontier to the North Sea. The building of the Maginot line stemmed from a collective cabinet decision, and the Belgians made it very difficult for the French to include them in their defensive thinking by declaring, in 1936, that they would be neutral in any future war. De Gaulle's failure to persuade the French to create a mobile striking force capable of deterring German aggression had very little to do with Pétain's own personal influence on French military thinking. It was the consequence, as de Gaulle himself makes clear in his *Mémoires*, of the obstacles which the governmental instability of the Third Republic placed in the way of any coherent and innovative defence policy. Neither should the German victory of 1940 be explained solely by the inadequacy of the French high command. In their tendency to masochistic self-centredness, this is what the French still tend to do, quite forgetting that victory in war, as on the games field, stems as much from the positive qualities in the winners as from the defects of the losers. It was foolish of Pétain to implement the decision to put the politicians of the Third Republic on trial at Riom in February 1942 on the grounds of having led France into a war for which they had not properly prepared. This enabled Paul Reynaud, Edouard Daladier and Léon Blum to point out, in their own defence, that theirs was an essentially shared responsibility in which the whole of the French high command, Pétain included, was inevitably involved. But since everybody turned out to be equally guilty for a war which the Germans then no longer seemed to be quite so certain of winning, it again made Pétain seem as much a victim of circumstances as everybody else. The only difference was that he had willingly agreed, in July 1940, to assume responsibility for a state of affairs which others apart from himself had helped to bring about.

There is also an important sense in which Pétain also became, with the passage of years, and in the judgement of politicians and historians, the victim of an ideology which he espoused but which he had not invented. This was very much the ideology of the French right, and one which Pétain shared with Weygand as well as with a large number of civilian politicians. He had made no secret during the 1930s of the fact that he disapproved of the free and easy atmosphere of the Third Republic, and went so far as to say in 1932 that the French could only profit from a little more suffering. The defeat of 1940 gave him a golden opportunity to impose this way of thinking on his fellow countrymen, and he made it quite clear why he thought the

Philippe Pétain: The Victim 83

French had – temporarily as it turned out – lost the war. 'I was with you in the days of glory', he promised in his broadcast to the nation on 18 June, in an obvious reference to the victory of Verdun, 'I shall remain with you in the days of darkness'. He then continued:

We shall draw the lessons of the battles we have lost. Since the victory (of 1918) the spirit of pleasure-seeking (*l'esprit de jouissance*) has taken precedence over the spirit of sacrifice. People have made demands instead of offering to serve. They have tried to avoid effort. Today, we have met with disaster.

The defeat, the French were told, was not the result of bad generalship or technological inferiority. It stemmed from a set of moral failings which had led the educated among them to read immoral authors such as Proust and Gide and to look indulgently at the irresponsible antics of the surrealist movement. It was the product of a selfishness and love of purely material advantages which had led the working class to go on strike for higher wages at the time of the Popular Front, and to demand paid holidays for everybody. The French had neglected their religious duties, and had been encouraged in their ungodliness by the secularisation of education in the 1880s and the separation of Church and State in 1905. As though to drive this point home, 1,328 *instituteurs* (primary school teachers) were subsequently dismissed from their teaching posts, partly because of their attachment to the secular ideal, partly to punish them for having gone on strike in 1938.[8]

The motion of 10 July which gave full powers to Marshal Pétain stipulated that these were to be used to establish a Constitution which protected 'les droits du Travail, de la Famille et de la Patrie'. Under Weygand's influence, there had even been a suggestion at one point that it would be appropriate to include a reference to God, but not even the supporters of what was to become the Vichy régime were prepared to go that far in rejecting seventy years of secular republicanism. But the proud, outward-looking motto of the French republic, *Liberté, Egalité, Fraternité*, was replaced by the more cautious, inward-looking slogan of *Travail, Famille, Patrie*. The Republic itself was abolished to make way for the neutrally named *Etat Français*, possibly in anticipation of a Europe of comparable 'States' under German leadership. The French were urged to think much of their duties and little of their rights, and to indulge in a policy of national repentance which also had the support of certain members of the Catholic Church. Cardinal Gerlier showed how grateful some mem-

84 French Caesarism

bers of the Catholic hierarchy were for the provision of government subsidies for Catholic schools and the attempt to reintroduce religious instruction into the hitherto strictly secular state system by stating clearly that 'Pétain c'est la France et la France c'est Pétain.' In an article published in *La Croix* on 28 June 1940, Monseigneur Saliège, who was later to show outstanding courage in helping Jews to escape from persecution and death, implored God to forgive the French for having earlier driven Him out of the schools, out of courtrooms and out of the nation itself, and asked the rhetorical but – for him – genuine question, 'What would we have done with an easy victory in 1940?'

This philosophy of national repentance has been given more permanent, albeit satirical form in the literature of the period. Both Jean-Paul Sartre's *Les Mouches* (*The Flies*, 1943), and Albert Camus' *La Peste* (*The Plague*, 1947) contain accurate and satirical versions of it. The first sermon delivered by Father Paneloux in Camus's novel exactly catches its tone. In it, the priest tells the citizens of Oran that the plague has been sent by God to punish them for their wickedness, and calls upon them to repent. It would nevertheless be a mistake to regard this attitude as an entirely new phenomenon in French national life, or to see Pétain as the sole person responsible either for using or for propagating it. The French have a well-established tradition of political masochism, and the decision to erect the Basilique du Sacré-Cœur on the heights of Montmartre in 1873 was intended to express the remorse which they felt over their recent defeat in the Franco-Prussian war, the excesses of the *Commune*, and their failure to save the Pope from imprisonment at the time of Italian unification:

Texte du Vœu National au Sacré-Cœur

EN PRESENCE DES MALHEURS QUI DESOLENT LA FRANCE ET DES MALHEURS PLUS GRANDS PEUT-ETRE QUI LA MENACENT ENCORE.

EN PRESENCE DES ATTENTATS SACRILEGES COMMIS A ROME CON-TRE LES DROITS DE L'EGLISE ET DU SAINT-SIEGE ET CONTRE LA PERSONNE SACREE DU VICAIRE DE JESUS-CHRIST.

NOUS NOUS HUMILIONS DEVANT DIEU ET NOUS REUNISSANT DANS NOTRE AMOUR DE L'EGLISE ET NOTRE PATRIE NOUS RECONNAISSONS QUE NOUS AVONS ETE COUPABLES ET JUSTEMENT CHATIES.

ET POUR FAIRE AMENDE HONORABLE DE NOS PECHES ET OBTENIR DE L'INFINIE MISERICORDE DU SACRE CŒUR DE NOTRE-SEIGNEUR JESUS-CHRIST LE PARDON DE NOS FAUTES AINSI QUE LES SECOURS

Philippe Pétain: The Victim

EXTRAORDINAIRES QUI PEUVENT SEULS DELIVRER LE SOUVERAIN PONTIFE DE SA CAPTIVITE ET FAIRE CESSER LES MALHEURS DE LA FRANCE NOUS PROMETTONS DE CONTRIBUER A L'ERECTION A PARIS D'UN SANCTUAIRE DEDIE AU SACRE-CŒUR DE JESUS.

Text of the Nation's Promise to the Sacred Heart

IN THE PRESENCE OF THE ILLS WHICH AFFLICT FRANCE AND OF THE PERHAPS GREATER ILLS WHICH THREATEN HER.

IN THE PRESENCE OF THE SACRILEGIOUS ACTS COMMITTED IN ROME AGAINST THE RIGHTS OF THE CHURCH AND AGAINST THE SACRED PERSON OF THE VICAR OF JESUS CHRIST.

WE HUMBLE OURSELVES BEFORE GOD, AND JOINING TOGETHER IN OUR LOVE OF THE CHURCH AND OF OUR FATHERLAND, WE RECOGNISE THAT WE HAVE BEEN GUILTY AND JUSTLY PUNISHED.

AND TO MAKE DUE AMENDS FOR OUR SINS AND TO OBTAIN FROM THE INFINITE MERCY OF THE SACRED HEART OF OUR LORD JESUS CHRIST FORGIVENESS FOR OUR SINS AND THE EXTRAORDINARY SUCCOUR WHICH CAN ALONE DELIVER THE SOVEREIGN PONTIFF FROM HIS CAPTIVITY AND BRING TO AN END THE SUFFERINGS OF FRANCE, WE PROMISE TO CONTRIBUTE TO THE BUILDING OF A SANCTUARY DEVOTED TO THE SACRED HEART OF JESUS.[9]

As though the architecture of the Sacré-Cœur were not already sufficient punishment, this vision of how wicked the French could allow themselves to be once they cast off the guiding spirit of the Catholic Church was linked in the ideology of Vichy with a view of France as essentially an agricultural country. 'La terre, elle, ne ment pas' (the earth does not lie), said Pétain in one of his eminently lapidary phrases, and this particular idea also presupposed a particular relationship between France and Germany. Germany would be the dominant, industrialised partner, supplied by France with food and perhaps with a little culture as well as with well-made, luxury articles. In view of the actual terms of the armistice of 1940, this was in fact the only way in which the French could think of themselves, and even then only with some difficulty. The so-called 'Zone Libre', the only one under the direct control of the Vichy government, contained less than a third of its industry and less than half its population. It also, unfortunately for this aspect of the Vichy ideology, included mainly the less fertile, wine-growing area of the South, and it is again difficult to associate an armistice which leaves over half the national territory under the direct control of the

86 *French Caesarism*

hereditary enemy with the normally triumphant associations of the word 'Caesarism'. But although this ideology represented the way of thinking both of Pétain himself and of another soldier, General Weygand, there is a further sense in which other people apart from them were also responsible for it. Indeed, it represented a way of thinking about France which formed part of a whole tradition of anti-modern and anti-revolutionary ideas. The works of novelists such as René Bazin, for example, are full of nostalgia for a supposedly more virtuous France which had remained unaffected by the industrial revolution, and the same view recurs in the more amusing works of a later author such as Marcel Aymé. The Revolution of 1789 had had the effect of splitting France into two nations, one which accepted the Revolution and one which did not. It was the one which did not that surfaced with surprising strength in 1940, and did so in a way that sometimes made Louis XIV look in retrospect like a model of an enlightened monarch with an equal concern for the welfare of all his subjects.

For the Vichy government did not show any particular reluctance in putting into practice the more obnoxious aspects of the Nazi régime. On 18 October 1940, before the Germans had asked for any such sign of agreement with their racialist philosophy, it promulgated its own legislation concerning the status of Jews in the unoccupied zone. They were not, as they were in the North of France, compelled to wear the yellow star, at least not until 29 May 1942. But while the Germans began by defining as a Jew in the part of France which they occupied anyone who professed the Jewish religion, the Vichy authorities adopted from the very beginning a set of purely racial criteria. A Catholic priest with two Jewish grandparents was thus considered Jewish. Shortly after the Vichy régime had been officially voted into power, a decree was issued on 17 July 1940 forbidding anyone whose father was not French from becoming a civil servant. From August 1940 onwards only someone with a French (i.e. non-Jewish) father could become a doctor, and the decree was subsequently extended to the legal profession. The Vichy régime also rounded up some 40,000 Jews who had not yet succeeded in taking out French nationality and placed them in special internment camps. Speakers on the state-controlled radio gloated over how good the fresh air and rigorous conditions of these camps were for the Jews thus interned, and had their wishes for an even harsher treatment satisfied when the Germans finally occupied the whole of France in November 1942. All that the Germans then had to do was transfer all

Philippe Pétain: The Victim 87

the Jews from the camps to the trains taking them to the gas chambers. On 16 July 1942 the Germans decided to arrest all the Jews in the Paris area. The Vichy government raised no objection to the French police being ordered to take part in an operation which grouped 13,000 Jews, children and women as well as men, in the *Vélodrome d'Hiver*. From there, they were transferred to a special camp at Drancy, to the north of Paris; and thence to the fate awaiting all the victims of the Final Solution.

The *Centre de Documentation Juive* has calculated that some 80,000 Jews were deported from France during the Second World War, out of a total Jewish population of 300,000. Compared to the 86 per cent of Dutch Jews murdered by the Nazis, this figure of 26 per cent looks – by the standards of the 1940s – relatively modest. But the Dutch Jews were almost all inhabitants of Amsterdam, and were easy to round up. Holland, moreover, was under direct German rule, with Queen Wilhelmina heading a government in exile in London. The Vichy government, in contrast, was supposed to be French, with the duty expected of any civilised government to afford equal protection to all its citizens. The fact that it did precisely the opposite, and selected particular social groups for persecution and death is what makes it indefensible. For Louis XIV merely billeted brutal soldiers on those of his Protestant subjects who were not prepared to convert to Catholicism, deprived them of their civil rights and forced them into exile. Pétain's government handed the French Jews over to certain death, and it is no reply to say that the French authorities had no choice but to co-operate in this as in other matters. Denmark also had a government which was, theoretically, committed to collaborating with the Germans. But King Christian made it very clear where his sympathies lay, and the example of how a systematic display of opposition from the head of state could influence behaviour lower down is well illustrated by what happened during the German occupation to the 7,000 or so Danish Jews. When, in September 1943, it became known that they were going to be deported to Germany, the Danish police co-operated with their Swedish colleagues and arranged for all of them to cross into Sweden. There was, it is true, no equally convenient haven for the French Jews. Neither, however, is there any evidence of a similar rescue operation being mounted by any organised group owing allegiance to the Vichy government. When the Catholic Church realised what was happening, it did indeed move away from the support which it had earlier given the Vichy régime. Its record for trying to protect Jews,

88 *French Caesarism*

especially by the generous provision of baptismal certificates, is a good one. But it had, by that time, become part of the opposition. In contrast to the twenty high-ranking officers from the army, only one representative of the clergy, Cardinal Liémont of Lille, came forward in Pétain's defence in the 1945 trial.[10]

In June 1941, in one of the first attempts to prove that Pétain alone was responsible for the events in France during the occupation, the playwright Henry Bernstein published two long articles in the *New York Herald Tribune*. In one of them, he claimed that antisemitism had no roots in France, and that the discrimination practised by the Vichy government against the Jews was directly modelled on the Nuremburg laws of the Nazis. The mere mention of the Dreyfus case, or of writers such as Charles Maurras or Léon Daudet, is enough to show how mistaken this view of Pétain's responsibility is. Indeed, here as elsewhere, there is even a case for seeing him as a victim of a set of peculiarly French attitudes for which he was not personally responsible. Ever since the 1880s, a particularly virulent strain of antisemitism had run through the whole of French life, and Pétain no more invented this than he invented the anti-republicanism which went with it. It is true that he did nothing to try to mitigate its effects. When one thinks of the immense prestige he enjoyed in 1940, and even as late as 1944, it is hard to believe that a single word or gesture by him would not have reduced the antisemitism of the Vichy government from the level of cholera to that of a mild head cold. But although he is reported to have said that while a Freemason is responsible for his choice, a Jew cannot be blamed for his birth, there is no record of his having made any attempt to enforce this distinction on the ministers who, as he frequently insisted, were responsible only to him. The Constitution which he hoped to impose on the French would have restricted the right to vote to French men and women who were born of French parents. Given the definition of who was and who was not French generally accepted by the Vichy government, this would almost certainly have meant the disenfranchisement of anyone regarded as Jewish as well as their exclusion from other areas of national life.

Perhaps it was not possible, given his age and background, for Pétain to have given the clear lead in moral matters which the modern reader expects of a responsible statesman. If there is no record of his ever having intervened to save a single Jew, the fault may lie as much with his class and country as with himself. After all, when he came to be put on trial, the examining magistrate (*juge*

Philippe Pétain: The Victim

89

d'instruction) responsible for preparing the case against him was a man called Pierre Bouchardon, who had earlier written articles in the violently antisemitic newspaper *Je Suis Partout*. The *procureur de la République* (counsel for the prosecution) at the actual trial, which took place between 23 July and 15 August 1945, was André Mornet. Three years earlier, as he was compelled to admit, Mornet had appeared on behalf of the Vichy government in the trial at Riom. He had also, from 6 September 1940 onwards, served as Deputy Chairman of the committee which Vichy had set up to make a close study of everyone who had recently acquired French nationality in order to discover and remove any Jews.[11] Pétain's readiness to endorse a distinction between good and bad French people on the grounds of race alone certainly marks him out in contrast to the other Caesars who took power in France. Napoleon I helped to heal the wounds of the first French Revolution by accepting service from anyone prepared to forget the past; de Gaulle welcomed in the 1940s anyone prepared to serve France. But as in other aspects of his career, Pétain's tendency to divide rather than unify the French stemmed as much from his education and background as from a deliberate and positive choice. There, as elsewhere, he was more of a victim than an instigator. It was, after all, Maurice Barrès, later to be elected to the *Académie Française*, who argued that since Dreyfus was a Jew, he belonged to a 'different species' from that of proper Frenchmen, and could not therefore expect to be judged by the legal system which provided protection for them.[12]

It is consequently not surprising that Pétain should remain the most controversial as well as the least successful of the French Caesars. Even nowadays there are few better ways of enlivening the discussion at a French dinner party than to suggest that his last wish be granted and his bones be allowed to rest in the cemetery at Douaumont with the other victims of the battle of Verdun. This is not only because the French, like the Irish, have long political memories. They are still divided among themselves on many issues involving the Second World War. Neither, unfortunately, is it always because of Vichy's treatment of Jews. It is also because Pétain left so little behind him by way of permanent achievements. For while the first Napoleon lives on in the *Code Civil*, his nephew in the physical appearance of Paris and Charles de Gaulle in the Constitution of the Fifth Republic as well as in the solution of the Algerian problem, there is little in France except controversy to show that Philippe Pétain ever existed as one of its rulers. It is true that it was under his rule that the French

90 French Caesarism

birth-rate, surprisingly enough, began to improve, and this may have been in response to the measures taken by the Vichy government. But a step had already been taken in that direction by the Third Republic with the introduction of family allowances and the promulgation of the *Code de la Famille* in July 1939. Pétain's technocrats may, as Theodore Zeldin has argued, have taken the first steps towards the economic planning of the Fourth Republic. But this would almost certainly have happened anyway under the influence of Jean Monnet and the general climate in post-war Europe. One of the quotations used to decorate the innumerable photographs of Pétain posted up on the walls of public and other buildings in France between 1940 and 1945 was the phrase: 'Je tiens toutes mes promesses, y compris celles des autres' (I keep all my promises, including those of other people). This is true in the sense that it was during the Vichy régime that old-age pensions were introduced in France, and that the first systematic, state-inspired attempt was made to limit the spread of alcoholism by forbidding anyone under the age of 18 from drinking in a public bar. You can still see the notices, dating from 1943, in the more remote areas of France. But it is hard, if not impossible, to see the Vichy government over which Pétain presided as leaving very much behind it except for endless controversy and a flourishing black market. There is certainly nothing which the Fourth Republic did not develop in a more permanent and acceptable form.

Yet Pétain still has defenders whose enthusiasm for him goes beyond the acknowledgement that he did, in 1940, play a useful role in preventing the French from plunging into absolute despair. Some remain enthusiastic supporters because of the attempt which Pétain made to repress the French Communist Party. Since it was frequently the members of the party, and other left-wing groups, who were most active in the purges which took place after the liberation of France, Pétain benefits in retrospect as the man whose supporters suffered most from this outbreak of apparently uncontrolled, but often carefully orchestrated, popular anger. The American historian Herbert Lottman has calculated that there were some 10,000 summary executions carried out in 1944, together with 767 following a formal trial.[13] Although considerably lower than the earlier estimates of 40,000, or even of 100,000, it is still a figure which explains why Pétain should have come to appear, in retrospect, a more providential figure than he actually was. This favourable impression is considerably strengthened when one reflects how much smaller Pétain's contribution to the defeat of 1940 was than that of the French

Philippe Pétain: The Victim   91

Communist Party. The ink had barely had time to dry on the non-aggression pact of 24 August 1939 between Nazi Germany and Soviet Russia before the Party began to denounce any war against Germany as an imperialist adventure. Maurice Thorez, its general secretary, showed what this attitude meant by deserting from the French army and going to live in Moscow. Pétain did, indeed, publicly shake Hitler's hand at Montoire on 23 October 1940 and called upon the French to collaborate. But *L'Humanité*, the official newspaper of the French Communist Party, had already shown him the way. Shortly after the Germans occupied Paris in 1940, it began to re-appear, and continued to do so until Germany invaded Russia on 22 June 1941.[14]

Other defenders of Pétain's attitude maintain that without the Vichy régime, over which he presided, the resistance movement would never have attained the dimensions that it did. Because the South of France was unoccupied, resistance groups would come into being much more easily under the indulgent eye of the French police than they would have done if the whole country had been ruled from 1940 onwards by the German army. It is a fact that most of these groups did begin life in and around the larger towns of the unoccupied zone, and it is always possible to argue that Pétain's denunciation of 'les mauvais Français' was just a blind put up to hide his real feelings from the Germans. If it was, then the claim which he himself put forward at his trial in 1945 of having been the shield of France while de Gaulle was its sword would have some basis to it. Pétain was certainly not keen on the para-military police force, *la milice*, which Joseph Darnand set up in January 1943 to fight against the resistance movement. On one occasion, he even asked Darnand how many Frenchmen he had killed today. But in his other conversations, he almost invariably referred to the members of the resistance movement as 'mutineers'. It was an indication of how much his mind still harked back to the days when he had had the task of suppressing the 1917 mutinies in the French army, and of how much he was, as de Gaulle suggested, also a victim of old age. 'La vieillesse est un naufrage', wrote de Gaulle in 1954, in the first volume of his *Mémoires de Guerre*, and added: 'Pour que rien ne nous fût épargné, celle du maréchal Pétain allait s'identifier avec le naufrage de la France.' (Old age is a disaster. To ensure that we would be spared nothing, that of Marshal Pétain was to be identified with the collapse of France.)[15]

Other defenders of Pétain put forward the geopolitical argument

92   *French Caesarism*

that Hitler allowed himself to be tricked by the armistice of 1940 into leaving the South of France unoccupied. This prevented him, it is alleged, from going down south quickly enough to secure complete mastery of the Mediterranean, and thus led to his defeat in the North Africa campaign. Alfred Fabre-Luce, one of Pétain's most consistent admirers, who published a book on him in 1945 entitled *Le Mystère du Maréchal*, even goes so far as to quote Winston Churchill as saying that the armistice of 1940 was, for this very reason, the greatest mistake that Hitler made. It is true that Churchill subsequently went back on this remark, but Fabre-Luce also maintains that Pétain had actually wanted to attack Germany in 1936, at the time of the remilitarisation of the Rhineland. The opportunity for doing so having been lost, argues Fabre-Luce, it would have been better for France not to have gone to war in 1939, ostensibly in defence of Poland but in fact without being able to do anything useful to prevent Germany from carrying out her aims. Instead, the French should have chosen a policy which allowed the Wehrmacht to 'waste itself in the Russian steppes' a year or two earlier than it did; thus completely avoiding the war in the West and the subsequent defeat of France.[16]

In such a reading of Pétain's intentions and achievements he is indeed credited with very considerable political acumen, albeit from a very right-wing and anti-Communist standpoint. He is not presented, as de Gaulle depicts him in the first volume of the *Mémoires de Guerre*, as a man incapable of seeing the Second World War as anything but a third round in the century-long conflict between France and Germany. Like Pétain's other admirers, Fabre-Luce also emphasises how acceptable Pétain was, initially at any rate, both to the Russians and to the Americans. In 1940, the Soviet Union had a mere *chargé d'affaires* representing her interests in the Paris of the Third Republic. When Pétain came to power, a full Ambassador was sent. It is equally clear from de Gaulle's *Mémoires* that the Americans were very happy to accept Pétain as a useful potential ally as well as the legal ruler of France. At the time of the allied landings in North Africa in November 1942, Roosevelt went out of his way to present the matter in as favourable a light as possible to Pétain, so much so that Churchill had to remind him of the obligations which already existed on the British side towards General de Gaulle. Neither do Pétain's admirers have any difficulty in producing evidence that Pétain retained his popularity with the mass of the French people until the very end, and that certain great French writers of the 1940s had an admiration for him that verged on idolatry. When, on

Philippe Pétain: The Victim 93

his 88th birthday, on 24 April 1944, the Germans allowed him to visit Paris, Pétain received almost as tumultuous a welcome as the one accorded de Gaulle some four months later. Paul Valéry, not normally famous for his credulity or intellectual indulgence, had prepared a text to be read out to him on arrival. This spoke of Pétain's victory at Verdun as being merely the prelude to an even greater destiny in which he took over a collapsing country in order to 'provide some kind of unity and some kind of future for it', and his remarks provide a curious echo to the words of a song sung in 1941 by André Lassarie and repeated, at regular intervals, by every schoolgirl and every schoolboy in France between 1941 and 1944:

> Une flamme sacrée monte du sol natal,
> Et la France enivrée te salue maréchal!
> Tous les enfants qui t'aiment et vénèrent tes ans
> A ton appel suprême ont répondu: 'Présent!'
> > Maréchal, nous voilà
> > Devant toi
> > Le Sauveur de la France!
> Nous jurons, tous tes gars,
> De servir et de suivre tes pas.
> > Maréchal, nous voilà!
> Tu nous as redonné l'espérance.
> La patrie renaîtra.
> > Maréchal, maréchal, nous voilà.
> Tu as lutté sans cesse pour le salut commun.
> On parle avec tendresse du héros de Verdun.
> En nous donnant sa vie, son génie et sa foi,
> Qui sauves la patrie une seconde fois.
> > Maréchal, maréchal, nous voilà etc.

(A sacred flame rises from our native soil, and France, exalted, salutes you, Maréchal! All your children who love you and venerate your great age have replied to your supreme call, saying: Maréchal! We are here! Before you, the saviour of France. We, all your young people, swear to serve and follow in your footsteps. Maréchal, here we are. You have given us back hope. The fatherland will come back to life. Maréchal, Maréchal, here we are. You fought ceaselessly for the good of all. People speak with emotion of the hero of Verdun, by giving us his life, his genius and his faith, has saved the fatherland a second time. Maréchal, etc.[17].

94 *French Caesarism*

As the words of this song suggest, with its praise to Pétain for having saved the fatherland twice (the first being Verdun), he enjoyed during the Vichy period an official adulation scarcely equalled even by the Napoleon to whom the new Catechism of 1803 was dedicated. Even François Mauriac, the one member of the *Académie Française* to take part in the resistance movement, wrote in June 1940 of how the words of Pétain's speeches 'emitted an almost timeless sound'. 'This old man', he continued, 'has been sent to us by the dead of Verdun and by the innumerable crowd of those who, for centuries, have been carrying the torch which our feeble hands have just let fall.'[18] One possible definition of Caesarism insists on the fact that a Caesar receives direct support from all classes of society, from the most numerous as well as the most cultured. It is certainly justified to study Pétain from this point of view. Precisely because he did incarnate a particular moment in French history with such accuracy, it is also possible to see him as being as much the victim of a set of peculiarly French attitudes as the man who, for a brief period, succeeded in profiting from them.

This is not to say that Pétain did not enjoy whatever authority he did possess or that he did not appreciate the adulation bestowed upon him. Neither does it involve the suggestion that he was reluctant to take power in 1940. At a cabinet meeting on 16 June 1940 Pétain threatened to walk out if there was any further talk of continuing the war from North Africa, and had to be persuaded to stay by the President of the Republic, Albert Lebrun. In his portrait of him in the first volume of the *Mémoires de Guerre*, de Gaulle speaks of 'une passion de dominer' which Pétain had long repressed before it was able to express itself in 1940, and there is no doubt that he believed in the ideology of the Vichy régime. But without the collapse of France in 1940, this side of his personality would never have found the opportunity to express itself. He certainly was a willing victim, in the sense that he propagated the ideas about the need to be absolutely French and insisted on the nefarious rôle played in the disintegration of French society by the Freemasons. But just as he was carried along by this ideology at the same time as he added to it, so the general historical circumstances in which he came to power made it almost inevitable that he would become the scapegoat for all the faults which were later seen as characterising his régime.

For in 1940, Pétain was an old man in an increasingly ageing country. One of the principal and most disastrous consequences of the slaughter of the First World War had been a dramatic decline in

Philippe Pétain: The Victim 95

the French birth-rate. This had already begun to fall in the nineteenth century, to the point where France had dropped between 1800 and 1900 from first to fifth place in terms of European population. This fall is sometimes explained by the articles in the Napoleonic Code which stipulated that all property should be divided equally among all children of a marriage. Faced with the need to keep the family property intact, it is argued, the French peasantry and property-owning middle classes restricted the number of their children in quite a dramatic manner. This may, of course, not have been the only reason, and 'le partage égal du patrimoine' was common practice in many parts of France before the first French revolution. The French cities of the industrial revolution were even less healthy places than their English counterparts had been some fifty years before. The failure of the French population to grow may thus have been due as much to a lack of hygiene as to Articles 745 and 913 in the Napoleonic Code. But an unfortunate consequence of the fact that there were, for whatever reason, only 45 million French people confronting almost 80 million Germans in 1914 was the decision of the French high command not to allow regular leave to men in the trenches. This meant that the birth-rate between 1914 and 1918 dropped so sharply that it was simply not possible, from 1936 onwards, for France to have had as large an army as Pétain and others would have liked. In that year, the number of deaths was so much higher than the number of live births that demographic projections predicted the virtual disappearance of the French by 1980. Céline was not just joking when he said, at the time of the French defeat of 1940, that it would be a miracle if any French word other than 'merde' still survived in 2940.[19]

Countries tend to have the army which reflects their general attitude. The ageing population of France, whose senior army officers were in 1940 some ten years older than their German counterparts, had two possible choices, neatly incarnated in the contrasting perso-nalities of Philippe Pétain and Charles de Gaulle. Either it could accept that wars were no longer possible; or it could decide to have a modern army which replaced men by machines. What it could not do, and this was amply proved by the battle of France in May–June 1940, was fight a war which involved heavy casualties. For in the five weeks that the campaign actually lasted, the French lost 84,000 soldiers and 80,000 civilians. It was a casualty rate that exceeded even that of 1915, when 309,000 French soldiers were killed over the whole year. The readiness with which the French surrendered can be seen almost

96 *French Caesarism*

as the biological reflex of a living organism threatened with extinction. Even more so than in 1917, Pétain drew his popularity from the fact of being the man who stopped the slaughter.[20]

It is true that the words he actually used to stop it could have been better chosen. By 15 May 1940, when Paul Reynaud summoned him from Madrid, Pétain saw fairly quickly that the situation was hopeless from a military point of view, and that any attempt to save the situation by a union between France and England could yield no practical results. It would perhaps have been possible for a large number of the French soldiers who were taken prisoner by the Germans to have avoided capture if Pétain had not announced, in his broadcast at midday on 16 June, 'It is with a heavy heart that I have to tell you today that we must stop fighting' (*C'est le cœur serré que je vous dis aujourd'hui qu'il faut cesser le combat*). A few hours later on the same day the message was altered to 'try to stop fighting', but by that time much of the harm had been done. But while more prisoners were taken by the Germans than was absolutely inevitable, Pétain would in any case have been faced, throughout his period as Head of State, with a situation in which over a million-and-a-half French soldiers were in German prisoner-of-war camps. The pessimistic side of his nature, which had come out at the time of the German offensive of March 1918 and led him to think that all was lost then as well, may well have led him in 1940 to give more of a hostage to fortune than he need have done. But in all his dealings with the Germans he was the victim of a situation which was not essentially of his making, and he could be very easily blackmailed by the promise to release prisoners of war or the threat to make their position worse. The defeat of France in 1940 had a large number of causes of which the inadequacy of the French high command was perhaps the most important. Pétain inherited this, just as he inherited the tradition whereby the French call in a soldier to find a solution for a problem which no civilian seems able to solve.

Another aspect of this situation was the failure of the kind of parliamentary democracy developed in the France of the Third Republic to provide the stable government necessary to deal with a crisis. When, for example, on 21 March 1940, Edouard Daladier resigned as *Président du Conseil* (Prime Minister) and Paul Reynaud was invited to form a government, he secured a majority of 268 votes against 156, but with 111 abstentions. In spite of the fact that the Radical Party had eleven ministers in his government, only 33 deputies from this party voted for him. The last government of the

Philippe Pétain: The Victim

Third Republic, like the régime itself, thus came into existence by a majority of only one vote. It was understandable, in the circumstances, that so many French politicians of the 1940s should have felt attracted by the apparent unanimous support which Hitler received from the Germans. On an emotional level, this attraction certainly explains a certain amount of the phenomenon known as collaboration. A touch of rigour, the 'slap of firm government', was what many politicians and intellectuals felt that the French needed, and Pétain was not averse to providing it. From the point of view of his reputation, and of the ultimate fate of France during the four years that he remained Head of State, it was nevertheless disastrous that he was able to obtain whatever power he had only by collaborating with a régime such as Hitler's. Alone among the French Caesars, he came to office through the intervention of a foreign country. The mandate with which he claimed to have been invested by the vote of 10 July 1940 in the French National Assembly was always open to the criticism that this vote had been taken under circumstances which precluded any genuine freedom of choice. A majority of 569 against 80 is certainly very impressive. If a régime is going to be allowed to vote itself out of existence, as the Third Republic did in July 1940, it could surely not be required to do so by a wider margin. The obvious disadvantage of Pétain's position was that the vote which gave him the authority to govern had been obtained in such extraordinary circumstances.

All Caesars do of course come to power because the normal machinery of government has broken down. If, by some historical miracle, the two Napoleons had been voted into office by free and fair elections scheduled in advance as part of a regular election timetable, and if the same had happened in the case of Pétain and de Gaulle, then the phenomenon of French Caesarism would not exist. From this point of view, and in spite of the insistence which each one of them placed upon his legitimacy, they can all be seen to some extent as usurpers. To call 'democratic' an election which takes place because the normal democratic system has broken down is a contradiction in terms. But while Charles de Gaulle escaped from the circumstances which enabled him to come to power, Pétain did not. He remained, from July 1940 to August 1944, the prisoner and victim of the military disaster which had originally inspired Paul Reynaud with the totally erroneous view that the best way of strengthening the French will to resist was by bringing Pétain back to Paris from Madrid. Pétain subsequently made matters worse for his own reputa-

98   *French Caesarism*

tion, if not necessarily for the French at the time, by constantly taking the initiative in insisting to the Germans on how ready France was to collaborate. It is true that his suggestions, unlike those of Admiral Darlan, did not seek to bring France into the war on Germany's side. The engagements in which French troops loyal to Vichy fought against Free French forces in Syria in the Spring of 1941, like the resistance of French troops to the allied landings in North Africa in November 1942, were not events which he deliberately tried to bring about. Pétain's attempts at collaboration were intended to improve living conditions for the French in France. His ideal in foreign policy was a France which remained neutral until the time came when it could emerge as a potential arbitrator. Even as late as 1944, at the time of von Stauffenberg's plot against Hitler's life, he was indulging in the pipe dream of serving as a go-between in an act of reconciliation between the new Germany and a revivified France. It is doubtful if he ever really understood the nature of the régime which von Stauffenberg was trying to overthrow, and the impossibility of reaching a genuine collaboration with it. That he pursued this policy with such insistence is a sign of the extent to which he was also, during the period in which he theoretically ruled France, the victim of illusions.

Thus he thought he was presiding over a nation that was undergoing a great moral revival. This was the whole point of the Vichy motto of *Travail, Famille, Patrie*, with its insistence on duties rather than rights. In fact, the largest growth industry in the France of 1940–1944 was the sending of anonymous letters to the authorities. At no other time in French history did so many French people write so many letters denouncing so many of their fellow citizens to the police – as Jews, Freemasons, resistance activists or sympathisers, black-market profiteers, listeners to the BBC, communists, socialists or trade unionists.[21] Pétain thought that his own prestige as a great military leader would impress the Germans and secure better terms for France. All that he managed to do was enable the Germans to economise on manpower by having the French police help to keep order. In 1940, it is true, at the time when the French were overwhelmed with defeat, and transformed by the attempt to flee from the victorious German armies into a nation of refugees, he did carry out a quite remarkable restoration of morale. But it was a temporary palliative, with all the disadvantages that palliatives traditionally present in treating symptoms rather than the disease. By persisting in the illusion, understandable in July 1940 but rapidly

Philippe Pétain: The Victim

invalidated, that Germany was going to win the war, he helped to bring about a civil war in France between the resistance movement and the supporters of the Vichy government. By dividing the French even more thoroughly against themselves, he went against his own deepest ambitions as a political leader.

What he was trying to do was restore in France the same kind of régime which had been overthrown by the Revolution of 1789, one in which people did what they were told because the government knew what was best for them. His model, in this respect, was President Salazar of Portugal; and it is a mark of the political underdevelopment of the Iberian Peninsula in the first two-thirds of the twentieth century that Salazar was able to remain in power for so long, from 1932 until his death in 1970. France, unlike Spain and Portugal, could not put the clock back in this way. As soon as the Germans were driven out of France, the Vichy régime disappeared without trace. France nevertheless needed, as the history of the Fourth Republic was to show, a fourth and final Caesar to carry out the paradoxical achievement of ensuring that Caesarism would no longer be necessary. It found him in Charles de Gaulle, who had served as a young second lieutenant in 1912 in a regiment commanded by Pétain; who had been helped in the early part of his career between the wars by Pétain's readiness to support him in 1927 as a lecturer at the *Ecole de Guerre*; who had, in 1932, dedicated his second book, *Le Fil de l'Epée* (*The Edge of the Sword*) to Pétain; who had originally set out to write what became *La France et son Armée* (1938) as a book intended to appear under Pétain's signature; who had been sentenced to death by the Vichy government in 1940; and who was, in 1966, in a speech at Verdun, to refuse the transfer of Pétain's remains to the cemetery at Douaumont.

4 Charles de Gaulle: The Winner

I

There is an obvious danger in writing about Charles de Gaulle: that of almost deifying for his achievements, courage and prose style a man whose methods, personality and underlying aims are sometimes as hard to understand as they are difficult to admire.

The case for seeing de Gaulle as the last and most successful of the French Caesars is nevertheless overwhelming. Like the hero celebrated in *Maréchal, Nous Voilà!* he did indeed save the fatherland twice. Verses praising him for doing this could have been sung with much more obvious justification about de Gaulle in 1962 than about Pétain in 1940, and he also performed the most difficult task confronting any great ruler: that of leaving his successor with a situation capable of constant improvement. None of the three previous French Caesars could do this, for they all left office as a result of an invasion of France which led to the fall of the régime over which they presided. De Gaulle left of his own free will, and the Constitution which he succeeded in having accepted by the French in 1958 has proved the most subtle and effective instrument for combining state authority with parliamentary democracy that his country has so far known. Predictions are the most dangerous form of activity for any historian, amateur as well as professional. The book published by General Chauvineau in 1936, under the title *Une Invasion Est-elle Encore Possible?* concluded that it wasn't. But it does seem, in 1988, as though the last of the French Caesars has put an end to French Caesarism by providing French civilian politicians with a democratic system that compels them to work together.

De Gaulle himself would have agreed with an assessment of his career which began with praise for his constitutional achievements. When he was brought back to power in 1958 as a result of the coup d'état organised by the French army and European settlers in Algiers, it was with the establishment of a new Constitution that he was primarily concerned. It was because he disapproved of the Constitution about to be established for the Fourth Republic that he

Charles de Gaulle: The Winner

had earlier left office on 20 January 1946, and it was in order to change this Constitution that he had launched the *Rassemblement du Peuple Français* on 30 March 1947. His remark in his *Mémoires d'Espoir, Le Renouveau*, in 1970, to the effect that by 1958 France had been deprived of stability and continuity for 169 years – that is to say, since the outbreak of the first French revolution in 1789 – overstates the case, and is an example of how Latin a statesman de Gaulle could sometimes be in his tendency to be carried away by his own rhetoric.[1] The Third Republic, for example, was a quite remarkably resilient régime, and the Second Empire was not wholly a failure. But both régimes failed because of their inability to stand up to a crisis. In the case of the Third Republic, in de Gaulle's contention, this failure stemmed as much from an inadequate Constitution as from an ill-equipped army.

In the first volume of his war memoirs, de Gaulle makes two main criticisms of the Constitution of the Third Republic: that it lacked an article enabling the President to react to a national emergency by taking special powers; that it was unable to take the kind of long-term decisions which might have prevented such an emergency from arising in the first place. In an attempt to compensate for this, Article 16 of the Constitution of the Fifth Republic does give the President 'when the institutions of the Republic, the independence of the nation or the integrity of its territory are seriously and immediately threatened and the regular working of the public constitutional powers is interrupted' the authority to 'take the measures required by the circumstances'. His right to do so is hedged about with a number of rules which the experiences of 9 November 1799 and 2 December 1851 make fully explicable: he must officially consult the Prime Minister and the Presidents of both legislative chambers, the *Chambre des Députés* and the *Sénat*; he cannot dissolve Parliament while the emergency powers are in operation; and he must inform the nation of what he is doing. But the powers are nevertheless considerable. Had President Lebrun possessed them in 1940, de Gaulle argues, he could have moved the French government to Algeria in order to continue the struggle from there. Had he also had the moral authority which the President of the Fifth Republic derives from being chosen by the nation as a whole and not simply by the *Assemblée Nationale*, it is indeed conceivable that Lebrun might have done this, though the de Gaulle of 1959 was less sanguine about the possibility. 'Basically,' he wrote in *Le Salut*, the third volume of his *Mémoires de Guerre*, two things were lacking in Lebrun as head of

102   *French Caesarism*

state: 'qu'il fût un chef; et qu'il y eût un Etat' (that he was a leader; that a state existed).[2]

But as the *Mémoires de Guerre* make clear, de Gaulle's objections to the Constitution of the Third Republic were more fundamental. On 14 October 1936 he was received by Léon Blum, Prime Minister of the newly formed Popular Front. It was, appropriately enough, on the very day that the King of the Belgians, Leopold III, had declared his country's neutrality in any future war, and abandoned its formal alliance with France. De Gaulle was thus able to use the event to impress upon Blum the fact that the purely defensive strategy embodied in the Maginot line could not even achieve its primary object of protecting France from invasion. The fortifications did not extend to the sea, and thus left the traditional invasion route through Belgium and the Low Countries wide open. More significantly, as de Gaulle also pointed out, the very existence of the Maginot line gave the clearest possible signal to the Germans that they had a free hand in Eastern Europe. Hitler could attack Czechoslovakia or Poland with total impunity. Whatever he did, France would wait behind the Maginot line until directly attacked herself.

Léon Blum listened with interest as de Gaulle developed the ideas which he had made public some two years earlier, in May 1934, in his most important pre-war book, *Vers l'Armée de Métier* (*Towards a Professional Army*). There, as in two shorter articles, he had put forward a concept of forward defence which sounds oddly like an anticipation of President Eisenhower's remark in 1952 about the ability of the United States to deter aggression by 'massive retaliation at a time and place of our own choosing'. For it would not be necessary, as de Gaulle pointed out to Blum, for the French to go all the way to the Vistula to help the Poles or all the way to the Danube to protect the Austrians; neither would the French have to indulge in the cumbersome exercise of general mobilisation. The constantly ready mobile striking force of 100,000 men and 3,000 tanks, advancing on a thirty-mile front, could attack the enemy where it wanted; breach his defences; and, by destroying his most vulnerable strategic points, bring down his whole state 'as a cathedral can sometimes be brought down by the destruction of one pillar'.[3]

Léon Blum listened with interest. Historical examples as well as a modern precedent were there to support de Gaulle's point of view, and to reinforce his argument. In 1867 Bismarck had acknowledged how concerned he had been, at the time of the war against Austria in 1866, lest the French army take up an offensive position on the

Charles de Gaulle: The Winner 103

Franco-German frontier. In January 1934, in an article entitled 'Forgeons une armée de métier' ('Let us create a professional army'), published in *La Revue des Vivants*, de Gaulle had spoken of the cost in blood and tears to the French of the Second Empire's mistake in 'allowing the battle of Sadowa to take place without bringing the army up on to the Rhine'.[4] On 7 March 1936, two years after the publication of this article, German troops broke one of the most important articles of the Versailles treaty by re-occupying the demilitarised zone on the left bank of the Rhine. Unsupported by London, unequipped to react quickly, France had done nothing. The then Prime Minister, Albert Sarraut, had said that his government 'would not allow Strasbourg to be in range of German cannon'. But no action was taken, and Hitler had succeeded in his first gamble.

Léon Blum gave every sign of agreeing with de Gaulle's ideas. But throughout the conversation the telephone kept ringing. Like all French governments of the Third Republic, the Popular Front was a coalition. This meant that the principal function of the Prime Minister was to keep the government together by persuading his partners not to withdraw their support. He could never stop himself from being threatened for long enough to concentrate on a single problem for more than five minutes, and de Gaulle's description in the first volume of his war memoirs is introduced in a most timely manner to reinforce the point which he makes earlier in the same volume by the account of his own career in the 1930s:

> At that time, I was appointed to the General Secretariat of National Defence, a permanent body at the disposal of the Prime Minister to enable him to prepare the state and the nation for war. From 1932 to 1937, under fourteen different governments, I was involved in the analysis of all the political, administrative and technical activity linked to the defence of the country.

What this revealed to de Gaulle, by enabling him to see matters from close to, was not only the extent of France's resources but also 'the weakness of the state'.

> Scarcely was he in office, than the Prime Minister was confronted with innumerable demands, criticisms, and exaggerated rival bids (*surenchères*), which required his complete attention but which he could never master. Parliament, far from supporting him, offered only ambushes and betrayals. His ministers were his rivals. Public opinion, the press, different interest groups, saw him as a target for

104   *French Caesarism*

every kind of complaint. Everyone, moreover – himself included – knew that he was there only for a short time. In fact, after a few months, he had to give up. As far as national defence was concerned, such conditions made it impossible for those in power to embark upon that solid body of consistent plans, of carefully considered decisions, and of measures taken through to their conclusion which is worthy of being called a policy (*cet ensemble de desseins continus, de décisions mûries, de mesures menées à leur terme, qu'on appelle une politique*).[5]

It is consequently understandable, with the traumatic experience of the defeat of 1940 behind him, that the de Gaulle of 1958 should have given absolute priority to constitutional questions. His decision to do so has proved the most fruitful aspect of his career, with the France of the Fifth Republic enjoying a series of stable governments unparalleled in its democratic history. The Constitution approved by the referendum of 28 September 1958 states clearly that the President appoints the Prime Minister (*il nomme le Premier Ministre*). It does not, it is true, say that this Prime Minister must be able to command a majority in the *Chambre des Députés*, but practice has always confirmed the implication that the head of a government in a parliamentary democracy must be able to win approval for his annual budget and for his major bills. When, in March 1986, the Socialist President François Mitterrand found himself with a right-wing assembly, he did not hesitate long before asking Jacques Chirac to form a government. This gave reality to a relatively new word in the French political vocabulary, 'la cohabitation', and the experience of having a left-wing President and a right-wing Prime Minister proved remarkably popular with the French public if not necessarily with professional French politicians. It enabled them to move away from what they themselves call the 'Manicheism' of French politics, the tendency of politicians to see one side as absolutely good and the other as absolutely bad. Perhaps more significantly, it also showed how wrong the earlier critics of the Fifth Republic had been to accuse it of totally subordinating Parliament to President, and of trying to run an effective modern democracy without political parties. For although the Constitution requires the President to ratify all laws with his signature, it also offers Parliament a neat way of making it awkward for him to refuse to do so. Article 49, section 3, allows the Prime Minister to make the approval of any government bill a question of confidence. The President can refuse to countersign a bill only if he is

Charles de Gaulle: The Winner 105

prepared to provoke a major constitutional crisis. Like Marshal Mac-Mahon in 1877, he must either submit or resign. He cannot veto parliamentary bills. The success of 'la cohabitation' between 1986 and 1988 also enabled the Anglo-Saxon observer to enjoy a slight but appreciative chuckle at de Gaulle's expense. From the early 1940s he was the most resolutely anti-American of all European politicians. 'La cohabitation' introduces into French politics what sometimes seems suspiciously like the established practice of American politics whereby a Democratic President has to govern with a Republican Congress, or a Republican President with a Democratic Congress. It is true that the differences between the two systems are considerable. The American administration is not directly responsible to Congress. There is no Prime Minister. There is no question of a vote of no confidence 'bringing down the government'. Party political lines are much less clearly drawn than in Europe. But the basic idea of having an executive and a legislature which belong to different persuasions is central to the American system, and the Constitution of the Fifth Republic has shown this can also happen quite easily in France.

There is also more than a touch of irony in the fact that François Mitterrand should have been one of the politicians to derive most benefit from the Constitution of the Fifth Republic. In June 1958, together with Pierre Mendès France, he was one of the 224 *députés* to vote against the motion granting de Gaulle special powers to govern for six months by decree and to introduce a new Constitution. He was active in opposing the acceptance of this Constitution in the referendum of 28 September 1958, and even more violently critical of the constitutional change which de Gaulle introduced in 1962. Originally, the President of the Fifth Republic was elected by a *Collège des Notables*, a body of 80,000 locally elected *conseillers généraux* and *conseillers municipaux* (county and town councillors). It was an improvement on the arrangements of the Fourth Republic, by which the President was elected by both houses of Parliament, the *Chambre des Députés* and the *Conseil de la République*. In December 1953, it had taken 13 separate ballots before René Coty was elected as successor to Vincent Auriol, and the prestige of the Presidential office was not increased by a selection process which enabled a book to be opened at the *Collège Franco-Britannique* – and probably elsewhere – with runners and prices. In 1958, there was nothing like this when de Gaulle was elected President by the *Collège des Notables*, and officially took up office on 8 January 1959. He secured 62,394 votes, as against 10,355 for a Communist, Georges Marrane,

106 *French Caesarism*

and 6,721 for the candidate of the democratic left, Albert Châtelet. But in September 1962, after he had narrowly survived the assassination attempt at Le Petit Clamart on 22 August, de Gaulle announced his decision to hold a referendum to endorse the proposed change whereby the President would be elected by universal suffrage. Among the innumerable politicians who denounced the change as unconstitutional and tyrannical, few were more vehement than François Mitterrand. Fortunately for the Mitterrand of 1981 – and, even more, for the Mitterrand of 1988 – de Gaulle won.

But 'la cohabitation' is not the only word which de Gaulle's Constitution enabled to take on a new meaning in French. Another, equally important one, is 'l'alternance'. The concept and practice which it describes are so much part of normal proceedings in Anglo-Saxon democracies that there is no single technical word to translate it. 'Buggins's turn' has been suggested, with the implication that since Juggins has had a number of years in power to show what he can do, he ought really to let Buggins have a go; after which, when Buggins loses the next election, Juggins will take over again. In the Third and Fourth Republics this never happened. Since no single party was strong enough to win a majority in the *Chambre des Députés*, all governments were coalitions. One of the main reasons for which parliamentary democracy became so discredited in France was that the voter could rarely see a direct connection between his decision to vote for a particular party and the policy which the government containing this party tried to put into action. This was especially noticeable in the two years immediately preceding the fall of the Fourth Republic. In January 1956, the predominantly left-wing coalition headed by Guy Mollet and Pierre Mendès France won a majority of seats. It nevertheless ended up pursuing a policy of keeping Algeria French, when most of those who voted for it wanted to put an end to the Algerian war.

De Gaulle himself may not have been personally responsible for the electoral system which has helped 'l'alternance' to take place, and to provide the French electorate with a clear choice between two political alternatives. *Le scrutin uninominal à deux tours* (single member two ballot system) was almost certainly proposed by Michel Debré, and it had been used in the Third Republic from 1889 to 1914 and from 1928 to 1936. But just as Napoleon I provided the authority under which the *Code Napoléon* could be drafted and adopted, so the presence of de Gaulle enabled the Fifth Republic to reinforce the tendency towards bipolarisation inherent in *le scrutin uninominal à deux tours.* At the first ballot, held as usual in France on a Sunday, electors vote for the candidate they really want. If he wins over half the votes cast, he is elected. If he does not – and only about one in five do – then there is a run-off on the following Sunday; preceded by a week of sometimes difficult negotiations in which the less favourably placed candidate on the left is persuaded to stand down in favour of his better placed ally and rival; while the same thing happens on the right. In the second ballot, the candidate obtaining most votes wins.

This system had not, it is true, produced 'l'alternance' until the Fifth Republic was 23 years old. Until 1981, France was governed by a right-wing or moderate centre alliance. From 1958 to 1967, the dominant element in this was the *Union pour la Nouvelle République* (UNR), the party formed when de Gaulle returned to power in 1958. In 1967, this party changed its name to that of the *Union des Démocrates pour la Ve République* (UDR), and in 1968 to the UDF (*Union pour la Défense de la République*). It is true that de Gaulle did not officially allow candidates to use his name. But there was no doubt that anyone voting for the UNR, the UDR or the UDF was voting for de Gaulle. When Jacques Chirac decided in August 1976 that he could no longer serve as Prime Minister under Valéry Giscard d'Estaing, he chose a very Gaullist set of initials to designate the party he then formed. The RPR (*Rassemblement pour la République*) sounded extraordinarily like the RPF (*Rassemblement du Peuple Français*), the organisation by which de Gaulle had tried to come back to power between 1947 and 1953. 'L'alternance' really began to work only when François Mitterrand was elected President in May 1981. He used Article 12 of the Constitution to dissolve the *Assemblée Nationale*, and obtained a Socialist majority of 46 over all the other parties combined. As Jacques Fauvet observed in *Le Monde*, the elections of 1981 had one undoubted winner: General de Gaulle. His Constitution had shown a combination of strength and adaptability which had enabled France not only to make a complete change of government without changing the régime – this had already happened in 1924 and 1936 – but to do so with some assurance that the new government would stay in power for a full five years. When, in the legislative elections of March 1986, the Socialists lost their majority – in spite of having changed the rules and introduced a system of proportional representation – there was again no problem in the arrangements whereby Juggins gave way to Buggins.

De Gaulle may not have wanted any of this to happen. He did not

108 *French Caesarism*

like politicians – indeed, there were times when he didn't really seem to like anybody, especially not soldiers – and one of his letters to his mother during the First World War strikes a note which enables one to understand why *The Times* of 8 June 1940, commenting on his entry as Under-Secretary for War in Paul Reynaud's cabinet, described him as 'rather aggressively right-wing'.

> Parliament (he wrote in December 1915) is becoming more and more hateful and stupid. The ministers literally have every single one of their days taken up by sittings in the House . . . They could not, even if they wanted to, find the time to administer their Department . . . We shall win the war as soon as we have driven out all this riff-raff (*dès que nous aurons balayé toute cette racaille*), and there is not a single Frenchman who would not shout for joy, the front-line soldiers in particular.[6]

But although there are plenty of other examples of de Gaulle's denunciations of what he called 'les politichiens' (J. R. Tournoux' *La Tragédie du Général* reports his description of them as 'les pisse-vinaigre, les tricheurs, les fuyards professionnels' – vinegar-pissers, cheats, professional cowards),[7] he never gave way to what must have been a temptation to devise a régime from which they would be totally excluded. In his very first book, *La Discorde Chez l'Ennemi*, published in 1924, he argued how essential it was, especially in wartime, for the naval and military authorities to remain subordinate to the civil power. It was, in his view, because Emperor William II of Germany proved incapable of imposing his authority on Admiral Tirpitz that the United States entered the First World War in 1917. Had William II succeeded in preventing the German navy from embarking upon a campaign of unrestricted submarine warfare, President Wilson might never have declared war. Germany would then have been able to obtain, through American mediation, a far more advantageous peace treaty than the one she finally had to sign at Versailles in 1919. Her disastrous defeat was, in this respect, a result of the failure to observe the 'great principle' of the subordination of military power to legally established civilian authority.[8] It was a principle which de Gaulle was to show himself both able and willing to put into practice when he came into conflict with the French army over the Algerian problem.

The Constitution of the Fifth Republic certainly tried to limit the influence of politicians, and even more of political parties. In particular, it gave the President the power to appoint a non-

Charles de Gaulle: The Winner 109

parliamentarian as Prime Minister. When de Gaulle made Georges Pompidou Prime Minister in 1962, Pompidou had never held elected office. Neither had Couve de Murville in 1968, and the same is true of Raymond Barre when he was made Prime Minister by Giscard d'Estaing in 1976. A *député* has to give up his seat in the *Chambre des Députés* on becoming a minister. His loyalty, in the Gaullist reading of the Constitution, is then to the government he serves, not to the party he represents. In its presupposition that there is an important way in which the state stands above party, this is a very Caesarian concept. It would certainly have appealed as much to Pétain as to the two Napoleons. It is nevertheless part of de Gaulle's greatness as the first Caesar really to come to terms with democracy that the Constitution he designed also accepts that the state and the parties should genuinely balance each other out. The former cannot wholly dominate the latter. The latter must accept the need to work within a coherent framework.

In 1958 the new Constitution was in fact much criticised for reducing the length of parliamentary sessions, giving the government virtually total control over the use of parliamentary time, and greatly limiting the opportunities for motions of censure. But there has never been any question of doing away with parliament, or trying, as Napoleon III did for the first 18 years of his reign, to restrict its opportunities for discussing the budget. It is perhaps arguable that de Gaulle never envisaged the possibility of his Constitution being used with equal facility by left and right. But there is no evidence to suggest that he intended to create a situation in which a right-wing President would perpetually dominate a subserviently right-wing Assembly. By French standards, and in spite of his occasional outbreaks of Anglophobia and nasty remarks about politicians, he was not in fact all that much a man of the right.

This is the first of de Gaulle's many paradoxes. In spite of its reluctance to involve itself in politics, the French officer class has traditionally favoured the right. It has done so with less virulence than the navy, whose nickname of 'la royale' is frequently a fair indication of its political attachments. But the army's behaviour at the time of the Dreyfus case did not stem solely from the natural reluctance of any organisation to go back on one of its own legal or administrative decisions. Although it made no concerted effort to overthrow the Republic, there is little doubt that its senior officers would have been happy to see a more authoritarian form of government replace what the right wing traditionally described as 'la gueuse'

110 *French Caesarism*

(the slut). The defeat of the campaign in favour of Dreyfus would have meant the triumph of the old, authoritarian France of the monarchy and aristocracy over the new, republican France, with its spirit of agnosticism, social equality and free enquiry. It would also, more disturbingly, have meant that France would have been the first country to fall victim to the new, antisemitic right of *L'Action Française*, with its passion for street violence, monarchism, and political hooliganism.

In his *Mémoires de Guerre*, de Gaulle describes his mother as 'bearing towards her country an uncompromising passion equal to her religious piety'. She had three sons, of whom Charles was the second, and was frequently congratulated on their achievements, intelligence and behaviour. She accepted the compliments with suitable modesty, and expressed only one reservation: 'They are all republicans'.[9] In the Lille of the 1890s and early 1900s, it was an unusual attitude to find among the sons of good Catholic families, especially if they also happened to have as father a man who taught in a private school. For the distinction, then as now, between private and state education in France was not, as it is in England and America, primarily one of class and money. It was one of ideology. From the moment that the Third Republic established in 1881 a system of national education that was free, compulsory, universal and secular (*laïque*), good Catholic families chose to keep their children away from what they called 'l'école sans Dieu'. De Gaulle's father Henri was in fact the only teacher not in holy orders at the *Collège de l'Immaculée Conception* in the rue Vaugirard, in Paris, where he taught until it had to close in 1901 as a result of laws forbidding certain religious orders to run schools. He subsequently founded another Catholic school, the *Ecole Fontanes*, and had little sympathy for the Republic. He agreed, apparently, with Joseph de Maistre in seeing the French Revolution as an undertaking that was 'satanic in its very essence',[10] and was a member of *L'Action Française* from its establishment in 1899 to its condemnation by the Vatican in 1926. But he did not believe that Dreyfus was guilty; and, at the time of the second trial, at Rennes, in August 1899, made his position clear to his wife, daughter and three sons.

Charles, born on 22 November 1890, was only 8 years old at the time. But the affair rumbled on until Dreyfus was finally rehabilitated in 1906, awarded the *Légion d'Honneur* and reinstated in the army with the rank of major. A belief in his innocence inculcated by the man so vividly and affectionately described on the first page of

Charles de Gaulle: The Winner

L'Appel is the first of many features which mark de Gaulle out from the very beginning as a heretic and a rebel to his class: 'Mon père, homme de pensée, de culture, de tradition, était imprégné du sentiment de la dignité de la France. Il m'en a découvert l'histoire.' (My father, a man of ideas, culture and tradition, was imbued with the feeling of the dignity of France. He revealed her history to me.) Many years later, in 1944, when he came back to liberated France as President of the Provisional French Government, he introduced a number of economic and social reforms which suggested to his admirers as well as to his critics that the Popular Front of 1936 was coming back to life in his person. Like almost everybody at the time, and certainly like everybody on the left, de Gaulle saw the state as needing to take an increasing and dominant role in the economic life of the country, and depicted it as being able to do so only by a systematic programme of nationalisation and economic planning. In 1945 he presided over the nationalisation of coal-mines, steel, and a good half of the banking system. It was while he was still in power in the immediate post-war period that the French social security system was established, and the Renault car factories taken into public ownership. He even followed some of the economic errors of the left, and contributed to the inflation which was to cause such problems to the Fourth Republic. In December 1944 he was called upon to adjudicate between Pierre Mendès France, a supporter of strict economic discipline, and René Pleven, who was in favour of a more relaxed approach. He sided with Pleven, and the inflation which Mendès France might have prevented proceeded to take off. It is not an unusual accompaniment to a left-wing government.

Julius Caesar found his most determined opponents among the aristocratic party in Rome; it was in order to prevent him from establishing a popular dictatorship that he was assassinated. It is a characteristic of Caesarism, as defined in this book, to establish as direct a link as possible between the ruler and the mass of those he rules, and to achieve this by reducing the number and power of intermediary bodies. This explains the importance of plebiscites and referenda in the Caesarist tradition, and is also consistent with de Gaulle's own hostility towards political parties. What he wanted to do, as he wrote in *Le Salut*, was derive his support from the people ('prendre appui dans le peuple'), rather than from the élites which 'tended to interpose themselves' between the people and him.[11] His concept of democracy, at least in theory, was a plebiscitary one. It is this as much as anything else which places him in the Caesarian

112 *French Caesarism*

tradition as a leader with a direct line to the masses. But there is a reassuring difference between the Constitution he left behind him, which has enabled a pluralist democracy in France to work, and this somewhat limiting concept of the leader who, in some semi-magical way, is the only person who understands what the people really need. In this particular aspect of his thinking, perhaps best defined as messianic, it is hard to take de Gaulle absolutely seriously.

Perhaps because he was half aware of this, de Gaulle was also exceptionally sensitive to criticism. During the whole of the Third Republic, there had been only six convictions under the law of 1881 making it an offence punishable by fine or imprisonment to insult the head of state; in the Fourth Republic, there had been only three. Between 1958 and 1968, there were over 350, and this can scarcely have been because de Gaulle was more frequently ridiculed than his predecessors.[12] But in spite of this similarity to Louis XIV, another ruler sensitive to *lèse-majesté*, de Gaulle was not right-wing in the way that Napoleon I, Napoleon III and Pétain were. Unlike the first two, he had no liking for military coups d'état. When, late in 1945, his authority was called into question by the Constituent Assembly, he did not for one moment envisage calling on the army. The *Discours de Bayeux*, which set out as early as 1946 the basic ideas which were to inspire the Constitution of the Fifth Republic 11 years later, specifically states that it is 'of the very essence of democracy that opinions should be expressed and that people should seek to use elections to direct public action and legislation in the way they choose'.[13] It also gives a definite rôle to parliament: 'It is clear, and plainly understood, that laws and the budget are finally approved by an Assembly elected by direct universal suffrage.' It could even be argued that the combination which he imposed on France of a strong Presidency governing in collaboration with an independently elected legislative assembly was the best possible way for his country to solve the basic dilemma of democracy. For this can function only if two conditions are fulfilled: that there is enough agreement on the basic Constitution for a change of government not to bring about a change of régime; and that there is enough disagreement between the competing parties for electoral contests to be meaningful. No major party in France, in the late twentieth century, wants to overthrow the Constitution of the Fifth Republic. In this respect, the situation is totally different from what it had been between 1870 and 1940 and between 1946 and 1958. France has become like the United Kingdom or the United States in that there is a general consensus about the

Charles de Gaulle: The Winner 113

kind of society, and the kind of Constitution, that most people want. Not all the credit for this, of course, need be given to de Gaulle. His critics point out that he himself, between 1947 and 1953, added greatly to the instability of the Fourth Republic. His decision in April 1947 to set up the *Rassemblement du Peuple Français* created the same kind of challenge from the right which had helped to bring about the downfall of the Third Republic. The RPF, an 'objective ally' in this respect of a powerful Communist Party on the left, placed the Fourth Republic in the uncnviable position of having more voters opposed to the régime than were actually in favour of it. If de Gaulle did not bring down the Fourth Republic, it was not for want of trying. Neither can he be given all the credit for reducing the major threat to French democracy: the strength of the Communist Party. This is partly the achievement of François Mitterrand, in succeeding from 1972 onwards in constructing a viable left-wing alternative; partly the result of the foreign policy of the Soviet Union; and partly the inevitable consequence of the surprising resilience, in France and elsewhere, of the capitalist system. What de Gaulle did was to create the conditions in which capitalism could work more efficiently in France and in which a democratic socialist party could, in 1981, translate its electoral appeal into a working majority.

If this was not precisely what he had in mind when he came back to power in 1958, it points to another of the similarities between literary criticism and historical analysis: neither discipline can limit itself to looking at intentions. A work of art always has a larger number of meanings than its author had consciously in mind at the time of composition. We read *Œdipus Rex* or *Hamlet* differently from Sophocles' or Shakespeare's contemporaries because our historical experience and world vision are different from theirs. Even if the authors were to come back to life and tell us what they 'really meant' this would not invalidate the interpretations which we place on their works today. The same is true of achievements of statesmen. In his heart of hearts de Gaulle may well have envisaged a political system in which parties were reduced to a consultative, subordinate rôle. The structure which he provided has nevertheless not worked that way at all. Presidents are elected on a party ticket, just as they are in the United States. Once elected, however, they are expected to rise above party politics, and the experience of 'la cohabitation' required François Mitterrand to do just that. De Gaulle may simply be benefiting, posthumously, from an extraordinary run of luck. It may be sheer chance that the system he left behind him is working so well.

114 *French Caesarism*

Or it may be that, by some stroke of intuitive and unconscious genius, he set up the right system for France. It would be pleasant to think so, for it would endorse his view that Providence has a particular eye for French interests. It would also mean, in S. E. Finer's terms, that France had finally become a mature political society. It is time to look at how de Gaulle did it.

II

By definition, Caesars are military men. There may indeed be a temptation, on first being asked to define the word in the context of French history and politics, to mention the names of Louis XIV and Clemenceau, or even of other notorious strong men such as Doumergue or Poincaré. But Louis XIV was an absolute monarch by divine right, and Clemenceau's majority in the *Chambre des Députés* from the moment he took up office in the First World War never fell below 213.[14] The element of illegality, indissociable from the first Caesar crossing the Rubicon at the head of his army without permission from the Senate, is quite absent from their careers, however much Louis XIV provided a model for de Gaulle's caricaturists and Clemenceau shared his impatience with French political parties. But it is not enough to be a soldier, even one exercising considerable power. Marshal Foch, in the closing stages of the First World War, may have acted at times like a dictator. His authority to give orders nevertheless stemmed from the fact that the man who appointed him had a majority in parliament. De Gaulle, in contrast, acquired such a majority in 1944 only after he had spent four years defying what was theoretically the legal government of France; and in 1958 only after an armed rebellion in Algeria had overthrown a government enjoying a majority in an assembly which had been quite legally elected only two years previously.

It is true that Napoleon III came to power without ever having faced men in battle. But his uncle's military achievements were considerable enough for him to present them as his own. He would certainly not have been elected President of the Second Republic without them. Had somebody else commanded the French armies at Verdun, Pétain would have died obscure and forgotten. De Gaulle's initial claim to represent France, like his later appeal, was inseparable from the fact that he was a soldier. Even after he had twice been elected President of France, he was rarely referred to as anything but

Charles de Gaulle: The Winner 115

'le Général'. Jean-François Revel, one of his most acerbic if not always accurate critics, once even accused him of failing to observe one of the typographical rules of French by referring to himself as le Général de Gaulle while placing the first letter of Giraud's or Catroux' title in lower-case type.[15] Almost all the photographs taken of de Gaulle, except the official ones of him as elected Head of State, show him in uniform. Apart from the curious affectations of Winston Churchill in wartime Britain, it is hard to think of an Anglo-Saxon equivalent, especially in a country where officers have, since the nineteenth century, discarded their uniforms when off-duty. De Gaulle's military achievements were real enough to provide a starting point for the increasingly political rôle which he played from 1940 onwards. They must nevertheless not be exaggerated.

Physically, as well as morally, de Gaulle was a very brave man. He was wounded in action three times in the first year of the First World War, and on the last occasion, on 2 March 1916, was reported as missing, presumed dead. The citation, composed by Pétain himself, read:

> Captain Charles de Gaulle, the company commander, widely known for his high intellectual and moral value, seeing that his battalion, subjected to a terrible bombardment, was decimated and that the Germans were overrunning his company from all sides, ordered his men to attack in a furious onslaught and bitter hand-to-hand fighting, the sole solution which he considered compatible with his concept of military honour. Fell on the field of battle. An incomparable officer, in every respect.

De Gaulle was not dead, of course. He had followed the very sensible tactic of anyone under heavy artillery fire and dived into a hole. There, covered with dirt and dead bodies, he had been stabbed in the left buttock by an enemy bayonet. Once captured, he showed great determination in trying to escape, and never lost his sense of dignity. When, on his third attempt, he was arrested by the German police, he told them very firmly to show him a little more respect. But he was taken back to Osnabrück, and spent the rest of the war in captivity. To end the war still a captain cannot have been anything but a great disappointment from a professional point of view; even if, unlike many others, he had the consolation of having survived.[16]

When the Second World War broke out, de Gaulle was still only a half colonel, and was never to have field command of anything larger than a division. He certainly had the right idea about tanks. Genera

116 *French Caesarism*

Giraud, in contrast, echoed the received wisdom of the French general staff by maintaining that they should be used only to accompany the infantry. In an exercise which took place in September 1937 he told de Gaulle quite categorically: 'As long as I am in command of the Region, you will link your tanks to the rhythm of the infantry.'[17] De Gaulle recognised the value of Liddell-Hart's concept of a rapidly moving, wholly mechanised, independently commanded armoured force. It was with such a force that Guderian was later to exploit Liddell-Hart's teaching in order to win the Battle of France in 1940, something which the Germans might perhaps not have been able to do if the French army had followed the advice of *Vers l'Armée de Métier*. With only 140 tanks at his disposal to support his six infantry battalions and six artillery groups, de Gaulle fought the one successful engagement against the Germans, at Abbeville, on 28 May 1940, taking some 300 prisoners. But although Guderian was worried about it for a short time, he did not regard the engagement as important enough to include in his report on the day's fighting, and there has even been some doubt as to whether de Gaulle's armoured striking force would have proved very successful in a sustained campaign. Liddell-Hart himself commented that the force described in *Vers l'Armée de Métier* would have been 'as far as can be deduced from his hazy outline ... a clumsy monstrosity impossible to manoeuvre'.[18] De Gaulle himself was so conscious of his failure to insist on the importance of air power that he gave a considerable hostage to fortune to his critics by modifying the 1944, Algiers edition of the book, in order to make himself appear in a better light.[19]

After he had been appointed as a junior minister in the War Ministry by Paul Reynaud on 5 June 1940, he never saw action again. Although he rarely appeared out of uniform, he was to all intents and purposes a politician, and to start with not all that successful or ambitious a one. His limitations as a man and leader are perhaps indicated by the fact that not a single one of the soldiers who had served under him at Abbeville came to join him in England. The largest single contingent came from the Ile de Sein, just off the coast of Brittany. The whole male population of the island turned up in London, presumably leaving their womenfolk to cope as best they ~ould. It is an interesting pointer as to the local enthusiasm which have greeted one of the projects which de Gaulle favoured for ~ in 1940, that of establishing a 'réduit breton'. This ᵼich might have held out for a short time, would ᵼed in practice only to more casualties, especially

Charles de Gaulle: The Winner 117

among the civilian population. De Gaulle's support for it does not provide very convincing evidence of his grasp of military tactics on a regional scale, any more than his choice of *Vers l'Armée de Métier* as the title for his 1934 book showed the political awareness needed in someone seeking to influence French political opinion. Had he chosen to give his book the French equivalent of the title under which it appeared in English translation in 1940, *The Army of the Future*, he might have encountered less resistance.[20] The words would not have evoked the vision of a professional army, potentially poised to become a Praetorian Guard. In 1850, General Romieu had explained to Louis Napoleon that he ought to carry out his coup d'état quickly, while France still had 'son armée de métier', a professional army.[21] The introduction of compulsory military service, he pointed out, would inevitably produce a socialist army opposed to any attempt to subordinate civilian to military power. De Gaulle's own experience in 1962 was to bear this out, when the conscript army of the Fifth Republic refused to obey the orders of their mainly professional officers and followed instead the orders of the President of the Republic. But in 1934, de Gaulle lacked the political skills he was to develop from 1940 onwards, and more especially from 1958. He did not, apparently, foresee the opposition which the idea of such a non-republican concept as a professional army calling itself by that name would arouse in French political circles.

It is nevertheless intriguing to read of the efforts that de Gaulle made in June 1940 to persuade somebody else to take over what he saw as the essential task of keeping France in the war. He would certainly have been happy to serve under Paul Reynaud. On 17 June 1940, the day before his famous broadcast, he actually sent a telegram to General Colson, the Minister for War in Pétain's cabinet, asking him for orders, and on 20 June he sent another telegram to Bordeaux declaring his readiness to serve under Weygand or 'any other French figure prepared to resist'. If he did become a Caesar in 1940, crossing the Channel away from his country as illegally as Julius Caesar had taken his army across the Rubicon in the direction of Rome, it was with more obvious reluctance than any of his three predecessors. Admittedly, on 18 June, he was already speaking 'au nom de la France'. When, in 1968, he spoke about 'cette légitimité que j'incarne depuis plus de vingt ans', he was not misrepresenting the way he rapidly took on the role of the saviour of France from 1940 onwards. But all the evidence at the time was that he did not want to do it. Few careers illustrate more clearly than that of General de

118 *French Caesarism*

Gaulle the fact that Caesarism can flourish in France only when civilian politicians either leave the Rubicon unguarded or refuse to ford it themselves.

For de Gaulle's admirers, of course, any suggestion that the government which he established in June 1940 was in any way illegal smacks of worse than impiety. It is positively sacrilegious. But although de Gaulle was quite right from a moral and political point of view, the legal and constitutional basis for his action was rather more shaky. If the majority of 569 to 80 which gave power to Philippe Pétain is not enough to alter one Constitution and establish a basis for a new one, it is hard to see how any democratic country is ever going to be allowed to change its form of government. The decision to take the vote may well have been morally and politically wrong. It is not a good idea to take decisions of this type when your country is being overrun by an enemy army. But it was not illegal. The constitutional law of 10 July 1940 was, as one of Petain's defenders observed, 'régulièrement promulguée, sous la signature du Président de la République, M. Albert Lebrun' – quite legally promulgated, and signed by the President of the Republic, Albert Lebrun.[22]

In 1940 de Gaulle's Caesarism was of an unusual and challenging type. It was based on fairly slender military achievements, and on an essentially Rousseauistic and almost Protestant idea that one man's intuition of what his country needs can outweigh any majority decision with which he happens to disagree. There is no lack of evidence to show that de Gaulle had this inner conviction. When Jules Jeanneney, the former President of the French Senate, insisted in 1942 that 'National sovereignty cannot be exercised either legally or materially by the Parliament in function. It is the Nation itself which has the right to assume it', de Gaulle agreed with him absolutely. Although by the end of 1940 he still had fewer than 7,000 men serving under him, de Gaulle was convinced that he was the incarnation of France. In September 1942, at the height of one of their innumerable disagreements about Syria, he told Churchill that he spoke in the name of France and was responsible to her.[23] One of the possibly ambiguous disadvantages of looking at de Gaulle in terms of the Caesarist tradition is to be reminded how very much this incarnation of Catholic France was a follower of Rousseau, Luther or even Cromwell. There de Gaulle stood – his conscience would allow him to do no other – beseeching his fellow countrymen to consider the possibility that they might be mistaken.

It is sometimes difficult, when reading the *Mémoires de Guerre*, to

Charles de Gaulle: The Winner   119

remember that de Gaulle was fighting the Germans. Far more pages are devoted to the way he thought he was being slighted by Churchill or Roosevelt than to the actual conduct of the war, and this is not simply how he saw matters in retrospect. To Daniel Mayer, arriving in London from occupied France in 1942, when Britain was considered as France's principal friend, a model democracy, and the haven of the world's liberty, de Gaulle's endless protests about his mistreatment by the Allies seemed sheer lunacy. Oliver Lyttleton also described what seems to have been a very common reaction among Anglo-Saxon if not French observers when he wrote that 'the General must have risen every morning saying to himself: "France is dishonoured. Where and when am I going to be insulted to-day?".'[24] De Gaulle suspected the British of wishing to take France's place as the leading European power in the Middle East, and quarrelled violently with Churchill over Syria. His principal object, it appears from the *Mémoires de Guerre*, was to ensure that it was the French and not the British who gave the Syrians independence. His relationship with Roosevelt was even more tumultuous, and led eventually to the situation where de Gaulle was not allowed to land in liberated France until a week after D Day. There seem, in this context, to have been as many faults on Roosevelt's side as on de Gaulle's – he is, after all, reported as saying at Casablanca in 1944 that France was 'a little child unable to look after itself' and commenting that 'in such circumstances, a court appoints a trustee to do the necessary'.[25] But if, almost fifty years later, de Gaulle occasionally seems to have been at one and the same time stiff-necked and narrow-minded, and to have lacked more than tact in dealing with his potential allies, his behaviour paid off amply in terms of French domestic policy when he came back to power in 1958. The Fourth Republic had been accused, by politicians on the right as well as on the left, of being at the beck and call of the Americans. When, on 8 February 1958, the French air force bombed the Tunisian village of Sakhiet, alleging it was being used as a base for Algerian *Front de Libération Nationale* guerrillas, an American diplomat was appointed by the United Nations to try to calm the situation down. But in Paris, the presence of Robert Murphy only exacerbated things, while providing de Gaulle's supporters with one of their key arguments in his favour: as his record in the Second World War showed, he was a stickler for national independence. With him, France would decide her own affairs.

   This remained one of his main attractions, illustrating how much

French Caesarism

more important he was as a politician than as a military leader. The kind of strike force which he envisaged in the 1930s may not have had the military qualities to repel an invasion. But its importance had always been more in its political significance, as a sign of the determination of France to adopt an aggressive stance in foreign affairs. France, as has often been argued, would have been liberated by the allied armies in 1944 whether de Gaulle had been there or not. The home-grown resistance movement certainly profited from his existence as an obviously identifiable leader, a name to provide a rallying point and the excuse for the more timid but linguistically conscious opponents of Vichy to express their support for him by carrying two fishing rods (*deux gaules* = De Gaulle). General Eisenhower paid this movement the compliment of attributing to it the importance of 15 divisions, and there is no discounting the rôle it played. But de Gaulle was not a Tito, a Ho Chi Minh or a Mao Tse Tung, a guerrilla leader who led his forces in the field and won battles on the ground. He was a politician who unified this movement from abroad.

This indeed was his main importance, both during the lifetime of the Vichy government and in 1944, at the time of the liberation of France. Left to themselves, the Americans might well have run into serious trouble with their plan to rule the country directly through AMGOT (Allied Military Government for Occupied Territories), with administrators who had, in Charlottesville, Virginia, 'learned in two months the art of being *préfet* in Chartres or *sous-préfet* at Carpentras'.[26] There would certainly have been difficulties between the allied armics and the left-wing elements in the resistance movement. One of the most important claims made for de Gaulle is that it was his presence which prevented the Communists from using the resistance as a springboard to a left-wing coup d'état which would have brought the whole of liberated France under their control. By his insistence, on 25 August 1944, in going directly to the War Ministry in the rue Saint Dominique, and not to the Hôtel de Ville, de Gaulle was asserting one of his most firmly held views: the predominance of the officially constituted organs of state over any forms of popular sovereignty which he personally did not control. Had he gone to the Hôtel de Ville and proclaimed the Republic in the way that the leaders wanted him to do, he could well have opened the door to an attempt at a political take-over by the left which might in turn have led, as it did in Greece, to a civil war with foreign intervention.[27] De Gaulle's insistence on re-establishing as quickly as

Charles de Gaulle: The Winner 121

possible the officially constituted organs of state also meant that some limit was placed upon the popular tribunals set up to punish collaborators, and here again he is well within the Caesarist tradition established by the first Napoleon in acting essentially as a national unifier. But he did this from a political and not from a military basis, and thereby revealed one of the many paradoxes in the French Caesarist tradition: although military men may take power in France as a result of the prestige they have won upon the field of battle, their more permanent achievements lie in their contribution to civilian rather than military life. From a military point of view, after all, Napoleon I left France with little more than the very dangerous myth that she was a great military power.

They also, of course, are successful in so far as they see themselves and are seen by others as unifiers. In the years of exile, between 1940 and 1944, de Gaulle showed an essentially eclectic attitude towards French politicians which recalls the readiness of the first Napoleon to accept service from anyone competent enough to offer it. Whatever *The Times* may have said about him being 'rather aggressively right-wing',[28] de Gaulle had no hesitation in taking left-wing and even Communist politicians into his government in exile. It was, admittedly, the right-wing Thierry d'Argenlieu who first adopted the Croix de Lorraine as a symbol for the Free French movement, thus creating what was to become a constant reference to Joan of Arc. But the majority of those who joined de Gaulle in London, and subsequently in Algiers, had served under the Popular Front government of 1936: Jean Moulin, Pierre Mendès France, André Philip, Pierre Brossolette, René Massigli, René Mayer. The Provisional Government which he formed in August 1943 worked out a programme which reproduced – and was later to put into action – many of the ideas inspiring the cult of nationalisation and state planning associated both with the Socialists of the 1930s and with the resistance movement. But just as de Gaulle had difficulty getting on with his Anglo-Saxon allies, so he found it a problem, once political life began to go back to normal after the liberation, to adjust to the idea of political parties. It was because of this difficulty that de Gaulle refused to take part in what he later called 'les jeux, poisons et délices du système' (the games, poisons and delights of the system) and why he was so easily out-manœuvred by the old parliamentary hand, Henri Queuille, in the 1951 general election.

De Gaulle had launched the *Rassemblement du Peuple Français* on 7 April 1947, and had done very well in the municipal elections in

122 *French Caesarism*

October of that year. The general election of June 1951 looked like his big chance to win power by wholly constitutional means, and thus establish something of a record. The two Napoleons, like Pétain, had needed a national emergency. But Queuille, seeing that the two largest parties in the Fourth Republic, the Gaullists and the Communists, were likely to increase their domination of the *Chambre des Députés*, and thus render France increasingly ungovernable, decided to introduce what was known as 'le système des apparentements'. In this, any group of political parties prepared to form an alliance was guaranteed all the seats in a particular constituency so long as it obtained over half the votes cast. It then divided the seats among its members according to a numerical formula decided in advance. This system created a great disadvantage for those parties which, like the Communists and de Gaulle's *Rassemblement du Peuple Français*, were compelled by their own intransigence and exclusiveness not to do any deals. Had it accepted the system, the RPF might have obtained between 160 and 186 seats, and become the largest party in the Assembly. As it was, it won only 120, and de Gaulle effectively lost the chance of coming to power by classic, parliamentary means. Just as General Boulanger had been made harmless by the simple constitutional device of changing the electoral rules to forbid multiple candidacies, so de Gaulle was foxed by an equally simple change in the rules in the classic parliamentary game. He was therefore compelled – and such is the nature of Caesarism – to wait until the political system of the Fourth Republic had broken down.

Without the Algerian problem, this might well never have happened. From 1952 onwards, France was caught up in the general movement towards greater prosperity which was a feature of the 1950s. In 1952, the insignificant-looking Antoine Pinay had engineered something of an economic boom, and in August 1954 Pierre Mendès France managed to end the war which France had been fighting since 1946 in order to try to keep Indochina out of Communist control. Had the French been able to introduce reforms into Algeria in time, and thus perhaps prevent the uprising which began on 1 November 1954, the Fourth Republic could have had as long a life as the Third. For most people were relatively happy with the system, in spite of its many failures. At the time of the defeat of Dien Bien Phu in 1954, for example, which had effectively put an end to French hopes of winning the Indochinese war, de Gaulle had tried to test the political temperature by announcing that he would go to the Arc de Triomphe in the afternoon of 9 May to welcome any Parisians

Charles de Gaulle: The Winner 123

prepared to support him. There was barely a tenth of the 100,000 people he had expected. Even General Boulanger, in the 1880s, had managed to collect more support than that in his attempt to come to power. Had there been a large enough crowd in May 1954, de Gaulle might have been tempted to try to take over France by extraparliamentary means four years earlier than he did, in spite of the scepticism he expressed on the value of *pronunciamientos*. All that these did, he observed in 1954, was to replace one sergeant-major by another. It is difficult to see so essentially dignified a man as de Gaulle doing anything visibly illegal. In a country like France, enjoying in the 1950s the benefits of an economic boom as well as of a developed if not a mature political culture, there has to be a very serious breakdown of the normal political process, as there certainly had been in 1799 and 1940. Otherwise, as de Gaulle commented in his customarily acerbic manner, 'tout va à peu près bien: le 3 pour cent se maintient, l'Inspection des Finances inspecte, les ministres offrent des déjeuners, les dirigeants organisent des conférences internationales. Rien ne va plus lorsque les circonstances s'aggravent' (everything works more or less satisfactorily: consols stay at 3 per cent, the *Inspection des Finances* inspects, ministers invite people to lunch, managers organise international conferences. Everything breaks down when circumstances get worse).[29] Algeria was to provide the breakdown and the necessary crisis.

Before it did so, however, the enforced leisure of the early 1950s enabled de Gaulle to write his *Mémoires de Guerre*. After its failure in the 1951 elections, the RPF gradually fell apart, and in July 1952 de Gaulle virtually retired from public life. This enabled him to devote his time to writing, and the first volume of the *Mémoires* appeared in October 1954, astonishing everyone by its success. Over 100,000 copies were sold in five weeks, and the two other volumes enjoyed comparable sales. De Gaulle did not, in fact, receive very much money for what was one of the great publishing triumphs of the post-war period, and died a relatively poor man. Towards the end of her life, a fund had to be opened to help his widow, Yvonne de Gaulle, to live out her old age with dignity. Unlike Napoleon I, who had a number of mistresses, Napoleon III, who was notoriously promiscuous, and Philippe Pétain, who enjoyed a great reputation as a womaniser and is said to have enjoyed his last act of physical love at the age of 80, de Gaulle was very much a family man. In particular, he was devoted to his younger daughter, Anne, who suffered severely from Down's Syndrome. She died in 1948, just before the age of 20,

124 *French Caesarism*

and was buried in the churchyard at Colombey. After the ceremony, when Yvonne de Gaulle was unable to tear herself away from the graveside, her husband took her gently by the arm with the words: 'Come along. She is like everyone else now.' Her death was followed by the establishment of the *Fondation Anne de Gaulle*, especially for handicapped children, and all the royalties from de Gaulle's books were given over to it.

In retrospect, the publication of *L'Appel*, the first volume of the *Mémoires de Guerre*, came at exactly the right moment in de Gaulle's political career. The memoirs kept him in the public eye at a time when his decision to dissolve the RPF in 1953 meant that he ceased to be a political figure. They reminded the French public of how right he had been in the 1930s and how vigorously he had defended French independence during the war. They showed him to be one of the great prose writers of French literature, with an eloquence and majesty of style that evoked all that was best in the classical tradition of the seventeenth century. They revealed him as a portraitist, and as a poet. The opening paragraphs, like the description of the French triumph at Bir Hakeim in June 1942, are classic passages in French literature. But most particularly, the *Mémoires* showed him as a highly skilled politician. He began with nothing, a bare £100 given to him by Paul Reynaud from the special government secret fund when he left for London on 17 June 1940. He had to depend absolutely on Britain for money. He had to overcome the fact that Churchill would have preferred Darlan, and Roosevelt Giraud. As Churchill put it:

> Admiral Darlan had but to sail in any one of his ships to any port outside France to become the master of all French interests outside German control. He would not have come, like General de Gaulle, with only an unconquerable heart and a few kindred spirits. He would have carried with him outside the German reach the fourth Navy in the world, and would have become the chief of French resistance with a mighty weapon in his hand.[30]

The Americans were equally prepared to look favourably at Darlan, and actually recognised him in 1942 as representing the French State in Algeria. While acknowledging that he was 'a deep-dyed villain', Eisenhower very realistically saw him as the man who could exercise effective authority, something which de Gaulle was not able to do in North Africa until he had very skilfully out-manœuvred General Giraud. There was indeed no shortage of potential Caesars in France in the 1940s, and it is again a reflection on

Charles de Gaulle: The Winner 125

the absence of French civilian politicians that de Gaulle's rivals should have been Admiral Darlan, Marshal Pétain, General Giraud and even, at one stage, General Noguès. But Darlan proceeded to show how fortunate France was to have been able to entrust herself to so relatively innocuous a leader as Pétain. He had, during the 1930s, shown considerable skill in building up the French navy to the point where it was the fourth largest in the world, immediately after those of Great Britain, Germany and the United States. This had involved him in spending more time on shore than at sea, and provides an interesting contrast with de Gaulle's failure during the same period to win effective support for his idea of an armoured strike force. But although he had achieved his aim of building up the navy by serving in a number of cabinets during the Third Republic, Darlan had little enthusiasm for the régime. In June 1940 he was swift to order the French navy to accept the armistice, and made no attempt to enable the ships under his command to continue the war by sailing to British ports. This refusal to follow what de Gaulle saw as the sole path of honour was as much a result of an obsessive Anglophobia as of a readiness to obey the Vichy government. He could not, apparently, allow any conversation to go on for very long without reminding everybody that his great-grandfather had been killed fighting against the English at Trafalgar in 1805. Churchill's decision on 7 July 1940 to attack the main force of the French fleet at Mers el-Kebir confirmed all his worst suspicions, but he seems to have done everything to make it inevitable.

The rest of the fleet which he had so skilfully built up scuttled itself in Toulon harbour on 27 November 1942 without ever having fired a shot at the enemy. Any historian or political analyst wishing to accuse de Gaulle of being right-wing should take a swift look at the career of Admiral Darlan in order to see what happens when people with really right-wing ideas try to play a part in French politics. Like that of the generals who were to rebel against de Gaulle's Algerian policy in 1961, Darlan's place in any account of French Caesarism is clearly marked. Like them, he provides a perfect illustration of how fortunate twentieth-century France was in the Caesars who did come to power. Had Admiral Darlan succeeded in his policies, France would have been an active ally of Germany before the end of 1941.[31]

De Gaulle was indeed fortunate that his actual or potential rivals for power in the 1940s showed so poor a grasp of political reality. General Giraud, who had managed a spectacular escape from a German prisoner-of-war camp in April 1942, was strongly favoured

126 *French Caesarism*

by the Americans, and until 1940 had had a more distinguished military career than de Gaulle. But he had given an embarrassing hostage to fortune by writing a letter to Pétain assuring him of his loyalty, and the popularity he enjoyed with the Americans did not endear him to the resistance groups in occupied France. He also totally lacked the kind of political vision that comes through both in what de Gaulle did and in his account of it in his *Mémoires*. When Field Marshal Keitel, on 9 May 1945, exclaimed in some exasperation at the surrender ceremony in Rheims, 'Oh no, not the French as well',[32] he was paying de Gaulle the greatest compliment he ever received. But although France would undoubtedly have been liberated in 1944 whether de Gaulle had been there or not, she would have had no great figure to turn to in 1958 when the Algeria problem threatened to cause civil war. De Gaulle's claim that he was France is in this respect fully justified. Without him, there would have been no incarnation of the national will that could give effective body to what the French actually wanted: a settlement in Algeria.

The impossible side of de Gaulle's character, which comes through in almost everything he wrote about his relationship with Churchill and Roosevelt, was also an advantage in the appeal he made in 1958. As awkward a person as this, it was argued, was not likely to neglect France's interests. If, in the view of his innumerable enemies on the right, he was eventually guilty of such neglect, it was also because he had the ability to see what was and was not politically viable. Having achieved what looked like the impossible miracle of giving France great power status again after the disaster of 1940, de Gaulle embarked in 1958 on the equally difficult task of bringing her down to the level of a medium-size European power whose interests lay in Europe and not overseas. He was able to do so because of his earlier triumphs, and there is in a way a curious parallel between the withdrawal he engineered from Algeria and the evacuation of the British army from Dunkirk in 1940. In both cases, a potentially disastrous recognition of the inevitable became the starting point for a great triumph, and an integral part of the myth of how this triumph was achieved.

III

The Algerian problem is as simple to explain as it was difficult to solve. France first occupied the town of Algiers in 1830, and

Charles de Gaulle: The Winner 127

colonised the rest of the country *ense et aratro* (by the sword and by the plough), under the vigorous leadership of Marshal Bugeaud, in the 1840s. In 1848 it officially became part of metropolitan France, but received little official attention during the Second Empire. Napoleon III was not particularly interested in colonisation. His belief in free trade did not encourage him to consider the advantages which colonies brought with them by way of captive markets. He also had a fairly modern attitude towards relationships between Arabs and Europeans, preferring to favour the interests of the former through the establishment in 1867 of the *Bureau des Affaires Arabes*. It was only after the defeat of France by Prussia in 1870 that colonisation really began, and it then did so for both political and military reasons. French families who did not wish to live in German-occupied Alsace and Lorraine were offered the chance of settling in French-speaking Algeria instead. To the end of his life, the Nobel prize winner Albert Camus was convinced that his ancestors belonged to such a family, when in fact his father's family had moved to Algeria from Normandy in the 1840s. It was especially important to families like them to see Algeria as an integral part of France. Economically, the Third Republic turned its back on the free trade principles favoured by Napoleon III, and embarked, under the leadership of Jules Ferry, on an ambitious programme of colonisation both in North Africa and the Far East. Just as it had been a civilian politician, Adolphe Thiers, who had engineered the massacres which ended the *Commune*, so it was under a civilian and not a soldier that France built up her overseas empire.

In 1873, the Europeans also introduced a land tenure system which enabled them to obtain possession of the lands previously held communally by the Algerian tribes. With a characteristically nineteenth-century indifference to the interests of the native population, they increased the amount of land used for wine-growing between 1878 and 1907 from 17,000 to 177,000 hectares. This was partly a result of the fact that it was possible to graft new wine stock from California, which was immune to the phylloxera bug, on to the shoots grown in Algeria, and there is a sense in which Algeria proved, in the nineteenth century, the salvation of the French wine-growing industry. But the Arabs obviously did not do very well from the system, since their religion forbade them to drink wine. The Europeans nevertheless prospered, and the original French inhabitants were joined by Italians, Spaniards and Maltese. They kept themselves rigorously apart from the Arabs and did not learn their

128 *French Caesarism*

language. Indeed, they did not even give Arabic an official status as an administrative language. Their numbers increased, and by 1954 there were over a million of them; but they faced some nine million Arabs.

This was the root of the problem. The Europeans had the same standard of living as the inhabitants of Marseilles or Toulon. The Arabs, in general, had that of Cairo. Left-wing commentators explained the difference in terms of colonialist exploitation. The Europeans had stolen the Arabs' land, and were using it to grow a product in which only they were interested. The Koran, after all, explicitly forbids the drinking of wine. At the same time, the Europeans provided a captive market for a French industry which was not competitive enough to sell its goods in an open, international market. The alternative view was to explain the economic gap between the two communities by reference to the coexistence of two cultures at different stages of development. It was nobody's fault, and the Arabs might perhaps have been even poorer if the Europeans had not been there. With a little more understanding on both sides, it was argued, the two communities could learn to live together, with the Europeans gradually bringing the Arabs up to their level. This analysis of the situation, in one way or another, provided the intellectual justification for the policy of keeping Algeria French. At the same time, there was the strong moral argument that France could not simply abandon the million or so Europeans, whose only home was in Algeria, to the not too tender mercy of the *Front de Libération Nationale*.

There were nevertheless a number of problems in accepting that Algeria ought to remain French. The French settlers had never agreed to implement any of the reforms aimed at giving the Arabs equal status. In May 1945 rioting broke out at the celebrations held at Sétif to celebrate the end of the war in Europe. Thousands of Arabs were killed, in response to the murder of just over a hundred Europeans. De Gaulle's memoirs barely mention the event. The French were, in this respect, colonialists of the old school, and the problem was made worse by the fact that most of them, by European standards, were poor. They could not allow themselves to sink down to the level of the Arabs, by whom they were always going to be outnumbered for purely demographic reasons. The Arabs, recognising the improbability of any change taking place except by force of arms, launched on the night of 31 October 1954 a campaign which had proved effective enough, by 1956, to require the French to keep half-a-million soldiers in Algeria. Most of these soldiers were conscripts, with the conscript's traditional ambition to go home as quickly as possible. But their officers, especially from the élite paratroop regiments, did not see matters in quite the same light. For France had not won a war by herself since the triumph of Napoleon's armies in the early nineteenth century. In the Crimea, she had had the British as allies, as she had also had the British and the Americans in the First World War. When facing Prussia alone in 1870, she had been defeated in less than six weeks; and the same thing had happened, even with British support, in May 1940. In 1954, Dien Bien Phu had been an equally disastrous defeat, and the French army had felt itself more keenly humiliated than the British by the failure of the Suez expedition of October 1956. Perhaps with some justification, the French had seen the possibility of a victory over Colonel Nasser as one way of defeating the Algerian *Front de Libération Nationale*, or at least of severely discouraging it. Colonel Massu, who was to play a leading role at different stages in the Algerian war, had been on the point of taking Alexandria when the order came for a cease-fire on 26 October 1956. After two more years in Algeria, in which his paratroops had made systematic use of torture to win the battle of Algiers, Massu and his brother officers were determined, in 1958, not to let metropolitan France steal the victory from them again by selling out to the FLN. For once, they were convinced, the French army could win a war.

The conditions were thus absolutely right for a classic military coup d'état. The army felt itself competent and morally qualified to perform a task which the politicians seemed unable to tackle: that of protecting the European population of Algeria and ensuring that Algeria remained French. The civilian power was weak and divided, with a parliament so constituted as to prevent the formation of any stable government. For the French parliamentary election of January 1956, organised on the proportional representation system introduced in 1946, had given a National Assembly in which only the Communist Party had more than a hundred members. The *Section Française de l'Internationale Ouvrière*, the main socialist party headed by Guy Mollet, had 95; the Radicals (an anti-clerical, anti-authoritarian, traditionally left-wing but non-socialist party) under the leadership of Mendès France, 91; the *Modérés* (the French equivalent of the conservatives), 91; the Catholic *Mouvement Républicain Populaire*, 83; the remnants of the RPF, Gaullist party, officially known as *Les Républicains Sociaux*, 22; and the new,

130 *French Caesarism*

aggressively right-wing *Poujadiste* party, 52. The parties differed on almost every issue except for the fact that only the Communists were prepared to say openly that the French ought to leave Algeria; and even the Communists were not prepared to use their considerable power in the shipping unions to hold up the supplies which were constantly crossing the Mediterranean. Plenty of journalists were saying that Algeria ought to become independent, including the very distinguished commentator, Raymond Aron. The columns of *L'Express*, *Le Monde*, *France-Observateur* and *Témoignage Chrétien* – to say nothing of Sartre's *Les Temps Modernes* – were full of articles setting out the case for a French withdrawal. But no politician would talk about anything other than *L'Algérie Française*. The presupposition was that France would stay there for a long time, if only because the Algerians were considered as incapable of looking after themselves.

Understandably, however, the army and settlers did not think that this desire to keep Algeria French was very strong in metropolitan France. After having accepted the American diplomat Robert Murphy as a go-between in the negotiations after the bombing of Sakhiet, the Prime Minister Félix Gaillard lost a vote of confidence on 15 April 1958, and it took three weeks before another politician could form a government. But Pierre Pflimlin, who set about the task on 8 May, was known for having at least suggested the possibility of holding talks with the FLN, and this was enough for the army and settlers in Algiers to launch their attempt at a coup d'état. The events of 13 May 1958 saw the establishment in Algiers of a *Comité de Salut Public*, headed by two army officers, General Massu and General Salan. The arrival of this news enabled Pflimlin to obtain 406 votes against 165 for his new government, the largest majority in the history of the Fourth Republic, but it was already too late. On 15 May, from the balcony of the government building overlooking the Forum in Algiers and at the suggestion of a civilian activist called Léon Delbecque, Salan shouted 'Vive de Gaulle', and the cry was taken up elsewhere. On 19 May, de Gaulle held a press conference in which he repeated the declaration which he had already made on 15 May when he said that he was 'ready to assume the powers of the republic'. By 1st June, at the urgent request of President Coty and under the threat of an actual invasion of France by French paratroopers from Algeria in what was known as 'Opération Résurrection', de Gaulle agreed to form his government. On 1 June, he appeared before the *Assemblée Nationale*, and received a majority of 105, with 329 for and 224

Charles de Gaulle: The Winner

against. Officially, he had had nothing to do with the events that began on 13 May, and this may well have been the case. But one of his closest associates, Jacques Chaban-Delmas, was moving between Algiers and Paris throughout the period, as was also Jacques Soustelle. It is hard to believe that de Gaulle did not know exactly what was going on, and he himself makes the situation quite clear in his *Mémoires d'Espoir*, the fourth volume of his memoirs. When the President of the Senate, André Le Troquer, raised an objection to one of de Gaulle's proposals, he received the reply that de Gaulle could always go back to his country retreat at Colombey-les-Deux-Eglises, 'en vous laissant vous expliquer avec les parachutistes'[33] (leaving you to sort things out with the paratroops). De Gaulle was not himself pointing a gun at the Fourth Republic; but he was in the position of being able to tell the person who was holding such a gun whether they should fire it or not. It was a coup d'état by proxy – the best kind if you then wish to disengage yourself from any possible obligation you might have incurred towards the people who helped you.

According to the American journalist Cyrus Leo Salzbergen, de Gaulle had shown no particular revulsion in 1957 at the idea of carrying out a coup d'état, observing that he had in fact carried out his first one in June 1940, when he established his movement in London, and his second in August 1944, on returning to Paris. The only point to note, he added, was that 'you can't carry out a coup d'état unless public opinion is asking you to do so (*vous réclame*). You must have the whole of public opinion behind you, as Napoleon did at the time of the 18 Brumaire.'[34] It is perhaps a broad definition of a coup d'état, in that it omits the idea of overthrowing the legally established authorities. But it does lay emphasis on the fact that none of the four successful French Caesars has ever found difficulty in obtaining retrospective electoral support for his seizure of power, and the result of the referendum whereby the French electorate approved the Constitution of the Fifth Republic on 28 September 1958 would suggest that de Gaulle was almost as popular then as he had been when he returned triumphantly to Paris in August 1944. If over 80 per cent of the voters expressed their approval for the new Constitution, this was probably not so much because they felt strongly about the doctrine of the separation of powers – under the Constitution of the Fifth Republic, *députés* have to give up their seats on becoming ministers – or really preferred a parliament which sat for only five months of the year. They were voting for or against de Gaulle, just as

132 *French Caesarism*

their ancestors had voted for or against the two Napoleons. But as far as the central problem of Algeria was concerned, nobody actually knew what de Gaulle intended to do, for the very good reason that he probably did not know himself. On 4 June 1958, he went to Algeria, where he received a rapturous reception at the Forum in Algiers itself. As he raised his hands in that characteristic gesture which transformed his whole body into a vast V for Victory sign, and declared 'Je vous ai compris', the crowd went delirious with excitement. It was only some four years later that his use of the essential ambiguity of language became clear. For he meant, not as had been thought at the time, 'I agree with you, and will make sure that Algeria remains French', but 'I can see what you want but very much doubt whether you are going to get it.'

De Gaulle's first priority for Algeria, as he makes clear in his *Mémoires d'Espoir*, was to make sure that France would not lose the war in purely military terms. This, given the wealth of France and the determination of the army, was not too difficult an aim. By 1961, the number of people killed in the rebellion had fallen from fifty a day to seven or eight, and by the time the cease-fire came into force, in March 1962, there were more safe areas in Algeria than at any time since 1956. But you can, as Napoleon I is said to have remarked, do anything with bayonets except sit on them. Where de Gaulle parted company with the people who brought him to power as well as with the French right in general, was in his view as to how long the bayonets could justifiably be considered necessary. The visits which he made to Algeria in 1958 and 1959 convinced him that French rule would never again be generally accepted there. Every Algerian whom he met outside the pre-arranged encounters told him the same thing: the Algerians wanted to take responsibility for their own affairs. On 16 September 1959 de Gaulle appeared on television to announce the existence of three possibilities for Algeria: secession, in which he said at the time that he did not believe; total integration into France, equally presented as impossible; the 'government of Algerians by Algerians', with an essentially federal structure in the country itself. This, clearly, was the solution he preferred.

It was his most important speech on Algeria, and marked the beginning of the central event in the early years of the Fifth Republic: the struggle between de Gaulle and the army. This was no new experience for de Gaulle himself. He had been against the military establishment in the 1930s, with his campaign in favour of an armoured force and against the Maginot line mentality. In the 1940s,

Charles de Gaulle: The Winner 133

when the majority of French professional soldiers preferred Pétain, he had also been a rebel against the military establishment. He was, in many ways, one of nature's rebels, and had never been wholly at ease in his relationship with the organisation which he had first joined in 1909. One of the many paradoxes about him was that he was a soldier who was at his best when defying the army, and the events of January 1960, like those of April 1961, added a new and attractive dimension to the general phenomenon of French Caesarism. For they showed de Gaulle, not as most military men who seize power in less developed countries tend to be, as the creature of the army, but as the man capable of defying it in order to provide the majority of the civilian population with what they really want. Successful Caesars are essentially unifiers, and there were two aspects to de Gaulle's achievement between 1958 and 1962. The first was to unify metropolitan France against the army and the Algerian settlers. The second was to change public attitudes in such a way as to make openly acceptable a readiness to abandon Algeria which had been only implicit or perhaps non-existent beforehand. For he also managed to grant independence to Algeria at a time when the majority of members of the political party most closely allied to him, the *Union pour la Nouvelle République*, resembled his Prime Minister, Michel Debré, in being supporters of *L'Algérie Française*.

The first test of wills between de Gaulle and the army came after an interview which General Massu gave on 18 January 1960 to the mass circulation Munich newspaper *Suddeutsche Zeitung*. In it, Massu suggested that the army had perhaps made a mistake in bringing de Gaulle to power, and could not understand why he was following a left-wing policy. In a scarcely veiled threat, Massu spoke of the strength which the army was holding in reserve, and the use which it might also make of the European para-military civilian forces which were well organised among the Europeans in Algiers. The challenge was a fairly open one, and expressed very much the same point of view as the comment made by Colonel Lacheroy in July 1958 when he told André Malraux that the army would probably in any case have preferred somebody like General Franco rather than an unorthodox personality such as de Gaulle.[35] Massu was immediately summoned to Paris, where he had a furious argument with de Gaulle. On 24 January, the European activists in Algiers ordered a general strike and a group of them occupied the university buildings. When the regular police, the *gendarmes mobiles*, tried to move against the demonstrators, shots were fired and 14 policemen were killed. So,

134 *French Caesarism*

too, were eight demonstrators, and two hundred people were wounded. It looked as though another military *putsch* might well follow the example of 13 May 1958, and with even more dramatic results.

De Gaulle did not react immediately. The European rebels were not in fact powerful enough to take over the whole city, and could only sit and wait: there was no second de Gaulle waiting in the wings. Then, on 29 January, he went on television to speak to the nation. Already, during the period in which he had led the Free French during the war, the microphone had been the weapon with which he had replied to the German tanks. What was then the complete state monopoly of radio and television in France was to be the decisive factor in his defeat of the European rebels – and, later, of the French army – in Algeria. In the name of the national legitimacy which, as he reminded his audience, he had now incarnated for over twenty years, he called on the French nation to support him and told the rebels to surrender. Both sides obeyed, and by 1 February it was all over. The army in Algiers proved loyal, and compelled the European rebels to evacuate the university buildings. Lagaillarde, the main leader, was arrested and brought to Paris. The other activists escaped to Spain. But although de Gaulle had won, he realised that the army was still not entirely on his side. On 3 March 1960, he set out on a tour of the units stationed in Algeria to remind them of their primary duty of defeating the enemy. At the same time, the first tentative negotiations began between the French and the representatives of the Arab nationalists.

There is no clear evidence as to when de Gaulle realised that Algerian independence was inevitable. In his press conference of 14 January 1960 he had spoken of 'l'Algérie algérienne'. In his whole career, he only once used the magical phrase 'l'Algérie française' in a public speech, and that was almost certainly a slip of the tongue. It was at Mostaganem, on 6 June 1958, on one of the rare occasions when he was influenced by the extraordinary atmosphere created by the army in its attempt by psychological warfare tactics to bring about the unification of the French and Arab populations in Algeria. To speak of 'an Algerian Algeria' was a clear sign that independence was inevitable, and the term recurred in another conference on 4 November. In total consistency with the Caesarist tradition of popular consultation, a further referendum was held on 8 January 1961 in which the French were asked an intriguing double question. Did they approve the draft bill concerning the right to self-

Charles de Gaulle: The Winner 135

determination for the different communities in Algeria? And did they approve of the organisation of the public authorities in Algeria before self-determination? They could not, in other words, say 'Yes' to Algerian independence, which by now the majority of the population in metropolitan France openly wanted, without confirming the considerable powers which the government enjoyed. The failure of the talks at Melun in June 1960 had led de Gaulle to recognise that no real solution was possible which did not acknowledge at least the long-term prospect of independence. The fact that 75 per cent of those voting replied 'Yes' in the referendum on 8 January meant that he could go forward to the next stage with the knowledge that his policy was what the French actually wanted and that he consequently remained, in a practical as well as a semi-mystical sense, the incarnation of the national will.

The next step came on 11 April 1961 when de Gaulle in another of his press conferences openly acknowledged for the first time, without any ambiguity, that Algeria would eventually become independent. When it was pointed out to him that both the USA and USSR might want to steal France's place in North Africa, he observed that he hoped they enjoyed the experience – 'à toutes deux, je souhaite d'avance bien du plaisir' (I hope they both enjoy it).[36] Another of the apparently minor aspects which distinguish de Gaulle both from the other three Caesars who took power in France and from those who failed to do so is the possession of a sense of humour. It also certainly marked him out from the four would-be Caesars who presented him with the greatest challenge in his Presidency, and whose attempt at a coup d'état in Algiers on 21 April 1961 once again brought out the difference between de Gaulle and the army. For Generals Challe, Jouhaud, Salan and Zeller were men who showed how seriously they accepted the demonology of the Cold War when they justified their attempted *putsch* by the question: 'Voulez-vous que Mers el-Kébir et Alger soient demain des bases soviétiques?' (Do you want Mers el-Kebir and Algiers to be the Soviet bases of tomorrow?) The object of what de Gaulle dismissively referred to as 'un quarteron de généraux en retraite' (a bunch of retired generals) was not, however, actually to take power. They recognised that de Gaulle would be a good deal more difficult to dislodge than Pierre Pflimlin had been in 1958. What they wanted to do, in so far as they had a plan ready in advance, was prevent him from putting his policy of independence for Algeria into action, and they knew that they could count on two forces: the European civilian population; and the regular officers in

136 *French Caesarism*

the French army, especially in the paratroop regiments. But they planned this action with an extraordinary lack of foresight. To begin with, they had no money. In a complex urban society, you can do little without a good deal of credit. Since Algeria was still – such indeed was the argument – an integral part of France, it was the French government which controlled the banks. 'Point d'argent, point de Suisses' (no money, no Switzers) as Petit-Jean observes in Racine's *Les Plaideurs*. In spite of the fact that Challe himself was an airman, none of the air force units stationed in Algeria came out on their side. Precisely because their object was to stop a policy and not to replace a government, the foursome had also made no real arrangements for support in metropolitan France. Because they were living in a technological age which de Gaulle understood but which they did not, they were unable to predict or control the reactions of the half-million or so French conscripts in Algeria.

For the conscripts had transistor radios. They did not have to rely, as they would have done twenty years earlier, on the mains-operated radio sets which were under the control of their officers. As de Gaulle put it in *Le Renouveau*, 'Un million de transistors ont fonctionné', and the conscripts were able to follow for themselves what was happening in France. In particular, they could hear how the general public – including the trade union movement – was reacting to de Gaulle's behaviour. This, predictably, was uncompromising, however great the note of panic may have been in Michel Debré's voice as he urged the population of Paris, on the night of 22 April, to climb into their cars and drive to the airports where the paratroops from Algeria were expected to land and 'convince these misguided soldiers how great their error is'. De Gaulle immediately suspended all air and sea links between metropolitan France and Algeria. This was something which Pierre Pflimlin had notably failed to do in May 1958, and points not only to the difference between the two men but also to the contrast between a charismatic military figure and a run-of-the-mill civilian politician. The former knows what he wants to do, and can rely on being obeyed. The latter, as was clear in 1958, has neither of these two advantages. Even if Pflimlin had given orders to isolate Algeria in 1958, few airmen, soldiers or policemen would have done as they were told.

Clemenceau, it is true, would have acted like de Gaulle and had the people in metropolitan France whom he suspected of complicity in a plot against the state immediately arrested. He would also, had the possibility been open to him, have used Article 16 of the

Charles de Gaulle: The Winner 137

Constitution to declare a state of emergency. The availability of this Article shows how right de Gaulle was to insist in 1958 on its inclusion. It gave him virtually dictatorial powers, and was again an immensely useful sign of the fact that he was indubitably in control. This indeed was the decisive factor, and his victory was essentially a psychological one, accomplished by his skilful use of the media of mass communications and without a single shot being fired. The revolt collapsed extraordinarily quickly. By 25 April, it was all over. The ultimate humiliation for the generals took place when they tried to harangue the crowd in the Forum, only to discover that somebody had cut off the electricity so that the microphones were not working. The most enthusiastic supporters of the *putsch* from within the French army, the Foreign Legion, marched back to barracks singing Edith Piaf's 'Non, je ne regrette rien', and the revolt was over. Independence for Algeria was now inevitable, the only problem to be solved being that of the European extremists who formed themselves into the *Organisation de l'Armée Secrète*. This exercised a reign of terror in the streets of the town of Algiers, and it caused more damage and casualties in the few months before independence than the FLN had done during the seven-and-a-half years of the war. In Algiers itself, the civilian authority of Ben Bella did not last long. On 19 June 1965 he was removed from power by a military coup d'état and replaced by Colonel Boumediene. It was not until after Boumediene's death in December 1978 that the army gradually began to lose power in Algeria, and the country was run, under President Chadli, by a predominantly civilian administration.

For de Gaulle, the violence of the OAS and its refusal to accept his solution to the Algerian problem went back a long way: to the opposition between Vichy and the resistance movement. It was, he suggests in *Le Renouveau*, an essentially anti-republican organisation, with ideological roots going deep into the traditions of the French right. The initials AF (*Algérie Française*) certainly showed a curious continuity with the *Action Française* of the 1890s. The attempt to make the French army into an anti-republican political force also links it with the opponents of Captain Dreyfus. It was a tradition to which de Gaulle had always been opposed, and his final victory in the confrontation with it marks a crucial and perhaps definitive stage in the development of French Caesarism. In spite of the description of him as 'Saint-Simon on horseback', and whatever his sympathy for the working class, Napoleon III resembled his uncle in being a man of the right. He was brought to power in order to

138 *French Caesarism*

ensure that the financial and social inequalities of mid-nineteenth-century France remained unaltered; and he succeeded. Pétain was even more closely linked with the anti-republican tradition of French right-wing politics, and the adoption of the term *L'Etat Français* involved a whole set of highly reactionary political attitudes. De Gaulle, in contrast, had always presented himself as an integral part of the republican tradition. At no point did he collaborate with the people who had brought him to power in 1958 in their wish to use the Algerian war to impose a more authoritarian régime in France. Far from being a man of the right, he carried out for the left the policy which it should have adopted but did not have the courage, the skill or perhaps even the desire to pursue.

Understandably, in this context, the most virulent attacks on de Gaulle for his Algerian policy came from the right-wing French press. Why, it was argued, had it been right for de Gaulle to refuse to obey Pétain in 1940 and wrong for Salan and the other generals to disobey orders in order to try to protect the French people in Algeria in 1961? Yet when a journalist commented in the royalist newspaper *Rivarol* on 7 June 1962 that 'if de Gaulle had not deliberately put an end to his career in 1940, he would be a five-star general – and would be in prison with the rest of them', he put his finger exactly on what distinguished de Gaulle from the other French military men who have tried to play a part in twentieth-century politics: he had enough common sense to tell which way the political wind was blowing. For the forecasts of national disaster which filled the right-wing press in 1962 all turned out to be wrong. The European Algerians were, ironically, welcomed back to France as 'des rapatriés' (homecomers), in spite of the fact that most of them had never set foot in mainland France before. Partly because of the activity of the OAS, but also because they did not trust the new Algerian government to keep its promise to respect their status, over 900,000 of the million or so Europeans living in Algeria in the 1950s did indeed move to France. But the prosperity of the 1960s, when there were fewer than fifty thousand people out of work in France, meant that they were quite quickly absorbed into French society, and they did not form an irredentist political party. The Evian agreements which brought the Algerian war to a close were approved in a referendum held on 8 April 1962 by over 90 per cent of those voting.

Paradoxical though it may seem to praise a military man for organising what was in fact a total defeat for the aims if not the performance of the French army, there is no doubt that de Gaulle's

Charles de Gaulle: The Winner 139

solution to the Algerian problem was an even greater achievement than his raising of France from defeat to victory between 1940 and 1944. He did, it is true, go against the tradition of 'la République une et indivisible' in giving up the Algerian *départements*. But it is hard to see how he could have done otherwise, and how any other politician, whether military or civilian, could have avoided the violence of the OAS. For the European Algerians were inspired by the not unreasonable feeling that they had been totally betrayed. They would undoubtedly have carried on their campaign for much longer, with even greater violence, against a ruler lacking de Gaulle's prestige and political skills. For once, the defence of a Caesar on the ground that he was a providential figure was fully justified. Caesar had beaten the army and broken the spell. Henceforth, in France, thanks to de Gaulle, it would be civilians who took both the initiative and the decisions.

IV

Had de Gaulle decided to leave power in 1962, behaving like a Roman dictator who goes back into private life once the crisis which led him to take over the state has ended, he might well not have found an overwhelming majority of French people trying to stop him. René Rémond even speaks of him being compared to a public receiver, brought in to liquidate a particular problem – as Pierre Mendès France had been brought in to end the Indochina war in 1954 – and who is then sent away again afterwards. De Gaulle knew that many people thought of him in this way, but was understandably determined to carry on. The narrowness of his escape from an assassination attempt on 22 August 1962 provided him with an excuse for the first of the major changes which showed that he was here to stay, and which has already been mentioned in another context: the election of the President of the Republic by universal suffrage.

Because the Constitution of the Fifth Republic had originally been so heavily criticised in 1958 for its similarities with the régime of the Second Republic, where the election of the President by universal male suffrage had made it easier for Napoleon III to carry out his coup d'état, the original arrangement in 1958 was for the President to be chosen by an electoral college of 80,000 'illustres inconnus', the locally elected politicians. De Gaulle did not think that this arrangement provided him with sufficient authority. He may well have

140 *French Caesarism*

thought that it made him, in the words of Jean Lacouture, merely 'Monsieur Queuille clad in the purple of the Caesars'.[37] Indeed, in a Presidential election held in an atmosphere not dominated by a national crisis such as the Algerian war, he might well have found few *notables* prepared to prefer him to Antoine Pinay. It was perhaps with thoughts of such a possibility in mind that on 20 September 1962, in a radio and television broadcast, he announced the holding of a referendum on the proposed change in the way the President was elected. Henceforth, it was to be by universal suffrage.

The number of criticisms to which this project was immediately subjected is an indication of how dispensable de Gaulle was thought to be now that the immediate danger was over. Virtually every political party, and almost every newspaper, found the proposal unacceptable and unconstitutional, with the President of the Senate, Gaston Monnerville, describing the political system such a change would produce as 'not the Republic, but a kind of enlightened Bonapartism'.[38] The *Conseil d'Etat*, the supreme body for administrative law, criticised the project on a number of grounds: that the announcement of the holding of a referendum should have been made by the Prime Minister and not the President, who was an interested party in the affair; that de Gaulle had kept Pompidou's government in power after 280 of the 480 members of the *Chambre des Députés* had supported a vote of no confidence in it; and that Article 89 of the Constitution was the one that ought to have been applied in any introduction of a constitutional change, and not Article 11, which de Gaulle himself had evoked. The average voter clearly found these mere technicalities. Until he lost his final referendum, in April 1969, de Gaulle was always able to appeal directly to the mass of the French people over the heads of their official representatives. This, again, is part of the essence of Caesarism, even though another aspect of de Gaulle's behaviour in the same year did not entirely fit in with his official vision of the President of the Republic as an arbiter placed above the contending political parties. After having, on 28 October 1962, won the referendum on the new mode of election of the President by 13,151,000 to 7,975,000, he openly supported the *Union pour la Nouvelle République* in the general election held later in the same year; and enabled it to win a comfortable majority.

Napoleon I had seized power in a coup d'état financed by bankers, and one of the immediate effects of *le 18 Brumaire* was to raise the value of government stock. The *Banque de France* opened a long line

Charles de Gaulle: The Winner 141

of credit for Louis Napoleon during the run up to the coup d'état of 2 December 1851, and the Stock Exchange rose with every sign of his popularity. French Caesars, at least in the early stages, are very good for business. The establishment of the Fifth Republic enabled France to profit from the increasing prosperity already visible in the last four years of the Fourth Republic. In spite of his earlier opposition to the European Defence Community in 1953, and to the European Iron and Steel Community in 1949, de Gaulle honoured the commitment made by the Fourth Republic to join the Common Market, and France abandoned her traditional protectionist policy for one of increasingly open international competition. This was what Napoleon III had done in 1860 with the Free Trade treaty with Britain. There are a number of other similarities between the Second Empire and the Fifth Republic as far as social and economic policy is concerned. The Second Empire had the railways, the Fifth Republic the *autoroutes*. The Second Empire, under Baron Haussmann, transformed Paris into a modern city. The Fifth Republic, under the inspiration of André Malraux, cleaned up its public buildings. Later, with the encouragement of Georges Pompidou, it embarked on a series of massive new building programmes, as well as on the unwise attempt to make Paris a capital suitable for motor cars to drive in. Neither régime, in the view of an anonymous critic in *The Times Literary Supplement* of 30 September 1965, was particularly distinguished for its cultural achievements, and in its early years the Fifth Republic was not noted for its tolerance either of greater freedom in artistic matters or of any political dissent which took the form of criticising the head of state. It confirmed the new middle class of managers and technocrats in its dominant role in French society, and put France back on the map in the international, diplomatic scene.

De Gaulle was a good deal better at publicising his achievements in this area than Napoleon III had been. The 1856 Paris conference did indeed put an end to the Crimean war, and without Napoleon III's intervention against Austria in 1859, Italian reunification might have been put off for decades. But his Mexican adventure of 1861 ended in total disaster, and his régime fell in 1870 as a result of a shattering military defeat. De Gaulle, in contrast, ensured by his refusal in 1963 and 1967 to allow Britain to join the Common Market that there would for decades be no serious political rival to France in Europe – the Germans, at the time, were still working their passage back to membership of the human race. On 1 July 1966 he removed French forces from the unified NATO command structure. But France still

142   *French Caesarism*

remained a political member, and in the two great Cold War issues of the 1950s and 1960s, de Gaulle adopted an impeccably hawkish line. His insistence on developing an independent French nuclear deterrent was not only a result of a nostalgia for a period in which France was a major international power. It was based upon a very acute awareness of how selfishly nation states behave. In 1949, the Americans had refused to include in the wording of the North Atlantic Treaty Organisation a clause stipulating that United States forces would automatically intervene in Europe if one of the European members of the alliance were attacked by the Soviet Union. Perhaps unjustifiably, he did not trust the Americans, in the last resort, to risk Chicago in order to defend Paris or Berlin. He pointed out to J.-R. Tournoux that you could judge the general value of international commitments by the fact that in 1938 Czechoslovakia had the fullest possible formal guarantees from Britain and France.[39] He refused, between 1958 and 1962, even to enter into discussions with the USSR about a possible change in the status of West Berlin, and told Mr Khrushchev in no uncertain terms, at the time of the abortive summit conference in Paris in 1960, that he did not believe in his threats. When Khrushchev tried to strengthen his hand in the Berlin negotiations by installing medium-range rockets in Cuba in October 1962, de Gaulle offered President Kennedy unwavering support. But he did so as an independent statesman who was in a position, if the Americans were to waver in their support of West Berlin, to threaten the use of the French nuclear deterrent as a trip-wire to bring everyone to their senses.

The early 1960s also saw one of the most dramatic changes in European politics with the ceremonies of reconciliation between de Gaulle and Adenauer and with de Gaulle's declaration in January 1963 that the understanding with Germany was the cornerstone of French foreign policy. In January 1964, he was the first Western leader to recognise Communist China, and in 1965 began his support for Vietnam and his campaign in favour of an American withdrawal. The preliminary meetings took place in Paris in the Spring of 1968, and when it was eventually Paris which was chosen in 1973 as the site for the conference which brought the Vietnam war to a close, de Gaulle's policy of highly critical independence towards the United States took on full if posthumous justification. One of the key words in French political discourse is that of Yalta, the 1945 conference which de Gaulle was not invited to attend, and whose decisions he constantly criticised on the grounds that they gave control of Eastern

Charles de Gaulle: The Winner 143

Europe to the Russians virtually on a plate. The rational basis for de Gaulle's opposition and hostility to the United States lay in the idea that circumstances might arise in which Western Europe might be abandoned in a comparable way, and that no country claiming sovereign status could possibly entrust its defence to a third party.

There were nevertheless times when de Gaulle's foreign policy took the form of a posturing whose ultimate utility seemed much less rational. In July 1967, for example, he visited Quebec, and made an extraordinary speech in which he compared the enthusiasm of the crowds who turned out to greet him to that of the French people welcoming the liberating allied armies in 1944. When, on 24 July 1967, he uttered his famous 'Vive le Québec libre!' from the balcony of the Hôtel de Ville in Montreal, it seemed that he was doing more than challenge the domination of the North American continent by those he always called 'les Anglo-Saxons'. He was also calling into question much of what had happened in the last two hundred years, and was apparently quite pleased when somebody told him that he had 'repaid the debt of Louis XV'.[40] The idea that one might seriously want to go back upon the consequences of the defeat of France in the Seven Years' War seems indeed almost incredible. De Gaulle nevertheless expressed a similar view in January 1963, after he had said 'No' for the first time to Britain's application to join the Common Market. For he then received a protest from his oldest political ally, Paul Reynaud, and replied by a brief telegram: 'If absent, please forward to Agincourt (Somme) or Waterloo (Belgium).'[41] The idea that a major country should conduct its foreign policy on the basis of resentments going back hundreds of years is really rather terrifying until you begin to reflect on another aspect of de Gaulle as a man: his tendency to perform the rôle of a mythical creature called 'De Gaulle'. He is said to have invented a number of anecdotes about himself to add to the many in spontaneous circulation – especially the one in which Jackie Kennedy said 'Vous savez, ma mère appartenait à une vieille famille française' and received the reply 'La mienne aussi, Madame' – and there may even have been an element of conscious self-satire in the speech which began: 'Je salue Fécamp, port de mer et qui l'entend rester.'

He certainly accepted and exploited the frequent identification of himself with Joan of Arc, to the point of using it to justify his refusal between 1947 and 1958 to take part in the official parliamentary activity of the Fourth Republic: 'Can one imagine Joan of Arc married, with children, perhaps with an unfaithful husband?' The

144   *French Caesarism*

ability to see himself as the incarnation of France was essential to his performance as a politician. For when, in May 1968, the student rebellion broke out in Paris and seemed about to overthrow not only the Fifth Republic but the capitalist state itself, de Gaulle seems to have entirely lost confidence in himself as a leader. He had begun to react with his customary force. On 18 May he refused to accept what he called in one of his characteristically vigorous phrases 'la chienlit' (balls-up; literally, fouling your own nest), and on 24 May he announced that a referendum would be held on the theme of 'La Participation'. But his proposal fell flat. François Mitterrand and Pierre Mendès France put themselves forward as respectively President of the Republic and Prime Minister; and on 29 May de Gaulle suddenly disappeared. The depressive side of his personality took the upper hand; and he lost, for once, the conviction that France and he were one and the same person.

He had, as it was subsequently revealed, gone to Baden-Baden in order to consult General Massu, the man whose dismissal had sparked off the first of the conflicts between de Gaulle and the army in Algeria. Massu, according to the account in his *Baden 68. Souvenirs d'une Fidélité Gaulliste*, provided de Gaulle more with psychological reassurance than with any promise that the army would be prepared to intervene on the side of the government if the need arose. De Gaulle returned to Paris on the same day. He summoned a cabinet meeting, made a broadcast on the radio in which he accused the Communists of being at the root of all the trouble, and announced that a general election was to be held. He was rewarded with the massive street demonstration in his favour that he had clearly been expecting on 24 May, when he announced the referendum, and on 30 June saw his Prime Minister, Georges Pompidou, transform his very narrow parliamentary majority into a very substantial one. But it was clearly the beginning of the end. Pompidou was seen as the person who had held firm and won the election, not de Gaulle. When, on 27 April the following year, de Gaulle announced what was in fact his fifth referendum, on a somewhat complex project to reform the Senate and introduce greater decentralisation, he lost, with a vote of 53 per cent against him. Faithful to his principles, he immediately resigned.

The writing had been on the wall since 1965, when de Gaulle had been forced to go to a second ballot in the Presidential election against François Mitterrand. His skill in the use of television enabled him to be re-elected, and his interview with Michel Droit on 13

Charles de Gaulle: The Winner 145

December 1965 was one of his best performances ever. But the election campaign had given the French the chance of seeing other politicians in action, and made them realise how completely what was then the state monopoly of radio and television in France had been taken over by the Gaullists. It is difficult for Caesarism, with everything that it implies by way of direct contact between the leader and the people, to survive in a complex society in which a large number of different interest groups have access to information and have the power to influence opinion. De Gaulle's attitude in Europe had alienated the fairly numerous voters who were opposed to his concept of 'l'Europe des Patries' and would have preferred France to support a more federal approach. His comment about the Jews at the time of the Six Day War in 1967 had also caused considerable disquiet. For his reference to them as 'un peuple d'élite, dominateur et sûr de lui-même' was more than a remark that could also be applied to de Gaulle himself. It awoke all kinds of echoes in the long history of antisemitism in France, to the point where it suggested that de Gaulle might, in his old age, be falling victim to the same kinds of attitude which had made Pétain so popular with the least attractive sections of the French population. De Gaulle's unremitting hostility to the Communist Party and to the trade union movement, his constant jibes at political parties, his obvious scorn for professional politicians, the cavalier way in which he dismissed and replaced his Prime Ministers, getting rid of Debré as soon as the Algerian war was over, placing Georges Pompidou 'en réserve de la République' after the events of 1968, all indicated that the force of character which had enabled him to triumph between 1940 and 1945 and between 1958 and 1962 had led to a kind of constant self-parodying, and to a hubris which was funny rather than frightening.

For the problem with Caesarism is that it is, in a developed country, essentially a transitory phenomenon. Military or protomilitary rulers may be essential when a country is going through a crisis, and the frequency with which Caesars crop up in France may be due to nothing more than its geographical position. For this exposes it to a larger number of crises than countries which, like America or Great Britain, are protected by the sea, or which have a range of mountains between them and the outside world like Spain or Italy. This geographical vulnerability explains the rise to power of both Pétain and de Gaulle, while the fact that revolutionary France was already involved in a land war with the rest of Europe is one of the major reasons for the initial rise of Napoleon I. The civilian politicians of

146 *French Caesarism*

the *Directoire* were looking for 'a sword' because they felt that the revolution was threatened from the outside as well as from within. Had Napoleon I, by some psychological miracle, been able to resist the temptation to go in for more and more conquests, his régime could well have settled down to the kind of liberal empire into which his nephew's empire began to relax in the 1860s. If this had happened, of course, Napoleon would have become redundant. The disappearance of both external and internal threats leads to a situation where the originally essential restorer of order becomes, as de Gaulle became in the 1960s, a figure driven to increasingly artificial and frantic posturing. In de Gaulle's case, this carried on even after he had left power. In 1970 he paid a visit to Ireland, and was about to deliver a speech in Dublin expressing, among other things, support for 'a fully united Ireland'. Fortunately, somebody had turned the microphone off.[42]

In the case of the first and the fourth Caesar, this geographical vulnerability is also linked to a set of historical circumstances which mean that France is peculiarly prone to what one might call the growing pains of progress. The French Revolution introduced a set of wholly new concepts into European history: nationalism, the doctrine of popular sovereignty, a belief in progress, the idea of universal equality before the law and the insistence on the rights as well as the duties of the citizen. It witnessed a major transfer of landed property. It marked the end of a political consensus going back to the Middle Ages and which saw the King as in some way God's minister on earth. It destroyed the idea of a divinely structured hierarchical society, and replaced it by one in which change was seen as not only endless and inevitable but eminently desirable. Like the seventeenth-century revolution in England, it gave the opportunity for the occasional expression of a doctrine of primitive communism and of complete social equality. It marked the beginning of a society in which religion played no official rôle, and added immensely to the organising and repressive power of the state. It was the most extraordinary explosion of energy ever to take place in any one country, and one which also involved an organised and systematic use of violence by the state against its own citizens which looks forward to the horrors of the first half of the twentieth century.

Yet although it all took place in what was the richest, most densely populated and intellectually developed country in the world, the strain was too much. After the frenzied activity of the first five years, culminating in the fall of Robespierre, there came the uncertainties

Charles de Gaulle: The Winner   147

and chaos of the *Directoire*. Somebody had to put an end to the disorder, and nobody was more obviously designated to do this than a soldier. Unlike the other social institutions of eighteenth-century France, the army had profited from the revolutionary period instead of being destroyed by it. Without Napoleon, the energy of the first French revolution might simply have run into the sands. With him, it was channelled, as far as the internal organisation of France was concerned, into a series of useful and durable courses.

The return to power of Charles de Gaulle in 1958 provided the solution for a double political crisis, one by which France was more deeply affected than any other European country. For the France of the Fourth Republic had to deal at one and the same time with two problems which occurred separately elsewhere. It had to face the problem of a large and vigorous Communist Party; at the same time, it had to decolonise. Italy had had to face the first problem, but not the second. Great Britain had to deal with the second but not the first, and had been able to do so in much more favourable circumstances. To give away from a position of strength is easy. With one or two hiccups like Kenya, Cyprus and Rhodesia, and not counting the million or so deaths resulting from the partition of India and Pakistan in 1947, Great Britain managed matters quite well. Because France emerged from the Second World War in the ambiguous position of a country which had been disastrously defeated but had nevertheless officially become one of the victors, it had great difficulty in coming to grips with the problem. Had it been clearly on the side of the losers in 1945, the problem would have been solved for it as it had been solved for Italy and Germany, who simply had their colonies taken from them. As it was, both Indochina and Algeria proved to be virtually insoluble problems because the French people genuinely did not know what they wanted: to hang on to their colonies as symbols of great power status; or to give them away and concentrate on domestic issues. De Gaulle helped them, one might almost say forced them, to make up their minds. At the same time, he offered a form of social and political unity which proved attractive to almost all classes in French society. From 1958 onwards, the appeal of Communism in France began to decline.

It is always possible to say that this would have happened anyway. Once capitalism had emerged from the crisis which had produced German and Italian Fascism, and had begun to work again in a reasonably satisfactory manner, Communist parties everywhere in the West began to lose their appeal. De Gaulle hastened the decline

148   *French Caesarism*

of the French Communist Party by the success which he achieved in solving the Algerian problem without causing a civil war. By doing so, he administered the proof that capitalist society could solve specific problems without total revolution. The fact that de Gaulle refused to give up power after solving the Algerian problem, and left France with a new and very effective Constitution, are signs of how difficult it is to set a limit to the solutions which Caesars are invited to impose. But at least the peculiarities of de Gaulle's foreign policy in the 1960s did not actually cause any deaths. There is also a sense in which his determination to keep an independent French nuclear deterrent provided more than protection against the Russians. It has also become a guarantee against the growth in France of an indigenous movement for unilateral nuclear disarmament. Nobody, in France, can use the campaign against nuclear weapons as a kind of smoke-screen for anti-Americanism, since the Bomb is French and nobody can be that unpatriotic. At the same time, since the President of the Republic is Commander-in-Chief of the armed forces, and as such the man with the power to set off the apocalypse, he becomes a kind of charismatic figure of national unity. In a curious, semi-mystical way, he is France, if only because he can in fact decide whether France – and the world – will continue to exist or not.[43]

Compared to Napoleon I and Charles de Gaulle, Napoleon III and Pétain are somewhat second-rate figures. The coup d'état of 2 December 1851 was almost certainly not necessary to prevent the Second Republic from degenerating into anarchy. Pétain played a major part in French national life only for a relatively short time. After 22 June 1941, when the Germans attacked Russia, and more especially after 7 December of the same year, when Japan attacked Pearl Harbor and Germany declared war on the United States, de Gaulle had been proved right and Pétain wrong. It was a world war and not the purely European conflict which Pétain's lack of historical imagination had made it seem to him. France had ceased to need a father figure, and Pétain became increasingly irrelevant. So, too, by the mid-1960s, was de Gaulle, except as a kind of myth. The frequency with which his memory is evoked continues to indicate how important this myth is, and it could perhaps be used as an argument in favour of some kind of restoration of the monarchy in France. De Gaulle himself certainly flirted with the idea towards the end of his life, and there is a sense in which a President who genuinely stood above political parties – which was de Gaulle's ideal – could fulfil the

Charles de Gaulle: The Winner

same sort of function as the monarchy in Britain. The restoration of some kind of monarchical system in France would be an interesting 200th-birthday present to the first French revolution.

Conclusion

The one feature common to the four French Caesars who took power is that the régimes which they established were all succeeded by some form of more conventional civilian government. None of them, in other words, was overthrown by another ambitious military man. When de Gaulle was faced by such a challenge in January 1960 by General Massu, and in April 1961 by Generals Challe, Jouhaud, Zeller and Salan, he shook it off without much difficulty. Napoleon I was succeeded by Louis XVIII's attempt at constitutional monarchy; Napoleon III by the parliamentary democracy of the Third Republic; Pétain by that of the Fourth; and de Gaulle by a succession of strictly civilian heads of state. This fact alone sets a gulf between France and the countries of Africa, South America or the Middle East, where the result of one military coup d'état is generally another coup d'état, followed by a third, fourth and fifth. From this point of view, as well as by the fact that French Caesars tend to rule through civilians and not through the army, the political stability achieved by France since de Gaulle's retirement in 1969 can be seen as the culmination of a general tendency. It is one which has been gradually growing stronger since the first French revolution of 1789 set out to establish what we now think of as a democratic type of government. The fact that it took a long time to achieve its final objective has been the main subject of this book.

The four interruptions in the development of parliamentary democracy in France point to the fact that the country of Montesquieu and Alexis de Tocqueville did remain, for quite a long time, what S. E. Finer in *The Man on Horseback* refers to as a developed political society rather than a mature one. On four occasions it proved vulnerable in a way that Scandinavian or Anglo-Saxon society has never done to a military man's ambition to show that he could manage affairs better than his civilian counterparts. On the first three occasions it needed an invasion of France to bring about a change of régime once this military man had established himself in power. But the very fact that the fourth of the French Caesars did leave power quite peacefully, as a result of losing a free election, points to another aspect of French Caesarism which makes it especially challenging to a systematically minded observer: it is virtually impossible to find any features in it which are genuinely shared by all four of its manifesta-

Conclusion 151

tions. Thus Napoleon III was not really a military man at all, but merely somebody who happened to be his uncle's nephew. The crisis which enabled Pétain to seize power was totally different from the one which provided Napoleon I with his opportunity. In 1940, France had just suffered a military defeat; in 1799, it had successfully fought off the threat of foreign invasion. Napoleon I governed with the support of the army, and encountered serious opposition only from civilians like Talleyrand and Fouché. De Gaulle's first four years in office were dominated by his struggle against the French army, and he received most of his support from civilians.

There are, admittedly, some marked similarities between Napoleon III and General de Gaulle: both adopted what could be seen as a left-wing, progressive policy on Algeria; both encouraged France to adopt free trade rather than protectionism; both presided over an industrial boom and over a series of changes which helped to make Paris a more impressive city. But while de Gaulle had the traditional Anglophobia of the French right, Napoleon III quite liked the English. These feelings were reciprocated by Queen Victoria, who thought him far too agreeable to be a Frenchman. He was, she said, much more like a German.[1] The only genuine similarity between Pétain and de Gaulle was that they were professional soldiers. On military matters, Pétain gave priority to defence, de Gaulle to attack. Pétain's vision of France was a profoundly reactionary one. He preferred agriculture to industry, and wanted to go back to the kind of organic society, free of conflicts among groups, which is sometimes seen as characterising the Middle Ages. De Gaulle's ambition was to drag France kicking and screaming into the twentieth century, and he very largely succeeded. Napoleon III had a similar effect on nineteenth century France, and also gave the French a Constitution which attracted favourable comment from English observers. Walter Bagehot described the Second Empire as 'the *best finished* democracy which the world has ever seen' and praised it for being an absolute government which, 'with a popular instinct', possessed 'the unimpeded command of a people renowned for orderly dexterity'.[2]

While de Gaulle was the only one to be a practising Catholic in his private life, each of the four French Caesars who actually took power also saw the Church as a useful barrier against social disorder. In this respect, they illustrate an interesting difference between Western and Eastern Europe, especially since the advent of Communism. One of the most striking features of Communist society is that while the army has tended to support the régime, the Catholic Church has not. But

152 *French Caesarism*

on the crucial issue of education, Napoleon I differed sharply from his three successors. Happy though he was to have the Imperial Catechism taught by the Church, he saw it as the privilege of the state to exercise a monopoly over primary, secondary and higher education. *L'Université Impériale* of 1808 provided a model for the very unCaesarian Third Republic by insisting on the right of the state to impose the syllabus, appoint staff and organise the time-table. What is known in French as 'le monopole des diplômes', the exclusive right of the state to grant recognised educational qualifications, from the *baccalauréat* to the *Doctorat d'Etat*, is one of the many signs which remind the Anglo-Saxon observer of how much more present and powerful the state is in France than in English-speaking countries. Although not introduced until 1879, it is a very Napoleonic concept.

The Catholic religion certainly was the official basis for the moral teaching of the Imperial University. But this was because Napoleon wanted it that way, not because there was any question of a Catholic education which would be different from the one provided by the state. The *lycées* were military establishments where pupils began and ended classes to the beat of a drum, and the principal aim of the *Ecole Polytechnique*, established by the Revolution but greatly developed under Napoleon, was to train artillery officers. Napoleon III, Pétain and de Gaulle, in contrast, all encouraged private, Catholic education, and thus tended to reduce the monopoly of the secular state. The desire of the French Socialist Party to establish what François Mitterrand called 'un grand service public laïc et unifié de l'Education nationale sans spoliation ni monopole' provided in 1982 a reminder of how the desire to extend the rule of the state is in France as much a characteristic of the left as of the right. The Russian aristocrats in *War and Peace* who spoke of 'Buonaparte' as a Jacobin were showing an appropriate recognition of how thoroughly he had taken over in this respect the desires of Robespierre and his followers to make the state play a central role in people's private lives. In educational matters, this was not something which Napoleon III, Philippe Pétain or Charles de Gaulle were interested in doing.

The causes which explain each successful Caesar's rise to power also differ quite radically from one case to another. In 1799 there was a genuine political crisis in the sense that the politicians of the *Directoire* could not agree amongst themselves as to whether France should become a radical republic, a constitutional monarchy, a conservative republic or an absolute monarchy. In 1799, as in 1795, Bonaparte acted at the invitation of civilian politicians seeking to

Conclusion 153

strengthen their own position. In 1851, there was no real political crisis. Napoleon III carried out his coup d'état with remarkably little support from civilian politicians. They may have wanted to use him, but he out-manœuvred them. It was through the army that he made himself Emperor, and the arrest of such impeccably middle-class conservatives as Thiers or Baze, or of more moderate soldiers such as Lamoricière and Charras, suggests that Marx was right to see Napoleon III, at least initially, as incarnating the class interests of the more retarded peasants of provincial France. Yet while this suggests a similarity between Napoleon III and Pétain, the latter's own performance shows how illusory such parallels can be. Whereas Napoleon III encouraged private capitalism, Pétain had little sympathy with big business. He preferred the old-fashioned France of the artisan to the large-scale, authoritarian capitalism which Napoleon III helped to develop during the Second Empire. Unlike the 'satrapist and sultanist militaries of Africa and the Middle East', criticised by Amos Perlmutter in *The Military and Politics* for failing to bring about political progress,[3] Napoleon III and Charles de Gaulle did help to modernise France. Pétain, in contrast, had neither the desire nor the opportunity to do so.

An attractive hypothesis for seeing more than an accidental and superficial similarity between the careers of the four men is nevertheless provided by the thesis that each of them came to power because of the inadequacy of French civilian politicians and as a result of a fundamental weakness of French political life. This hypothesis is linked to the doubt which I mentioned in the Introduction to this book as to whether France is a country genuinely suited to democratic government. Both the Third and the Fourth Republics, it has been argued, disappeared more as a result of euthanasia, or even of suicide, than through the impact of a violent and well-organised plot. In the case of the Third, Jean-Pierre Azéma and Michel Winock go so far as to speak of 'la faiblesse profonde de la vie politique française',[4] and to suggest that the ultimate cause lies in the exhaustion of the ideology which had inspired the triumphs of this Republic during the first fifty or so years of its existence. For while the enthusiasm for secular republicanism and for the rôle of France as a country capable of bringing civilisation to all men did have the effect of linking French people together in the unity which enabled them to win the First World War, ideas of this kind became increasingly irrelevant to the society of the 1920s and 1930s. Neither did the specifically French version of socialism inspire much resistance to the transformation of

154   *French Caesarism*

the Third Republic into a corporate state on the model of Mussolini's Italy or the Portugal of Salazar. Of the 104 *députés* belonging to the *Section Française de l'Internationale Ouvrière*, 94 voted on 10 July 1940 in favour of giving full powers to Marshal Pétain; and they had all, four years earlier, supported the Popular Front government of 1936. Although their leader, Léon Blum, personally voted against, he did not try to organise an opposition group because he was afraid of splitting the party.

It is also true that Pétain was given his chance to come back to power by Paul Reynaud. But once in Paris, Pétain then began to behave in a way that Reynaud had not anticipated, and was no more prepared to accept the Prime Minister's authority than the other soldier who was playing a major part in French politics at the time, General Weygand. He, too, hankered after a more authoritarian régime and would have been quite prepared to take over in France if Pétain had been unavailable or unwilling to do so. It is even alleged that he had an army division ready at Clermont-Ferrand in July 1940 to sweep away the National Assembly if its members did not vote in favour of the motion abolishing the Third Republic.[5] But since there was no resistance, and no civilian politician of any stature anxious to assume responsibility at the time of the defeat in 1940, the case that the Third Republic collapsed because it ran out of steam and supporters is quite a strong one. But in 1958, when de Gaulle became the fourth French Caesar to take over the state, there was plenty of opposition from established politicians, Pierre Mendès France and François Mitterrand among them. If they did not succeed, it is because there are limits to what even the most determined civilian politicians can do without widespread popular support in the face of the reality or even of the convincing threat of military force. In 1940, with French casualties running at almost 20,000 a week, the galvanising effect of a Churchill or a Clemenceau might well have been a bloodbath which would have made Verdun or the Somme look insignificant in comparison. In 1958, a powerfully led movement of republican resistance could have easily given rise to a civil war. In both cases, one might well argue that the absence of powerful civilian politicians was an advantage rather than a drawback. Even when the clumsy brutality of Napoleon III is taken into consideration – 300 or so casualties in the fairly aimless shootings which followed the coup d'état of 2 December 1851 – military take-overs in France are relatively economical, at least in the first instance, in human lives. The actual events accompanying or succeeding them – the defeat of

Conclusion 155

1940, Napoleon's military campaigns – may be murderous. Between 1803 and 1815, a million-and-a-half Frenchmen died in the Napoleonic wars, 200,000 more than between 1914 and 1918. But the take-overs themselves were fairly bloodless; especially when compared to the slaughter of 20,000 Parisians instigated by the strictly civilian Adolphe Thiers when he put down the *Commune* in 1871.

If, then, it is the fundamental weakness of French political life that makes France so vulnerable to Caesarism, this is not always and entirely a bad thing. Paradoxically enough, the two French Caesars who took power in the twentieth century are best known for bringing wars to an end, and thus saving human lives: Pétain in 1940 and Charles de Gaulle in 1962. But the case for explaining French Caesarism by invoking the weakness of French political life is by no means an overwhelming one. It is true that the July Monarchy, like the Restoration Monarchy which preceded it, fell because of its inability to make the necessary reforms in time. It is equally true, and perhaps more significant, that the Second Republic collapsed because its leaders were incapable of dealing with Napoleon III. But both the Third and the Fourth Republics were quite capable of running their affairs with moderate competence until some kind of crisis supervened. Any English historian or political scientist who accuses the French of being unable to run parliamentary government properly forgets the fortunate geographical position of the British Isles. Only if the British parliamentary system had been tested by invasion could we be absolutely sure that we were better at politics than the French. For without the defeat of 1940 France would have been faced neither with the reproach of having given supreme power to an 84-year-old soldier, nor with the failure to decolonise in time which was the ruin of the Fourth Republic. The British, from this point of view, had things relatively easily, for it is not too much of a problem for a country to be generous when it has just been rather spectacularly victorious. Even if one takes matters further back in history, and compares the immediate origins of parliamentary government in the two countries, it is remarkable how the English revolutions of the seventeenth century profited from the fact that Britain is an island. Scottish intervention contributed to the victory of the Parliamentarians at Marston Moor in 1644, but could do nothing for Charles II in 1650 and 1651. Whatever sympathy the monarchs of France and Spain may have felt for Charles I, they could not translate this into effective military support. In 1655, the French had to agree to the expulsion from France of the exiled court of Charles II; and General

156 *French Caesarism*

Monck carried out the Restoration of 1660 with an army of English and Scottish soldiers. William of Orange's victory over James II at the battle of the Boyne in 1690 marked the end of a French attempt to intervene which failed partly because of problems of supply. Northern Ireland is, after all, some distance away from France. From 1792 onwards, in contrast, the French Revolution was faced with the prospect of foreign invasion and interference which made it almost inevitable that the army would assume a major and permanent rôle.

One of the dilemmas to confront any historian, whether amateur or professional, is well summed up by two quotations from French authors: Pascal's remark that if Cleopatra's nose had been shorter the whole face of the earth would have changed; and Montesquieu's observation that if a particular incident was the immediate cause of the fall of an empire, this was because the empire was doomed to fall anyway. Had Cleopatra been less beautiful, Mark Antony would not have fallen in love with her. He would not then have lost the battle of Actium; and he would thus have been able to prevent Augustus from bringing the whole Roman world under the unified control of one leader. Christianity might then not have spread with the ease afforded to it by the existence of a single empire in the East and West, and the unity of what we now think of as Europe might have a very different form. In the debates on the origins of French Caesarism, one might similarly explain it by the geographical accident of France having a common frontier with Germany, of Napoleon I being born in 1769 and not in 1779, of Pétain and de Gaulle having the good fortune to survive the First World War. De Gaulle, in this respect, is a disciple of Montesquieu rather than of Pascal, what historians of philosophy call an essentialist rather than an existentialist. He shares the view of Napoleon I that there is some inherent quality in the French which condemns them constantly to disagree amongst themselves, and thus to need a firmer form of leadership than other, essentially more united peoples. When he describes France, in *L'Effort*, the fourth volume of his *Mémoires*, as 'a country which, since the time of the Gauls, is periodically the theatre of those "sudden and unexpected upheavals" which already astonished Julius Caesar', he is taking up an idea already put forward in the first volume. There, he argues the need for 'de vastes enterprises' to 'compenser les ferments de dispersion que son peuple porte en lui-même', and clearly sees France as a kind of living individual with inner and inescapable characteristics, characteristics which are the

Conclusion 157

cause rather than the consequence of the historical events which actually take place.[6]

It is obviously not possible to prove a semi-poetic vision of this kind. Nations may well have inherent personalities, and there may well be an immanent destiny which shapes their ends, rough-hew them how they will. On the other hand, there may not, and there are fairly precise historical reasons for what de Gaulle ('quel joli pseudonyme', André Lapié is said to have remarked when his first book appeared in 1924) also referred to as 'notre vieille propension gauloise aux querelles et aux divisions' (our old Gallic propensity towards quarrels and divisions). On the political left, for example, the divisions between the various parties which prevented the Fourth Republic from keeping the promises of its bright dawn all had very explicable if slightly complicated origins. The left-wing Catholic party, the *Mouvement Républicain Populaire*, was a welcome novelty, in the sense that organised Catholicism had, since 1789, tended to favour the right. But the MRP could not agree with the socialist party, the SFIO, on the question of whether or not the state should provide subsidies for Catholic schools. The members of the *Section Française de l'Internationale Ouvrière* maintained that the state needed to provide only one educational system out of the tax-payers' money, just as it provided only one army and one police force. The MRP took the opposite view. It argued that it was unjust to require practising Catholics to pay taxes to support a wholly secular educational system while at the same time refusing to allocate any part of these taxes to subsidise the schools to which such Catholics wanted to send their children. The Radicals, the oldest of the French political parties and the one most concerned with protecting the individual citizen against both Church and State, agreed with the Socialists – the SFIO – on refusing state subsidies for Catholic schools. They nevertheless disagreed with the Socialists' view that the best way to solve the country's economic problems was by nationalisation. They supported the continued existence of privately owned firms, especially if these happened to be small. The Communists agreed with the Socialists in wishing to extend the economic rôle of the state, but disagreed with them – as with everybody else – in persistently supporting the foreign policy of the USSR. In 1920, at the Congrès de Tours, the original SFIO had been unable to agree on whether or not to ally itself with the Third International founded by Lenin in 1919. The majority had decided in favour of such an alliance, and formed itself into the *Parti Communiste Français*. The minority refused and

158 *French Caesarism*

kept the old name of the SFIO. But it tended to attract mainly schoolteachers and office workers. It was the PCF, skilful in exploiting the understandably bitter memories of the *Commune* and the June Days of 1848, which won the support of the industrial working class. Here, again, it was the weight of the past which created the divisions of the present, and a more existentialist view of French history will explain by reference to specific and often accidental events the multiplicity of parties which essentialist historians see as the product of an inherent national character. After all, it was de Gaulle himself, by the creation in 1947 of the *Rassemblement du Peuple Français*, who added yet another division to French political life; and it is hard to argue that the acts of one man are the expression of a whole nation's collective personality.

At times, when you think about yourself, everything that has happened to you seems to form part of a pattern. This pattern itself strikes you as the product of an inherited disposition, and you feel that your present situation has been brought about by inner forces over which you have no control. So, in looking at a country such as France, the recurrent pattern of military men taking over at moments of national crisis sometimes seems the inevitable outcome of in-built tendencies over which individuals have no power. A country with so marked and repetitive a tendency to be divided against itself has to call in a providential saviour from time to time, and a country with so quarrelsome a disposition inevitably summons a soldier. At other times, when you think about yourself, you realise that you have built up what you think of as your essential character by a series of separate, individual decisions. Each of these could have been different, and each of them had to be taken in circumstances that were often entirely accidental. So, in the case of France, an existential reading of her history will see the two Napoleons, Pétain and de Gaulle as the products of that combination between chance and free choice which so frequently strikes us as characterising individual human experience. De Gaulle himself said that 'History does not teach fatalism. There are moments when the will of a handful of free men breaks through determinism and opens up new roads. People get the history they deserve',[7] and his essentialist view of France as a country predestined to divisions went hand in hand with a belief in free will that would have done credit to the early Jean-Paul Sartre himself. For the existentialism of *L'Etre et le Néant*, *Baudelaire* and *Réflexions sur la Question Juive* presented human beings as constantly able to alter by new acts the personality created by the free

Conclusion 159

decisions they had taken in the past. It was an attractively optimistic doctrine, and there is pleasure as well as paradox in the reflection that the French politician who most successfully put it into practice was the exact opposite in so many other ways of everything that Sartre stood for. At a time when the French left was increasingly unable to translate into practice the principles set out in *La Déclaration des droits de l'homme et du citoyen*, a soldier came along and did it for them. It is – let us hope – the triumphant end of French Caesarism.

Notes

INTRODUCTION

1 The figures for these and other plebiscites and referenda are taken from *Quid* (Paris: Laffont, 1985) p. 626.

2 See J.-R. Tournoux, *La Tragédie du Général* (Paris: Plon, 1967) p. 470. The full quotation illustrates the permanence of de Gaulle's vision of the nation state and of nationalism as decisive forces in world politics: 'Napoleon, the greatest captain of modern times, was defeated from the moment when, instead of using a national army against royal armies, he found himself facing nations with the name of Spain, Prussia and Russia.'

3 See Albert Soboul, *La Révolution Française* (Paris: PUF, 1965) 'Que sais-je?', p. 116. It is very comforting, after reading the account in William Doyle (see note 12 to Chapter 1) of how Anglo-Saxon historians have cast doubt on all the received wisdom about the French Revolution, to turn back to a historian who considers that the Revolution did take place; that it did destroy the remnants of the feudal system; that the French nobility did enjoy fiscal privileges; that it was a closed caste; that the nationalisation of the Church lands did create a class of peasant small-holders; that the Revolution itself was (p. 114) an 'étape nécessaire de la transition générale du féodalisme au capitalisme' (a necessary stage in the general transition from feudalism to capitalism); that it was therefore a Good Thing; especially since the rising middle class would shortly be giving way to the triumphant proletariat. For a more up-to-date and less traditional account of what really mattered in the French Revolution, see T. C. W. Blanning, *The French Revolution: Aristocrats versus Bourgeois?* (London: Macmillan, 1987). This emphasises how large the French aristocracy was – about 25,000 families, as against 250 members of the Peerage in eighteenth-century England – and what benefits an enterprising noble – not distinguishable in this respect from a member of the middle class – could derive from the disappearance of the *ancien régime*. Pointing out how much damage the Revolution – to say nothing of the Napoleonic wars – did to the French economy, Dr Blanning also observes (p. 47) 'that it seems an odd sort of revolution which can inflict so much damage on the most advanced sector, economically speaking, of the bourgeoisie'.

4 This aspect of Louis Napoleon's constitutional position is rarely mentioned, and Article 45 of the 1848 Constitution also insisted that neither the President himself nor his Vice-President nor any of his relatives were re-eligible. However, the constitutional lawyer Armand Marrast published in *Le Moniteur Universel* for 31 August 1848 a long analysis of the Constitution in which he made the point that the President could stand again for office once a four-year period had

Notes to pp. 2–12 161

elapsed after the end of his first mandate. See Maurice Deslandres, *Histoire Constitutionnelle de la France de 1789 à 1870* (Paris: Armand Colin, 1932) p. 367. For the remark about liberty, see J. M. Thompson, *Napoleon III* (Oxford: Basil Blackwell, 1954) p. 251.

5 See Raymond Aron, *Mémoires* (Paris: Julliard, 1983) p. 234. Aron had originally said in a lecture that the French carried out revolutions but not reforms. De Gaulle, in a conversation that took place in 1947, corrected him by reminding him of the reforms carried out after the liberation of France in 1944.

6 In a speech given on 13 December 1850. See R. P. T. Bury and R. P. Tombs, *Thiers. A Political Life* (London: Allen and Unwin, 1986) p. 123.

7 *De l'Ancien Régime et la Révolution*, Collection 'Idées' (Paris: Gallimard, 1952) p. 236.

8 See S. E. Finer, *The Man on Horseback* (London: Pall Mall Press, 1962) p. 88. France, in this analysis, falls into the category of what Finer calls 'developed political culture', in the sense that 'the legitimacy of the procedures for transferring political power and the question of who or what should constitute the sovereign authority are both in dispute'.

9 The plebiscites were: (1) 10 May 1802, on Bonaparte being Consul for life; (2) 15 May 1804, on the establishment of the hereditary Empire; (3) 22 April 1815, on the Additional Act to the Constitution of the Empire (introducing a more liberal régime during the Hundred Days); (4) 2 December 1851, on Louis Napoleon being President for ten years; (5) 21 November 1852, on the re-establishment of the Empire; (6) 8 May 1869, on the liberal reforms introduced into the Second Empire.

The referenda were: (1) 28 September 1958, on the Constitution of the Fifth Republic; (2) 8 January 1961, on self-determination for Algeria; (3) 8 April 1962, on the Evian agreements putting an end to the Algerian war; (4) 28 October 1962, on the election of the President by universal suffrage; (5) 27 April 1969, on the reform of the Senate and regionalisation.

The first of the series in which the question asked by the Executive received the answer 'No' was also the last of the series.

10 For Nordlinger, see his *Soldiers in Politics. Military Coups and Governments* (New Jersey: Prentice Hall, 1977) p. 210. For Tournoux, see his *Secrets d'Etat* (Paris: Plon, 1960) p. 449.

For a comparable use of the adjective, see Jean Lacouture, *De Gaulle* (Paris: Seuil, 1969) p. 185, where de Gaulle is described as being 'l'agent nécessaire d'une brusque mutation vers l'âge industriel: une opération qu'on qualifierait volontiers de "césarienne"' (the necessary agent for a harsh change introducing the industrial age. An operation which one might well call 'Caesarian').

For uses of the word Caesarism by English-speaking historians, see *Soldiers and Statesmen*, edited by Peter Dennis and Adrian Preston (London: Croom Helm, 1976), in which Adrian Preston's Introduction describes the elevation of Wellington to Prime Minister as 'a clear

162 *French Caesarism*

invitation to Caesarism or to civil war' (p. 9), and quotes Michael Howard in 'The Armed Services as a Political Problem' as talking about 'Caesarist ambitions' (p. 12). In 1879, General Wolseley was suspected of trying to establish an independent Indian Army, an attempt described as 'the closest thing to a drift towards Caesarism that the Victorian age experienced' (p. 31).

Not all French people – nor all French historians and political commentators – immediately recognise or spontaneously use either the term 'Césarisme' or its associated adjectives. A frequent reaction, on hearing the word explained, is to talk about 'l'homme providentiel'. De Gaulle expresses a similar idea on pp. 22–3 of his *Mémoires d'Espoir* (*L'Effort*, Paris: Plon, 1971) when he writes, describing his own return to power in 1958: 'Une fois de plus, il serait arrivé que, devant un drame national ayant pour cause première l'incapacité des partis, ceux-ci auraient feint d'abdiquer entre les mains d'un démiurge tout à coup chargé du salut – ainsi: en 1914, Joffre; en 1917 Clemenceau; en 1940 Pétain; puis, l'erreur reconnue, de Gaulle; en 1958 de Gaulle encore.'

(Once again it has happened that, faced with a national drama whose primary cause is the incapacity of political parties, these have pretended to abdicate into the hands of a demiurge suddenly entrusted with the task of ensuring salvation – thus, in 1914, Joffre; in 1917, Clemenceau; in 1940, Pétain; then, the mistake acknowledged, de Gaulle; in 1958, de Gaulle again.)

11 *Le Fil de l'Epée* 1932 (Paris: Plon, 1971) p. 100.

12 *Carnets II* (Paris: Gallimard, 1964) p. 340.

13 For Paxton see his *La France de Vichy, 1940–1944*, translated from the English by Claude Bertrand (Paris: Seuil, 1973) p. 253. The enthusiasm which some very clever people felt for the Vichy régime is illustrated by an anecdote on p. 463 of J.-B. Duroselle's *L'Abîme 1939–1945* (Paris: Imprimerie Nationale, 1982). Jean Bichelonne, who had graduated from the *Ecole Polytechnique* with the highest number of marks ever awarded in the history of the institution, collaborated enthusiastically because his knowledge of mathematics enabled him to prove the inevitability of a German victory.

For Weygand, see Henri Amouroux, *La Grande Histoire des Français sous l'Occupation*, Vol. ii, *Quarante Millions de Pétainistes* (Paris: Laffont, 1977) p. 344.

14 *En France* (Paris: Julliard, 1965) pp. 42–3. The quotation is preceded by the remark: 'Le général de Gaulle a parfaitement raison de croire qu'il incarne la France, il a tort de croire que cela soit flatteur pour lui' (General de Gaulle is quite right to see himself as the incarnation of France, where he is wrong is to think that this is flattering for him).

Notes to pp. 11–27 163

CHAPTER 1

1 See Corelli Barnett, *Bonaparte* (London: Allen and Unwin, 1978) p. 48. This envigoratingly hostile account of Bonaparte's career nevertheless attributes most of his victories to good luck. There are said to be over 100,000 books on Napoleon, among the most recent the *Dictionnaire Napoléon*, edited by Jean Tulard (Paris: Fayard, 1987) with 1,769 pages. This contains the interesting information that one of the first accounts of Napoleon's career appeared in 1816, in Chinese. The permanence of the hostility towards him characteristic of French liberal and left-wing thinkers can be seen in Roger Caratine's review of the *Dictionnaire Napoléon* in *Le Nouvel Observateur*, 1209 (1988). He describes Napoleon's career as a 'national disaster' for France, but stops short, for reasons obvious to any reader in the closing years of the twentieth century, at the frankness of disapproval which led *The Morning Post* to call Napoleon, in the early nineteenth century, 'an indefinable being, half-African, half-European, a Mediterranean Mulatto' – quoted on p. 93 of Felix Markham, *Napoleon* (London: Weidenfeld and Nicolson, 1963).

2 See Thomas Carlyle, *History of the French Revolution* (1837), Vol. III, Book VII, Chapter VII, in which 'the quellers of Sans-culottism were themselves quelled, and the sacred right of Insurrection was blown away by gunpowder; wherewith this singular eventful History called *French Revolution* ends'.

3 I have no printed source for this anecdote, which was told to me by an Italian. The figures for Bonaparte's plunder are from a French source as hostile to him as Corelli Barnett, Henri Guillemin's *Napoléon Tel Quel* (Paris: Editions de Trévise, 1969) pp. 48–55. Even a more objective historian such as Jacques Godechot, however, emphasises the way in which 'les contributions de guerre levées en Italie, en Allemagne et en Suisse, de 1796 à 1798, permirent à la France de rétablir son équilibre budgétaire et d'abandonner les assignats pour revenir à la monnaie métallique', and points out that the French budget was balanced between 1803 and 1814 solely as a result of levies raised in conquered countries. See *Occupants–Occupés, 1792–1815*, *Actes du Colloque qui s'est tenu à Bruxelles, les 29 et 30 janvier, 1968* (Université libre de Bruxelles, 1969) pp. 27–8. In this respect, as in others, Napoleon could legitimately say: 'I am the Revolution.'

4 Finer, p. 213.

5 See Jacques Godechot, *Napoléon. Le Mémorial des Siècles* (Paris: Albin Michel, 1969) p. 161.

6 Lynn Hunt, *Culture, Politics and Class in the French Revolution* (Berkeley: University of California Press, 1984) p. 2.

7 Alfred Cobban, *A History of Modern France* (Harmondsworth: Penguin Books, 1957) p. 109.

8 For Weidlé, see his *La Russie absente et présente* (Paris: Gallimard, 1949).

9 See Donald Greer, *The Incidence of Terror during the French Revolution* (Cambridge, Mass.: Harvard University Press, 1935) p. 135. Greer

164 French Caesarism

also observes on p. 108 that it was the people from the upper reaches of society who were most likely to be guillotined, and discounts the view that the Terror formed part of a systematic attempt to enforce economic controls. There is, he writes on p. 124, 'irrefutable evidence that the Terror was used to crush rebellion and to quell opposition to the Republic'.

10 See *French Liberal Thought in the Eighteenth Century* (London: Turnstile Press, 1954) p. 1.

11 Estimates of historians vary on this point. André Latreille, in *'Eglise Catholique et la Révolution Française* (Paris: Hachette, 1948), says on p. 10 that it owned between 6 per cent and 10 per cent of the national territory, but points out that this varied from 4 per cent in the West to 20 per cent in Picardy.

12 For a full treatment of the now much disputed question of whether or not the French nobility did enjoy genuine fiscal privileges, see William Doyle, *Origins of the French Revolution* (Oxford University Press, 1980) pp. 117–18. While nobles were certainly not exempt in the way that the Church was – it paid only a *don gratuit*, made after negotiations with the Crown which took place every five years – they did feel themselves threatened in the privileges which they still had by the proposal in 1787 to levy a new tax in kind at the moment of harvest.

See also Part I of Doyle's book, 'A Consensus and its Collapse: Writings on Revolutionary Origins since 1939' for the view that there was no genuine conflict between the nobility and the Third Estate, since both nobles and bourgeois belonged to (p. 19) 'a single propertied élite'. What is hard to understand, if this is so, is why the Declaration of the Rights of Man laid so much emphasis on the need for formal social equality. See also above, note 3 to the Introduction.

13 See Henri Calvet, *Napoléon* (Paris: PUF, 1964) p. 69. William Doyle argues in his discussion of the bourgeoisie that there was no fundamental conflict of interest between nobles and bourgeois before 1787, and (p. 136) 'before 1788, little evidence of widespread, conscious bourgeois hostility to the idea of nobility'. The ambition of rich, middle-class families, he argues, was to become noble. But once the events of 1789 had begun to develop, he suggests, middle-class hostility to the nobles becomes more acute (pp. 137–8).

14 See Felix Markham, *Napoléon*, p. 135.

15 See *Secrets d'Etat* (Paris: Plon, 1960) pp. 230–370 and 449.

16 See Jacques Godechot, *Napoléon. Le Mémorial des Siècles* (Paris: Albin Michel, 1969) p. 361. The calculation was made in a letter to *The Times* by 'Probus' on 7 July 1815. The discussion as to what to do about Napoleon after his final defeat in 1815 occupied a good deal of space in the correspondence columns of *The Times*. The wide variety of points of view expressed, which often included considerable sympathy for him and doubts as to what right the British had to exile him, is in marked contrast to the unanimity about the treatment to be meted out to twentieth-century tyrants.

17 For Freud, see *Standard Edition of the Complete Psychological Works of Sigmund Freud* (London: Hogarth Press, 1935) pp. 196–8.

Notes to pp. 27–52 165

18 For Macmillan, see Bernard Letwidge, *De Gaulle* (London: Weidenfeld and Nicolson, 1982) p. 260.
19 Corelli Barnett, *Bonaparte*, p. 110.
20 Letwidge, *De Gaulle*, p. 170.
21 For further discussion of this point, see Amos Perlmutter, *The Military and Politics in Modern Times* (Yale University Press, 1977) pp. 267–92.
22 Se Arthur-Lévy, *Napoléon Intime* (Paris and London: Nelson, 1893) p. 141.

CHAPTER 2

1 See Maurice Agulhon, *1848 ou l'Apprentissage de la République*, Vol. 8 in *La Nouvelle Histoire de la France Contemporaine* (Paris: Seuil, 1973) p. 217.
2 Thus Raymond Aron observes on p. 174 of his *Immuable et Changeante. De la IVe à la Ve* (Paris, 1959) that the French army never took the political initiative in the nineteenth century and that Louis Napoleon had difficulty finding generals to execute his enterprise against the Assembly. The matter is further discussed in Paul-Marie de la Gorce, *The French Army. A Military–Political History* (New York: George Braziller, 1963) and in Olivier Girardet, *La Société Militaire dans la France Contemporaine* (Paris: Plon, 1953). See also Alfred Cobban's remark on p. 242 of Vol. ii of his *History of Modern France*: 'Of all the revolutions or coups d'état between 1815 and 1958, none was made and none was prevented by the army. The initiative had to come from civilians.'
3 For Napoleon III's financial problems and solutions, see Henri Guillemin, *Le Coup d'Etat du 2 Décembre* (Paris: Gallimard, 1951) pp. 267–8. Cyril Pearl, in his *The Girl with the Swansdown Seat* (New York: Signet Books, 1956) says on p. 133 that the 'often repeated' figure of £320,000 which Miss Howard is supposed to have lent him is 'obviously absurd', even for a girl of her potentialities; and suggests the much lower figure of £13,000, still a considerable sum for the period. To the modern reader, who has to judge the appearance of the man whom General Changarnier dubbed 'the melancholy parrot' by photographs and portraits, such munificence is inexplicable on the grounds of sexual attraction. Miss Howard's generosity nevertheless paid off, and the wages of sin were high. In 1853, when Napoleon III reluctantly jettisoned her to marry Eugénie de Montijo – who was not rich, but also had red-gold hair – the Emperor created her Countess of Beauregard, repaid her loans, and bestowed on her an annual income of £20,000.
   For Pétain's financial situation, see Herbert R. Lottman, who points out in his *Pétain. Hero or Traitor?* (London: Viking Books, 1985) that in 1941 Pétain's declared earned income totalled 1,893,000 francs, over $250,000 in US currency. Between 1941 and 1944, some two million francs were deposited to his wife's account in Antibes.

166   *French Caesarism*

4   Admirers of Marcel Proust will immediately recognise the man so incomprehensibly seen by Madame de Varanbon as one of the close relatives of the Narrator in *A la Recherche du Temps Perdu* (Paris: Pléiade, 1954) Vol. II, p. 498.

5   For the figures illustrating the economic inequalities of mid-nineteenth-century France, see Theodore Zeldin, *Histoire des Passions Françaises*, Vol. IV, *Colère et Politique* (Paris: Seuil, 1983) p. 226.

6   See *Les Luttes de Classes en France 1848–1852 et Le 18 Brumaire de Louis Bonaparte* (Paris: Editions Sociales, 1848) p. 241.

7   See Henri Guillemin, *Le Coup d'Etat du 2 Décembre* (Paris: Gallimard, 1951) p. 324. Guillemin is also not very fond of Thiers, and in 1952 published in Sartre's *Les Temps Modernes* a series of articles arguing that Thiers deliberately tricked the Parisian working class into the rebellion of the *Commune* in 1871 in order to provide himself with the opportunity of having them massacred. On p. 358 of *Le Coup d'Etat du 2 Décembre* he says that when Thiers was arrested in the early morning of 2 December 1851 he was unable to control his bowels.

Guillemin's hostility towards Napoleon III is not an exclusively French phenomenon. On 2 March 1946 a vigorously worded review of Albert Guérard's *Napoleon III* (Cambridge, Mass.: Harvard University Press, 1943) was published in *The Times Literary Supplement*. It described Napoleon III as 'a plebiscitary Caesar', and wrote that his 'taciturn, shadowy, impassive figure' has 'puzzled the century which has gone by, as the shrieking, convulsive, hysterical figure of Hitler will puzzle the one to come'. The Second Empire, it argued, with 'its strictures on sectional interests', its 'bombast about the integration of all truly national interests' was the forerunner of the single party totalitarianisms of the modern age. 'The pulling down and rebuilding of capitals', it continued, in an obvious reference to the work of Baron Haussmann, 'is again a recurrent feature in the history of despots and dictators, from Nero to Mussolini and Hitler.'

Albert Guérard's book in no way tried to put forward a critical account of Napoleon III's career. Although quoting Metternich's comment that there was a good deal less in him than met the eye, it presented Napoleon's III's brand of 'Caesarian democracy: a single leader endorsed by a plebiscite' as a régime that brought France prosperity. The remark on p. 172 that Napoleon III was 'unmilitary in his ineradicable gentleness' is also a reminder that he was so upset by the spectacle of the carnage at Solferino that he founded the International Red Cross.

The rule of anonymity then governing contributions to the *TLS* was still in force when a comparably hostile account of Napoleon III appeared on 12 January 1962 in a review of T. A. B. Corley's *Democratic Despot. A Life of Napoleon III* (London: Barrie and Rockliff, 1962). However, the remark that 'There is something tawdry and utterly banal about the man, about his Court, about his standards and about his woolly and confused thinking' points to the possibility of a common authorship. The 1962 review evoked a reply on 9 January 1962 from Ernest Weal, Honorary Secretary of the *Société d'Histoire*

Napoléonienne and of the *Souvenir Napoléonien* in England. He also inserted a notive in *The Times*: 'In respectful memory of a beneficent and far-sighted man, died January 9, 1873. He has found peace; one day he will find true justice.'

On 15 December 1966, a Mr Ernest Weal also wrote to the *TLS* in his capacity as Secretary of the Fire Protection Association.

8 For Gladstone, see J. M. Thompson, *Napoleon III* (Oxford: Basil Blackwell, 1954) p. 301. Thompson also quotes the British Ambassador in Paris, Lord Lyons (p. 288) as hoping in July 1870 that France would not win against the Prussians since 'a thoroughly successful war would simply give His Majesty a fresh lease of "Caesarism" and adjourn indefinitely the liberal institutions which he considers essential to the desirability of the dynasty'. J. M. Thompson is much more favourably inclined to Napoleon III than many other historians, and prefaces every chapter of his book with a quotation from *Hamlet*, who resembles Louis Napoleon in being 'a brave and wise young prince, called to mend a deep wrong done to his house, and born to set right a world that is out of joint, finds that the task is too much for him, and that he has not yet the strength to make his dreams come true'.

9 Quoted on p. 254 of Frederick H. Seager, *The Boulanger Affair. Political Crossroads of France 1886–1889* (Ithaca, NY: Cornell University Press, 1969). On p. 45, Lord Lyons, still British Ambassador in Paris, is quoted as asking in 1886 'whether Boulanger is aiming at being a Cromwell or a Monck' (i.e. wishing to establish his own Commonwealth or bring back the monarchy) and as commenting that 'the Republic here has lasted sixteen years, which is about the time the French take to tire of any form of government'.

10 In an article published in *Le Petit Marseillais* on 9 February 1941.

11 See J.-B. Duroselle, *L'Abîme 1939–1945. Politique Étrangère de la France* (Paris: Imprimerie Nationale, 1982) p. 218.

CHAPTER 3

1 For Laval, see Robert Paxton, *La France de Vichy, 1940–1944*, translated from the English by Claude Bertrand (Paris: Seuil, 1973) p. 288. For Pétain, see Marc Ferro, *Pétain* (Paris: Fayard, 1987) p. 562.

2 See Ferro, *Pétain*, p. 637, for details of these events and for a full version of the prepared statement read out by Pétain on the first day of his trial on 23 July 1945. In this statement, he repeated the phrase about making a gift of his person, first broadcast on the French radio at 12.30 p.m. on 16 June 1940 in the same speech in which he told the French that they should stop fighting. In late 1940, a slim volume entitled *Le Maréchal Pétain. Appels aux Français* was published in the 'Editions de services d'information – Vice-Présidence du Conseil'. This contained the text of all the speeches given that year by Pétain, with the phrase 'il faut tenter de cesser le combat' replacing 'il faut cesser le combat'. On 16 June the announcer introducing Pétain anticipated the

168 *French Caesarism*

forthcoming constitutional change by talking about 'les services de radio de l'Etat Français'.

In the summer of 1979, a remarkable series of broadcasts were made on *France-Inter*, in which the journalist and historian Henri Amouroux presented the main findings of his monumental *La Grande Histoire des Français sous l'Occupation* (Paris: Laffont, 1976–1983). The repeat of Pétain's broadcast was made on 9 July 1979.

See also Herbert Lottman, *Pétain. Hero or Traitor?*, p. 368. Marc Ferro also gives details of the voting at Pétain's trial, stating on p. 653 that 'the vote for mercy was carried by 17 votes to 13, while the vote for the death penalty was carried by 14 votes to 13'. It is difficult to see how the first vote was arrived at, if there were only 24 jurors and three judges. Ferro points out that all 12 resistance jurors voted for the death penalty.

3   For figures of French tanks and aeroplanes, see J.-B. Duroselle, *L'Abîme 1939–1945. Politique Étrangère de la France* (Paris: Imprimerie Nationale, 1982) p. 20. For a full account of the defeat of 1940, see Alistair Horne, *To Lose a Battle* (London: Macmillan, 1979). On p. 100 Mr Horne quotes an instructive anecdote about Napoleon. When one of his marshals brought him a plan of campaign in which the French army was neatly and evenly drawn up from one end of the frontier to the other, Napoleon asked him if he was trying to stop smuggling. As the best book on Napoleon as a military man, David G. Chandler's *The Campaigns of Napoleon* (London: Weidenfeld and Nicholson, 1978), points out, he was a specialist in the blitzkrieg technique developed by the Germans in the early years of the Second World War, and especially the technique of carrying out a highly concentrated attack at the enemy's centre of gravity (*Schwerpunkt*). Like Brigadier Ritchie-Hook in Evelyn Waugh's *Men at Arms*, Napoleon was in favour of biffing the enemy – as, too, was de Gaulle.

4   See Ferro, *Pétain*, p. 644.

5   The question of Pétain's involvement in a plot to overthrow the Republic is naturally a controversial one. The most that the formal act of accusation could find to say in 1945 was that Pétain was prepared to have his name used by various right-wing groups who were, in the 1930s, undoubtedly trying to overthrow the Republic (Ferro, *Pétain*, pp. 626–30). But both Ferro and Paxton point out that Pétain was very careful about formally endorsing any political movement, and the mention of his name was frequently unsolicited. The charge that Pétain used his period as Ambassador in Madrid to make contact with Hitler was based upon the uncorroborated evidence of Raphael Alibert, whose readiness to lay the blame on his former leader smacks of a minor criminal trying to escape prosecution by turning Queen's evidence. Alibert was not cross-examined, so that the inherent improbability of the charge remained untested. Alibert was Justice Minister (*Garde des Sceaux*) in the Vichy government, and took much of the initiative in introducing antisemitic legislation. Henri Amouroux, in *Quarante Millions de Pétainistes* (Paris: Laffont, 1977), pp. 36–43, also discusses the accusation that Pétain was involved in a plot – and rejects it. He nevertheless points out how much Pétain enjoyed power once he

Notes to pp. 76–91 · 169

6 Jean Zay, quoted by Jean-Pierre Azéma and Michel Winock, *Naissance et Mort de la IIIe République* (Paris: Calmann-Lévy, 1970) p. 291.

7 Paul Johnson, *History of the Modern World from 1917 to the 1980s* (London: Weidenfeld and Nicolson, 1983) p. 365. Ferro, *Pétain*, p. 374, and pp. 375–81 for details of Pétain's thinking on military matters. See also Alistair Horne, *To Lose a Battle* (London: Macmillan, 1969) p. 62: 'But what is really important, as far as Pétain is concerned, is that during the years when the really irreparable damage was done to the French military machine – 1936 to 1940 – the old Marshal's influence had been largely removed from the Councils of War.'

8 See Ferro, *Pétain*, p. 265. Ferro points out that this information is not to be found in French historians of the period, but only in Anglo-Saxon scholars such as Robert Paxton in his book on Vichy and W. D. Halls in his *The Youth of Vichy France* (Oxford: Clarendon, 1981).

9 The text of *Le Mémorial* is on a bronze plaque just inside the Cathedral and is also sold as a postcard to visiting tourists.

10 For details about Vichy's treatment of the Jews, see Henri Michel, *Pétain et le Régime de Vichy* (Paris: PUF, 1978) pp. 49–51. See also Amouroux, *Quarante Millions* . . . , Vol. II, pp. 466–89. The dramatic nature of the persecution of the Jews by Vichy as well as in the occupied zone was very well rendered by the Henri Amouroux broadcasts on 2 August 1979, 'L'anti-sémitisme', and on 10 August, 'La chasse au Juif'. For details about the treatment of Jews in Denmark, see Ferro, *Pétain*, pp. 413–14. For Bernstein, see Ferro, pp. 681–4. For the details of Pétain's proposed Constitution, see one of the hagiographic volumes published in 1956 to celebrate the centenary of his birth, Gérard Hering, *La Vie Exemplaire de Philippe Pétain, Chef de Guerre – Chef d'Etat – Martyr* (Paris-Livres, 1956) pp. 144–8. On paper, this was quite a liberal Constitution, guaranteeing freedom of speech, equality before the law, protection of property and free elections. By giving two votes to the father of a family with more than two children, it tried to improve the French birth-rate. As in the Constitution of the Fifth Republic, the President was to appoint the Prime Minister, who would moreover be responsible to him. Laws were to be voted by a National Assembly of 500 members elected by universal suffrage – women as well as men – every ten years.

11 For details about Bouchardon and Mornet, see Ferro, *Pétain*, p. 630, Amouroux, *Quarante Millions* . . . , Vol. II, p. 377, and Alfred Fabre-Luce, *Le Mystère du Maréchal* (Geneva/Paris: Editions du cheval ailé, 1945) p. 138.

12 For a full discussion of Barrès' attitude on this matter, see pp. 126–9 of *Les Ecrivains et l'Affaire Dreyfus, Actes du Colloque organisé par l'Université d'Orléans et le Centre Péguy*, Collection Université d'Orléans (Paris: PUF, 1973).

13 Lottman, *The People's Anger* (London: Viking Books, 1986), quoted by Ferro in *Pétain*, p. 618.

14 See Amouroux, *Quarante Millions* . . . , Vol. II, pp. 415–61 for details

170 French Caesarism

about the absence until June 1941 from the columns of *L'Humanité* of any attacks on Hitler or the German occupation of France; of the acts of resistance by individual Communists; and of the sudden change which followed the invasion of Russia by Germany on 22 June 1941.

15   De Gaulle, *Mémoires de Guerre, L'Appel* (Paris: Plon, 1954) p. 61.

16   Alfred Fabre-Luce, *Le Mystère du Maréchal*, Paris/Geneva: 1945) pp. 23, 34 and 73. For Churchill's comment, see *Their Finest Hour* (London: Cassell, 1949) p. 196: 'One day when I was convalescing at Marrakesh in January 1944, General Georges came to luncheon. In the course of casual conversation, I aired the fancy that perhaps the French Government's failure to go to Africa in June 1940 had all turned out for the best. At the Pétain trial in August 1945, the General thought it right to state this in evidence. I make no complaint, but my retrospective speculation on this event does not represent my considered opinion either during the war or now.' On p.121, Fabre-Luce tells an interesting anecdote about a French lieutenant who in 1939 built tank barriers across two of the narrow roads which the Germans were to use when coming through the Ardennes in 1940, but was told to take them down. On p. 167, Fabre-Luce also quotes a passage from Pétain's *Testament Politique* which makes the Edmund Burke of *Reflections on the Revolution in France* sound like a revolutionary anarchist: 'The authority of the State is independent only when it is handed down by a law free from the arbitrary interference of anyone who pleases (*une loi étrangère au bon vouloir de quiconque*), a law which is in some way superhuman. You need historical heredity, that is to say the designation made by birth within an authority whose usefulness has been proved by history.'

17   The song is vigorously rendered in the programme of *Les Français sous l'Occupation* broadcast on 18 July 1979, 'La devise de Vichy'. I owe the transcription of the words to my friend and colleague, F. C. C. Todd.

18   See *Le Centenaire du Maréchal Pétain, 1856–1956*, edited under the auspices of the Association pour Défendre la Mémoire du Maréchal Pétain (Paris, 1956) p. 253.

19   See Paxton, *La France de Vichy*, p. 23.

20   For casualty figures, see Henri Michel, *Pétain et le Régime de Vichy* (Paris: PUF, 1978) p. 24, and Amouroux, *Quarante Millions . . .* , Vol. ii, p. 337.

21   See André Halimi, *La Délation sous l'Occupation* (Paris: Alain Moreau, 1983).

CHAPTER 4

1   *Le Renouveau, Mémoires d'Espoir* (Paris: Plon, 1970) p. 23.

2   *Le Salut* (Paris: Plon, 1959) p. 23.

3   *L'Appel* (Paris: Plon, 1954) p. 9.

4   Republished in *Articles et Ecrits* (Paris: Plon, 1975) pp. 308–14, especially p. 309. On p. 266 of his *Napoleon III*, J. M. Thompson

Notes to pp. 91–116 171

quotes Bismarck as saying that the appearance of 15,000 French soldiers on the Rhine in 1866 would have made him lose the war against Austria.

5   *L'Appel*, pp. 3–4.

6   Quoted in Jean Lacouture's three–volume biography of de Gaulle, Vol. ɪ, *Le Rebelle* (Paris: Seuil, 1984) p. 67.

7   See *La Tragédie du Général* (Paris: Plon, 1967) pp. 84–5. On p. 161 Tournoux also reports him as saying 'Mon candidat est Cornu. Il couronnerait si bien le régime.'

8   *La Discorde Chez l'Ennemi* (Paris: Plon, 1924; Livre de Poche, 1973) pp. 29–59, especially p. 59.

9   See Lacouture, *Le Rebelle*, p. 16.

10 *Le Rebelle*, p. 15.

11 *Le Salut*, p. 8. See p. 21 for his view of the inevitable conflict between 'cette légitimité de salut public' and 'la démagogie des partis et l'ambition des communistes'. On p. 307 of *L'Unité*, the second volume of the war memoirs (Paris: Plon, 1956), he also writes that 'il suffit que la masse et moi nous nous trouvions ensemble pour que notre unité l'emporte sur tout le reste'.

12 See Don Cook, *Charles de Gaulle. A Biography* (London: Secker and Warburg, 1984) p. 379, with the comment that 'apart from the period of Pétain and Vichy fascism, not since Napoleon III in the mid nineteenth century, was the law so assiduously applied to shield a head of state from public offense'.

13 The text of the Bayeux speech, delivered on 16 June at the first town to be visited by de Gaulle after the invasion of 1944, is in the *Documents* section of the first volume of the *Mémoires de Guerre, L'Appel*, pp. 646–52.

14 See David Robin Wilson, *Clemenceau. A Political Life* (London: Eyre Methuen, 1974) p. 279. His weakest position was on 18 January 1918 when he had a majority of 368 to 155.

15 See his *De Gaulle* (Paris: Seuil) p. 187.

16 For all these incidents, see Lacouture, *Le Rebelle*, pp. 70–2.

17 *Le Rebelle*, p. 265.

18 See Cook, *Charles de Gaulle . . .* , p. 49.

19 When *Vers l'Armée de Métier* was republished in 1971, the extreme right-wing *Minute* was delighted to pick up this particular point in the review it published on 12 November. The equally right-wing, royalist publication *Rivarol* also argued on 19 November that the view of the use of tanks put forward by de Gaulle in 1934 was 'profoundly unrealistic', since his armoured striking force would simply have been destroyed by the German artillery and crushed by dive bombers. The hostility to de Gaulle by the extreme right-wing press in France is a constant feature of his career, and one of the best illustrations of how sound his political views were. For a further discussion of the rôle of air power in *Vers l'Armée de Métier*, see *Le Rebelle*, pp. 233–4. Alistair Horne points out that de Gaulle's attack on the Germans at Abbeville in May 1940 failed largely because of his lack of air support, and shares de Gaulle's view of the havoc which a well-organised mobile striking

172 *French Caesarism*

force could have wrought on the German supply and support columns, perhaps forcing Guderian to break off his attack.

20 Published by Hutchinson and Co., London, 1940. No translator's name given.

21 Guillemin, *Le Coup d'État du 2 Décembre*, p. 323.

22 See the insistence placed upon this point by Gérard Hering, *La Vie Exemplaire de Philippe Pétain*, p. 91.

23 *Le Rebelle*, pp. 543–4 and p. 567.

24 For Daniel Mayer, see *Le Rebelle*, p. 725. For Oliver Lyttleton, see *Soldiers as Statesmen*, edited by Peter Dennis and Adrian Preston (London: Croom Helm, 1976) p. 163. Other remarks about de Gaulle reprinted in this volume include Churchill's 'There's nothing hostile to England that this man might not do once he gets off the chain', coupled with the recognition that he is 'perhaps the last survivor of the warrior race'; Sir Alexander Cadogan's 'I can't tell you anything about de Gaulle; except that he's got a head like a pineapple and hips like a woman'; and Lyndon Johnson's exasperated appeal to Maurice Schumann: 'For God's sake, tell me once and for all what General de Gaulle wants.'

25 See Cook, *Charles de Gaulle . . .*, p. 191.

26 *Le Rebelle*, p. 748.

27 De Gaulle himself certainly thought that it was the Communists' intention to organise such a take-over. See *L'Appel*, pp. 231–2, and *L'Unité*, pp. 2, 50, 51, 254, and especially 291, where they are accused of trying to establish 'the so-called "dictatorship of the proletariat"'. Robert Aron argues in his *Histoire de la Libération de la France, Juin 1944–Mai 1945* (Paris: Fayard, 1959) that this was indeed the ambition of Charles Tillon and his FTP (Francs–Tireurs–Partisans), but that he was dissuaded from making the attempt by Thorez and Duclos after de Gaulle had visited Stalin in Moscow in December 1944.

28 On 8 June 1940. See *Le Rebelle*, p. 326.

29 Quoted by Tournoux, *La Tragédie du Général* (Paris: Plon, 1967) p. 200.

30 *Their Finest Hour* (London: Cassell, 1949) p. 202. Churchill's verdict that, instead, Darlan 'went forward through two years of worrying and ignominious office to a violent death, a dishonoured grave, and a name long execrated by the French Navy and the nation he hitherto served so well' is well borne out by the facts. De Gaulle is equally scathing about Darlan on pp. 67–9 of *L'Unité*, accusing him of placing the interests of the French fleet before those of France. He nevertheless also uses the example of Darlan to emphasise the importance of having a strong state: 'Comme d'autres malheurs insignes qui avaient fondu sur la France, les fautes de l'amiral Darlan, le triste sort de notre flotte, l'insondable blessure portée à l'âme de nos marins, étaient les conséquences d'une longue infirmité de l'Etat'. (Like other notorious misfortunes which had rained down upon France, Admiral Darlan's faults, the sad fate of our fleet and the fathomless wound inflicted upon the pride of our sailors were the consequences of years of disease within the state.) Translated by Richard Howard, *Unity* (London: Weidenfeld and Nicholson, 1959) p. 74.

Notes to pp. 117–58

31 See J.-B. Duroselle, pp. 175–9 and pp. 300–81 for a more detailed account of Darlan's behaviour, especially of his readiness to bring France into the war on Germany's side.
32 *Le Salut*, p. 177.
33 *Mémoires d'Espoir, Le Renouveau* (Paris: Plon, 1980) p. 30. See also Lacouture, *Le Rebelle* vol. II, *Le Politique*, p. 482. It is understandably difficult to find any commentators who believed that de Gaulle knew nothing of what was going on, and Raymond Aron comments in his *Mémoires* (Paris, 1983), p. 377, that although legal forms had been respected, the Fourth Republic had surrendered to a rebellion of the army, 'rébellion à laquelle de Gaulle n'était pas entièrement étranger'. As Arthur Hugh Clough's *The Latest Decalogue* might have put it, he 'did not kill; but did not strive officiously to keep alive'.
34 See *Le Point*, 2 October 1972.
35 *Le Politique*, p. 534.
36 Quoted on p. 493 of *Le Politique*.
37 *Le Politique*, p. 592.
38 Quoted by de Gaulle on p. 70 of *L'Effort*.
39 *La Tragédie du Général*, p. 335.
40 See Bernard Letwidge, *De Gaulle*, p. 265.
41 Lacouture, *Le Rebelle* vol. III, *Le Souverain*, p. 338.
42 Letwidge, *De Gaulle*, p. 374.
43 For a discussion of de Gaulle's defence policy, see *Defence and Dissent in Contemporary France*, edited by Jolyon Howarth and Patricia Chilton (London: Croom Helm, 1987).

CONCLUSION

1 Cobban, *A History of Modern France*, vol. II, p. 159.
2 Quoted in J. M. Thompson, *Napoleon III*, p. 253.
3 Yale University Press, 1977, p. 67.
4 See *Naissance et Mort de la IIIe République* (Paris: Calmann-Lévy, 1970), pp. 327 and 297.
5 Paxton, p. 35.
6 For the sudden changes of mood which astonished Julius Caesar, see *L'Effort*, p. 5. See p. 1 of *L'Appel* for 'les ferments de dispersion que son peuple porte en lui-même', 'the ferments of disintegration inherent in her people' (*The Call to Honour* (London: Collins, 1955, p. 1). For Napoleon, see Theodore Zeldin, *Histoire des passions françaises*, vol. II, *Orgueil et Intelligence*, (Paris, 1980) p. 3. For the *Discours de Bayeux*, see *Le Salut*, pp. 647–8. For the pseudonym, see *TLS*, 30 September 1963.
7 Quoted by Letwidge on the cover of his *De Gaulle*.

Appendix A Selected Events in the French Revolution, the Consulate and the First Empire

This Appendix concentrates on home affairs. Appendix B concentrates on foreign affairs.

It is convenient to regard the Revolution of 1789 as beginning with the convocation of the Estates General on 5 May 1789 and ending with Napoleon's coup d'état on 9 November 1799 (*18 Brumaire*). The Consulate then goes from 9 November 1799 to 2 December 1804 and the establishment of the First Empire. This lasts until 11 March 1814 when Napoleon abdicates. The episode known as the Hundred Days begins when Napoleon escapes from Elba on 26 February 1815 and ends with his defeat at Waterloo on 18 June 1815 and departure for his final exile on the island of St Helena on 7 August 1815.

The Revolution itself can be seen as going through three principal stages, described here under I, II, III.

I 5 MAY 1789 to 21 SEPTEMBER 1792: ATTEMPT AT A CONSTITUTIONAL MONARCHY

1789

5 May	Convocation of Estates General.
17 June	The Estates General declares itself to be a National Assembly, and by the Tennis Court Oath of 20 June refuses to separate until a Constitution is established. It is consequently sometimes referred to as the Constituent Assembly.
14 July	Fall of the Bastille.
17 July	Louis XVI is welcomed in Paris by the National Guard (created 13 July) and accepts the Tricolour Flag, in which the traditional white of the House of Bourbon is placed between the red and the blue of the Commune of Paris as a symbol of national unity. The King's brother, le Comte d'Artois, leaves France. He is followed by a number of aristocrats in the gradually increasing movement known as the emigration.
4 August	The National Assembly officially abolishes most feudal dues and seigneurial rights, and declares those based upon individual contracts to be open to repurchase.

174

Appendix A   175

26 August	Proclamation of the *Déclaration des droits de l'homme et du citoyen*.
5 October	A large crowd of Parisians, worried by the increasing shortage of bread created partly by hoarding of flour and partly by the poor harvest, goes to Versailles to bring back 'le boulanger, la boulangère et le petit mitron' (the baker, the baker's wife and the little baker's boy, i.e. Louis XVI, Marie-Antoinette and the Dauphin).
2 November	On Talleyrand's proposal, the lands of the Church are declared national property and made available for sale.

1790

12 July	The National Assembly adopts the *Constitution Civile du Clergé*. Each of the 83 *départements* in which France has now been divided for administrative reasons is given its own bishop, who is to be elected and then consecrated by the Metropolitan Archbishop. Priests are also to be elected, and the Assembly sets aside the sum of 77 million francs to replace the income earlier derived from the nationalised Church lands. Initially Louis XVI is reluctant to approve of this attempt to create an elective clergy, but finally agrees on 24 December 1790. On 27 November 1790, the National Assembly decides that all bishops and priests shall take an oath of allegiance to the Constitution. If they do not do so within a week, they will be dismissed. This accentuates the division, already begun by the nationalisation of the Church lands, into a traditionally Catholic France hostile to the Revolution, and a France which is favourable to the Revolution but increasingly hostile to the Catholic Church. The decision by Pius VI to condemn the *Constitution Civile du Clergé* in March 1791 widens the gap, which is not bridged until the Concordat of 1801.
14 July	To commemorate the fall of the Bastille, all the local federations come together in Paris on the Champ de Mars to celebrate *La Fête de la Fédération*. Talleyrand says mass, and the King swears to accept the Constitution.

1791

21 June	Louis XVI tries to escape from France, but is recognised at Varennes and brought back under escort to Paris.
17 July	In order to protest against the reluctance of the National Assembly to condemn Louis XVI for his attempted escape, the Paris municipality decides to organise a meeting on the Champ de Mars, at which the people of Paris are invited to sign a petition calling for the King's dismissal. The situation gets out of hand, and the National Guard fires on the demonstrators. *Le massacre du Champ de Mars* reveals the existence of a further division in France, between the moderates, headed by La Fayette, and the people of Paris, orga-

176 French Caesarism

nised by the various clubs, who would like the Revolution to continue and intensify.

September The National Assembly votes in favour of the Constitution of 1791. This gives the future Legislative Assembly the sole power to initiate legislation, to declare war, to propose a budget and approve treaties. This Assembly is elected by limited suffrage, in two stages: four million tax-payers choose 50,000 electors, who then choose the members. The King cannot dissolve the Assembly and can use his veto only to suspend legislation. The National or Constituent Assembly originally established two years earlier, on 17 June 1789, declares that its own members are ineligible for election to the new Legislative Assembly. This meets for the first time on 1 October 1791, theoretically for a two-year period. It has 745 members, 263 of them moderate, Constitutional monarchists, and 136 Jacobins, soon to be divided between the more moderate Girondins, or Brissotins, and the more radical followers of Robespierre. In the middle are 300 uncommitted members of the *Marais*, the swamp or plain. The Declaration of Pillnitz, published by Frederick William of Prussia and the Emperor Leopold II of Austria on 25 August 1791, had threatened the revolutionaries with foreign intervention in order to restore Louis XVI to his traditional rights. This creates a war psychosis in France, and helps to explain the deteriorating situation of 1792 and the end of the attempt at a constitutional monarchy in the summer of that year.

1792

20 March Law approving use of guillotine passed by the *Assemblée Nationale*; as a humanitarian and democratising measure, extending the privilege of *décollation* (being beheaded) to all sorts and conditions of men (and women; see Olympe de Gouges, article X of *Déclaration des droits de la femme et de la citoyenne*, 1792: 'la femme a le droit de monter sur l'échafaud; elle doit avoir également celui de monter à la Tribune, pourvu que ses manifestations ne troublent pas l'ordre public établi par la Loi.')

2 April The Legislative Assembly declares war on Leopold II, described as 'the King of Hungary and Bohemia'. Louis XVI wants war to re-establish his authority after what he imagines will be the revolutionaries' failure to control the situation; the Girondins in order to unite the country and compel Louis XVI to choose between France and his foreign allies. Robespierre opposes the war.

25 April Guillotine first used; on a highwayman.

20 June The war begins badly, and the King uses his veto to suspend the measures against any priest refusing to subscribe to the *Constitution Civile du Clergé*. The crowd invades the Tuiler-

Appendix A   177

	ies, insults the King, who nevertheless puts on the Phrygian bonnet of liberty and drinks a glass of wine with them. This scene is witnessed by Napoleone Buonaparte.
11 July	The Legislative Assembly declares 'la patrie en danger'. Detachments from provincial sections of the National Guard arrive in Paris, many of them from Marseilles. They sing what then becomes the French national anthem *La Marseillaise*, composed by a royalist called Rouget de L'Isle.
1 August	News of 'Le Manifeste de Brunswick', originally published on 25 July at Coblenz, arrives in Paris. This threatens, if any harm comes to the King or Queen, to hand Paris over to 'military execution and total subversion', as an act of 'exemplary and unforgettable vengeance'.
10 August	The crowd invades the Tuileries. The King is deposed and power entrusted to a Council of six ministers, headed by Danton. The Legislative Assembly, less than one year old, is dissolved and replaced by a National Convention.
17 August	Adoption of the guillotine for political crimes.
2 September	Verdun falls to the Prussians. Some 2,000 priests and other suspects are massacred in the prisons of Paris and elsewhere, with the connivance of Danton if not on his specific instructions.
20 September	The Legislative Assembly meets for the last time. The French win the battle of Valmy, a victory later described by Goethe as marking 'a new epoch in the history of the world'. The events of Summer 1792 mark the end of the attempt to create a constitutional monarchy, and the beginning of the most violent stage of the French Revolution.

II 21 SEPTEMBER 1792 to 9 JULY 1794: LA CONVENTION: ATTEMPT AT A DEMOCRATIC REPUBLIC

1792

21 September	Declaration of the Republic, first meeting of the Convention. The Girondins, the more moderate group, are confronted by the Jacobins, so called because they meet in the old Jacobin convent in the rue St Honoré.
19 November	The Convention declares that it will 'offer fraternal assistance to all peoples wishing to recover their liberty'.
20 November	Discovery of the 'armoire de fer' (iron wardrobe) containing the alleged correspondence of Louis XVI and the foreign powers, including the *émigré* army, threatening the Revolution.
11 December	Louis XVI is tried and found guilty of having conspired against the nation. 387 members of the Convention vote for the death penalty, and 334 for exile.

178   *French Caesarism*

1793

21 January Execution of Louis XVI. Spain declares war; Great Britain breaks off diplomatic relations.

10–11 March Beginning of the rising in the West against the attempt to recruit 300,000 men for the revolutionary armies. This marks the beginning of a civil war in La Vendée which will continue on and off until Napoleon signs a peace treaty with the royalist and Catholic leaders in February 1800.

April In order to reinforce its control over the provinces, the government establishes the *Représentants en mission*. It also takes the first step towards the Terror by setting up the revolutionary tribunal.

2 June The struggle between the Girondins, the more moderate party associated with decentralisation, and the centralising, more radical Jacobins, ends with victory for the latter when the National Guard surrounds the Assembly and the Girondin leaders are arrested. They are executed on 31 October.

4 September Official proclamation of *La Terreur à l'ordre du jour*.

17 September The *loi des suspects* demands the immediate arrest of 'all those who, by their actions, their acquaintanceships (*leurs relations*), their speech or writing, have shown themselves in favour of tyranny and federalism and enemies of liberty'. 5,000 arrests.

29 September Attempt to control prices and wages through the *loi du Maximum*, thus beginning of breach between the Jacobins and the Paris crowd, which wanted control only over prices.

October–November Execution of the Girondin leaders, of Marie-Antoinette, of 'Philippe-Egalité', brother of Louis XVI and father of future King Louis-Philippe. Attempt to dechristianise France, introduction of Revolutionary calendar and of ten-day week. Military victories through the reforms and new organisation of the army by Carnot.

1794

14 March Robespierre, by now virtual dictator in France through his dominance among the Jacobins, destroys left-wing opposition by having the leaders of the extremist party, the *Hébertistes*, arrested. They are executed on 24 March, and the revolutionary army of Paris is disbanded.

30 March Robespierre destroys the more moderate faction by having Danton and his friends arrested on the charge of corruption and collaboration with the enemy. They are guillotined on 5 April. During the period which begins on 4 September 1793 with *La Terreur à l'ordre du jour* and ends with the fall of Robespierre on 27 July 1794, 2,639 people are guillotined in Paris, and some 40,000 executed in the provinces, often in a very summary fashion.

27 July *Le 9 Thermidor*. Robespierre, having made a speech in which almost everybody is accused of preparing to betray

Appendix A 179

him, is overthrown in the Assembly, arrested, and guillotined on the following day with 22 of his supporters, including Saint-Just. This marks the end of the Terror, and thus of the movement of the French Revolution towards the left.

III 1795–1799: LE DIRECTOIRE: ATTEMPT AT A MODERATE REPUBLIC

1794

8 November	Closure of the Jacobin Club.
December	Abolition of the *loi du Maximum*.

1795

1 April The crowd attempts to surround the Assembly, but is dispersed by the National Guard. On 20 May the army intervenes for the first time against the crowd, and disperses it. The revolutionary army wins important victories, enabling France to occupy Holland and have the Rhine accepted by the treaties of Bâle and of The Hague (April, July 1795) as the 'natural frontier' of France.

5 October Bonaparte disperses the royalist demonstration which is threatening to invade the *Convention*, now in its last days. This is Carlyle's 'whiff of grapeshot', referred to in French history as *le 13 Vendémiaire, an III*.

25 October Official beginning of *Le Directoire*, a constitution in which five *Directeurs* are chosen, one retiring each year, by two elected chambers: *le Conseil des Cinq-Cents* and *le Conseil des Anciens*. The suffrage is much narrower than in the *Constitution de l'an II*, officially adopted by the *Convention* on 24 June 1793, but never put into practice.

1796

7 February The *Directeurs* use Bonaparte to close down the *Club du Panthéon*, in which Babeuf's *Conspiration des Egaux* meets. On 10 May 1795 Carnot succeeds in arresting Babeuf, who is executed on 27 May. The potential success of his conspiracy is explicable by the increasing gap in the society of the *Directoire* between rich and poor.

1797

4 September (18 Fructidor, an V) When the elections to the *Cinq-Cents* and the *Anciens* produce a majority of royalists, Barras uses General Augereau, sent by Bonaparte from Egypt, to surround the Assembly and declare the elections in 49 *départements* null and void.

180   *French Caesarism*

1798
11 May
(22 Floréal)

The Jacobins win a majority in the elections; the *Directeurs* declare 108 results invalid, thus keeping a majority in favour of a moderate policy.

1799
18 June
(30 Prairial)

In an act of revenge the two *Conseils* compel three of the *Directeurs* to resign. A more successful prosecution of the war against the Second Coalition leads to the defeat of the Austro-Russian army in Switzerland and of the English in Holland. But Sieyès is determined to change the constitution of the *Directoire* so as to produce a stronger executive. This leads to the *coup d'état du 18 Brumaire*, 9 November 1799, and to the *Constitution de l'an VIII* and the *Consulat*. Most historians see this as marking the end of the Revolution.

DOMESTIC POLICY OF THE CONSULATE (1799–1804) AND OF THE FIRST EMPIRE (1804–14) (*For foreign policy, see Appendix B.*)

1799
9 November
(*18 Brumaire*)
24 December

Coup d'état overthrows *Le Directoire*. Power to a provisional triumvirate: Bonaparte, Sieyès, Roger Ducos. *Constitution de l'an VIII*. Bonaparte first consul, Cambacérès, Lebrun second and third consuls. The Tribunate discusses laws but does not vote them; the *Corps Législatif* votes without discussion. *Le Conseil d'Etat*, established on 2 November 1799, plays the central rôle of discussing the wording of new laws, and especially *Le Code Napoléon*.

1800
3 January

New Constitution approved by a majority of 3,911,107 to 1,579 with four million abstentions in a public plebiscite.

18 January

Establishment of the *Banque de France*. Creation of the *franc Germinal*, the currency unit which will last until the First World War, after which, in 1925, Poincaré establishes the new franc at one-fifth of its value.

18 February

A *préfet* is appointed at the head of each of the 83 *départements* into which France is now divided. He is directly responsible to the central government. As the number of *départements* grows to 130 in 1810, the same system is applied.

13 August

Appointment of Tronchet, Bigot de Préameneu and Portalis to begin work on the *Code Civil*. Tronchet had attempted to save Louis XVI from execution by requiring a three-quarters and not a two-thirds majority; Préameneu had been a moderate member of the Legislative Assembly; Portalis was

Appendix A 181

a progressively minded lawyer who had defended the validity of Protestant marriages in 1771, argued in favour of the freedom of the press under the *Directoire*, and returned to France from exile in Switzerland only after Napoleon's coup d'état. He was later to play a major role in preparing the text of the *Concordat*.

1801
15 July
Signing of the *Concordat*, the agreement whereby the state appoints bishops and the Pope consecrates them.

1802
6 April
Official approval of the *Concordat* by the *Corps Législatif*; followed by a *Te Deum* on Easter Day to celebrate both the *Concordat* and the Peace of Amiens.

10 May
Bonaparte Consul for life – 3,568,185 votes for, 9,704 against. Extension of powers of First Consul.

15 May
Establishment of *La Légion d'Honneur*.

1803
9 April
Installation of the first *auditeurs* at the *Conseil d'Etat*.

14 April
Banque de France granted monopoly for issuing bank notes.

1 December
Institution of the *livret ouvrier*, the document on which the employer wrote his comments on the conduct and attitude of the worker, and which was necessary to secure employment.

1804
21 March
Publication of final text of the *Code Civil*, subsequently the *Code Napoléon*.

18 May
Napoleon proclaimed *Empereur des Français*, with right to transmit his title to male descendants. Approved by plebiscite of 3,321,615 to 599; abstentions and spoiled ballot papers counted as 'yes' votes. Beginning of First Empire.

2 December
Ceremony at Notre Dame at which Napoleon crowns himself Emperor.

1806
4 April
Publication of *Le Catéchisme Impérial*.

1807
2 March
Decrees setting out the legal situation of practising Jews, and regulating their choice of names. While reinforcing the control of the state over the synagogue, Napoleon did provide Jews with the protection under the law refused them under the *ancien régime*.

16 September
Establishment of *La Cour des Comptes*.

1808
10 May
Establishment of *L'Université de France*, also known as

182 French Caesarism

L'Université Impériale. On 2 September 1808 granted a monopoly on secondary and higher education, not to be broken until the *loi Falloux* of 1850. 1808 also sees the institution of the *agrégation.*

1810
12 January — Napoleon's marriage to Joséphine annulled.
1 April — Napoleon marries Marie-Louise d'Autriche.

1811
20 March — Birth of Napoleon's son, the 'Roi de Rome'.

1812
15 October — *La Comédie Française* officially established by decrees published in Moscow.

1814
6 April — Abdication of Napoleon I. End of First Empire. Le Comte de Provence, born in 1755, recalled to the throne with the title of Louis XVIII.

Appendix B Selected Events in the Life of Napoleon Bonaparte

This Appendix concentrates on foreign affairs. Appendix A concentrates on home affairs.

1769
15 August — Birth at Ajaccio of Napoleone Buonaparte, second son of Carlo-Maria de Buonaparte and his wife, *née* Letizia Ramolino.

1779
March — Napoleone leaves Corsica for Autun, and after six months, goes on to Brienne.

1784
October — After five years at Brienne, moves to the *Ecole Militaire* in Paris.

1785
September — Placed 42nd out of 58 in the *concours de sortie*. Commissioned in October as Second Lieutenant. Posted to Valence.

1786
September — On leave in Corsica. The frequency with which the young Buonaparte took leave and spent it in his homeland has led historians hostile to him to point out that his original ambition was to follow out the plans of the nationalist leader Paoli and dedicate himself to Corsican independence. At the time Napoleone also expressed strong anti-French emotions.

1788
June–September — In Auxonne, with his regiment.

1789
September — Again in Corsica, where he stays until February 1791. His views have now changed, and he is a supporter of the Revolution and against Paoli. He spends a further period in Corsica, from Autumn 1791 to May 1792.

184 French Caesarism

1792

In Paris, where he witnesses the invasion of the Tuileries by the mob and the humiliation of Louis XVI on 20 June, as well as the events of 10 August, in which the *Commune* of Paris overthrows the Legislative Assembly.

1793
March–
April

Again in Corsica, then in Provence, where in August he writes *Le Souper de Beaucaire*, a dialogue expressing support for the ideas of the Jacobins.

16 September

Given command of the artillery in the siege of Toulon, occupied by the English. Toulon falls in December of the same year. Augustin Robespierre, Maximilien's brother, offers him the command of the army in Paris, but Buonaparte refuses, preferring to be Inspector of the Coasts of France. This position enables him to keep his family with him. In July 1793 they all had to leave Corsica for France, after their house had been sacked by Paoli's supporters. In keeping with Latin and Mediterranean tradition, Napoleone sees himself as responsible for providing for his whole family – as will be seen.

1794
April

Appointed *Général d'Artillerie* in the *Armée d'Italie*.

27 July
(*9 Thermidor*)

After the fall of Robespierre, Buonaparte is briefly in prison as suspected of sympathy with the Jacobins. On 20 August, he is released, restored to his command, but stays in Paris.

1795

Buonaparte declines to go and serve against the rebels in Vendée; and is placed on indefinite leave.

5 October
(*13 Vendémiaire*)

At Barras' instigation, disperses royalist demonstrators who are about to attack the *Convention*, now in its last days. Carlyle's 'whiff of grapeshot'. Barras becomes one of the *Directeurs*; Buonaparte is given command of the Army of the Interior, with the task of closing the Jacobin Club.

1796
9 March

Buonaparte marries Joséphine de Beauharnais, who is six years older than he is, having been born in Martinique in 1763. *Née* Tascher de la Pagerie, she married Eugène de Beauharnais in 1778 and had two children by him: Eugène, whom Napoleone would later make Viceroy of Italy, and Hortense, who in 1802 was married – against his wishes – to Napoleone's younger brother Louis (born 1778) and became the mother of the future Napoleon III. Joséphine's husband had been guillotined in 1794, and

Appendix B   185

	she had been Barras' mistress. It was nevertheless on his advice that she married Buonaparte, and he was a witness at the civil marriage.
10 May	Buonaparte defeats Austrians at Lodi.
15 May	Triumphant entry into Milan. Compulsory levies of money and art treasures on all Italian princes within his sphere of influence. Creates Cisalpine republic.
17 November	Victory of Arcole over Austrians.

1797

14 January	Victory of Rivoli enables Bonaparte to take Mantua.
Easter	Anti-French riots in Verona provide Bonaparte with excuse to overthrow Venetian republic.
Summer	Joséphine, accompanied by her lover, Lieutenant Charles, joins Bonaparte at the castle Mombello, near Milan.
4 September	*Coup d'etat du 18 Fructidor.* Bonaparte sends his deputy Augereau to support the Republican *Directeurs* in their overthrow of the new monarchist majority in the *Conseil des Anciens* and the *Conseil des Cinq-Cents.*
17 October	Peace of Campo-Formio, between France – in fact, Bonaparte – and Austria. France is recognised as having her natural frontiers along the left bank of the Rhine. Austria also recognises the Cisalpine republic, and receives in part-exchange the former republic of Venice. This treaty marks the revival by revolutionary France of the same kind of territorial policy which characterised the *ancien régime*; there is no question of consulting the populations concerned.
10 December	Triumphant return of Bonaparte to Paris.

1798

| 19 May | Bonaparte's expedition sails to Egypt, captures Malta on 10 June, wins the victory of the Pyramids on 21 July, but is cut off by Nelson's victory at Aboukir Bay on 1 August. |

1799

February	Bonaparte enters Syria, fails to take St Jean d'Acre, defeats Turks near Aboukir Bay, leaves Egypt on 22 August. His army is subsequently repatriated by the English after the peace of Amiens in 1802.
9–10 November	*Coup d'état du 18 Brumaire.* Power taken from the *Directoire* and its two assemblies and entrusted to the provisional triumvirate of Bonaparte, Sieyès and Roger-Ducros.
24 December	*Constitution de l'an VIII:* Bonaparte first Consul; Cambacérès and Lebrun second and third. *Le Tribunat* can discuss laws but not vote; *Le Corps Législatif* votes without discussion.

186 French Caesarism

1800

15 May — Bonaparte crosses St Bernard pass into Italy.

14 June — Battle of Marengo, against the Austrians; a half-victory, presented as a triumph in the war bulletins.

1801

8 January — Peace of Lunéville. Acceptance by Austria of earlier treaty of Campo-Formio.

1802

January — Bonaparte becomes President of the Cisalpine Republic, henceforth known as the Italian republic.

25 March — Peace of Amiens with England, Egypt restored to Turkey, but England refuses to recognise France's 'natural frontiers' and insists upon the French evacuation of Malta.

1803

Worsening relations with England lead to the departure on 11 May of the Ambassador, Lord Whitworth, and the concentration in December of the *Armée d'Angleterre* near Boulogne.

30 April — Louisiana purchase. For 15 million dollars, the United States receives from France, who had it from Spain, most of what is now Arkansas, the Dakotas, Iowa, Kansas, Missouri, Montana, Nebraska and Oklahoma.

1804

21 March — Execution of the Duc d'Enghien, the incident described by Talleyrand as 'more than a crime, a mistake'. Enghien was the son of the Duc de Condé, and was probably involved in a royalist conspiracy to overthrow Napoleon. He was kidnapped, court-martialled and shot within 24 hours.

2 December — Self-coronation of Napoleon at Notre Dame.

1805

26 May — Napoleon crowns himself King of Italy, at Milan.

9 August — Austria joins British–Russian alliance; beginning of Third Coalition.

20 October — Defeat of Austria at Ulm.

21 October — Nelson destroys French fleet at Trafalgar.

2 December — Victory of Austerlitz against the Austro-Russian army under the joint command of Joseph I of Austria and Alexander I of Russia. End of Third Coalition.

26 December — Peace of Pressburg, whereby Austria cedes Venice to Napoleon's Kingdom of Italy. The Holy Roman Empire is dissolved.

Appendix B 187

1806

30 March	Napoleon makes his elder brother Joseph King of Naples and Sicily, in spite of the fact that the Bourbons, in Sicily, are protected by the British navy.
5 June	Napoleon makes his younger brother Louis King of Holland.
12 July	Establishment under Napoleon's protectorate of the *Confédération du Rhin*, replacing what was earlier the Holy Roman Empire.
15 September	Beginning of Fourth Coalition: England, Russia and Prussia.
14 October	Prussian armies destroyed by Napoleon at Jena-Auerstaedt.
11 November	Beginning of the Continental System with Decree of Berlin. This declares the British Isles to be in a state of blockade, and forbids any port under French control or under the control of one of its allies to allow an English ship to unload her cargo.

1807

8 February	Bloody and indecisive engagement between French troops and the combined armies of Russia and Prussia at Eylau. 40,000 killed. The Russians and Prussians withdraw, but Napoleon does not succeed in his ambition of destroying their armies.
14 June	Decisive victory at Friedland over the Russians and Prussians.
24 June	Meeting of Napoleon and Alexander I of Russia on a raft in the Niemen. Russia agrees to take part in the Continental System, and to declare war on England if a peace treaty is not signed by 1 October. In return, Russia is given a free hand in Sweden. The Grand Duchy of Warsaw is expanded at the expense of Alexander's former ally, Prussia.
24 August	Napoleon makes his brother Jérôme King of Westphalia.

1808

2 May	Riots in Madrid, bloodily suppressed by Murat. Both Charles IV and his son Ferdinand agree to submit their rights to the Spanish throne to Napoleon. Joseph is made King of Spain, and makes a triumphant entry into Madrid on 20 July. On 30 July, he leaves rapidly.
August	British troops land in Portugal; beginning of the Peninsular War.
November	Napoleon enters Spain, and recaptures Madrid on 4 December.

1809

	Fifth Coalition. Britain and Austria. Russia remains neutral.

188 French Caesarism

May	In face of Pope Pius VII's refusal to break with England, Napoleon annexes the Papal States and imprisons the Pope at Fontainebleau.
6 July	Victory of Wagram against the Austrian troops under the command of Archduke Charles. 50,000 Austrian casualties; 34,000 French. Napoleon, visiting the battlefield on the morning after, is reputed to have said: 'Une nuit de Paris réparera tout cela' (One night in Paris will restore all this).
14 October	Peace of Vienna. Austria cedes Illyria (modern Albania) to Napoleon.
December	Dissatisfied with the way his brother Louis is administering Holland, given to him in 1806, Napoleon threatens the independence of that country, and demands annexation.
15 December	Joséphine, unable to have children by Napoleon, publicly announces that she will accept a divorce. Napoleon, seeking for a 'royal womb' (*un ventre*) asks Caulaincourt to demand of Czar Alexander I the hand of his sister Catherine.

1810	
8 February	Napoleon organises military administration of Spain, where a guerrilla war is still operating against the French troops.
9 February	Napoleon asks for hand in marriage of Archduchess Marie-Louise, daughter of Leopold I of Austria and niece of Marie-Antoinette.
9 July	After a series of partial annexations, Napoleon occupies the whole of Holland.
31 December	Alexander of Russia confirms by ukase that he is in favour of British trade. This defiance of the Continental System marks the beginning of the events which will lead to the invasion of Russia and Napoleon's eventual downfall. The period of 1807–1810 marks the height of Napoleon's achievement as conqueror, and of France's predominance. France has 130 *départements*, and the election on 20 August of Bernadotte as Royal Prince of Sweden means that French influence extends from the North of Europe right through to Spain.

1811	
20 March	Birth of Napoleon's son, François Charles Joseph Bonaparte. Immediately proclaimed *Roi de Rome*.

1812	
24 June	Napoleon, faced with Alexander's refusal to apply the Continental System, invades Russia with his *Grande Armée* of some 500,000 men. The Russians fall back,

Appendix B 189

	fighting him at Borodino, on 7 September, and allowing him to take Moscow in September. But Moscow catches fire, and on 18 October Napoleon's army begins to retreat. His Grand Army is now reduced to some 50,000 men, and between 25 and 29 November, crosses the Berezina.
5 December	Napoleon leaves his army and returns to Paris. His 29th Bulletin describes the retreat from Moscow and ends with the words: 'His Majesty's health has never been better.'
1813	
19 October	Napoleon loses the battle of Leipzig, against the Austrians, the Prussians, the Russians and the Swedes. He retreats into France, and declines the peace offer from the allies which would have left France with the Rhineland and Belgium.
1814	
January– February	The allied armies invade France, and after a long resistance by Napoleon, take Paris on 31 March.
6 April	Napoleon forced to abdicate; given sovereignty of the Island of Elba. On 7 April, Louis XVIII is invited to return to France as King.
1815	
26 February	Napoleon escapes from the Island of Elba.
1 March	Lands at Golfe-Juan.
18 June	Defeated at Waterloo. Exiled to St Helena, described in one of the geography notes at Brienne as 'petite île'.
1821	
5 May	Napoleon dies, probably of cancer of the stomach.

Appendix C Selected Events in the Life of Louis Napoleon; of the Second Republic; and of the Second Empire

1808
21 April

Birth in Paris of Charles Louis Napoleon Bonaparte, third son of Louis Bonaparte, Napoleon I's third brother, and Hortense de Beauharnais, daughter of Joséphine de Beauharnais by her first marriage. There seems little evidence to confirm Napoleon III's own doubts – and Victor Hugo's accusation – that he was not his father's son; or that his real father was Napoleon I.

1815

After the fall of the First Empire, Louis Napoleon is brought up by his mother, in Switzerland, where his tutor is Philippe Le Bas, son of the revolutionary leader. He trains as an artillery officer, and is commissioned in the Swiss army.

1831

Travels in Italy. Strong sympathy for the Italian *carbonari* and their support for Italian unification. The death on 22 July 1832 of Napoleon I's son, *le Roi de Rome*, makes Louis Napoleon the sole legitimate heir to the Bonaparte dynasty.

1836
October

Failure of Louis Napoleon's attempt to seize power by a military uprising at Strasbourg. Expelled from France.

1839

Publication of *Les Idées Napoléoniennes*. Argues that Napoleon I was a man of peace whose main considerations were the liberty and security of the French.

1840
6 August

Failure of attempt to seize power by a military uprising at Boulogne. Sent to prison at the fortress of Ham. Writes *L'Extinction du Paupérisme*, arguing that his can be achieved

Appendix C

only by state intervention in the economy. Escapes in the clothes of a man called Pinget, whose nickname of Badinguet will later be taken up as a term of abuse by Victor Hugo. Goes to live in London, where his mistress, Elizabeth Howard, lends him a large sum of money. On 10 April 1848 he appears as a special constable in Piccadilly at the time of the uprising expected to occur when the Chartist movement presents its petition.

1848

25 February Proclamation of the Second Republic, after the revolution of 22–24 February has driven out Louis-Philippe. The provisional government dissolves the *Chambre des Députés* previously elected on a very narrow franchise of 250,000 and organises elections to a Constituent Assembly at which all men aged over 25 years – nine million people – can vote.

23 April First meeting of the Constituent Assembly, consisting of 450 moderates, 200 *Orléanistes* and only 200 republicans.

22–26 June Closure of the *ateliers nationaux*, established in February 1848 to provide work for everyone and solve the unemployment created by the Hungry Forties. The attempt at an uprising is put down by General Cavaignac.

10 December Election by universal male suffrage as first President of the Second Republic of Louis Napoleon Bonaparte.

1849

13 May Election of Legislative Assembly. *Le parti de l'ordre*, grouping Catholic conservatives favourable to a restoration of the monarchy but divided between *Orléanistes* and *Légitimistes* obtains 500 seats; the *Montagnards*, or left-wing republicans, 180; and the moderate republicans 75.

13 June A second attempt at an uprising, inspired by hostility to the despatch of French troops to Rome to protect the Pope, is firmly put down and Louis Napoleon warns that 'the time has come for the wicked to tremble and the righteous to feel reassured'.

1850

15 March The *loi Falloux* breaks the state monopoly established by Napoleon I and allows qualified individuals and organisations – for the most part priests and religious orders – to open secondary schools. The readiness of the *Assemblée Législative* to approve the measure confirms the general movement to the right of the Second Republic. In this respect, there is little hostility to the establishment of a more authoritarian régime as such; the problems arise as to the manner in which it was done.

31 May Law restricting the right to vote to people able to prove that they had lived in the same place for at least three years. Since

192   *French Caesarism*

many workers changed their residence frequently, this measure disenfranchised some 30 per cent of the electorate.

1851

2 December — *L'opération 'Rubicon'* informs the Parisians that the National Assembly has been dissolved and the law of 31 May 1849 suspended. A brief attempt at armed resistance is rapidly crushed.

20 December — A plebiscite gives Louis Napoleon a vote of 7,499,916 in favour of his coup d'état, with 646,737 against and 1,500,000 abstentions.

1852

12 January — Official adoption of a new Constitution which gives Louis Napoleon power for ten years. A legislative chamber, elected by universal male suffrage, votes laws proposed solely by 'le Prince–Président'.

20 November — A plebiscite on the 'restoration of the Imperial dignity in the person of Louis Napoleon' receives a vote of 7,839,532 against 253,145 with 2,062,798 abstentions.

2 December — Official proclamation of the Second Empire. 15 August is officially declared the French National Day. The freedom of the press is severely restricted. In contrast to the middle-class monarchy of Louis-Philippe, the Imperial Court imitates the splendour of the First Empire.

1853

30 January — Napoleon III marries Eugénie de Montijo.

1854

14 September — In alliance with Great Britain, France fights the Crimean War against Russia. Victory at the battle of the Alma (20 September) and Malakoff (September 1855).

1855

Exposition de Paris. Five million visitors.

1856

February — Treaty of Paris marks end of Crimean War.

16 March — Birth of Napoleon III's son, *Le Prince Impérial*.

1859

24 June — Battle of Solferino. A murderous encounter between French and Austrian troops which inspired Henri Dunant, encouraged by Napoleon III, with the idea of the Red Cross. The technical victory won by the French drives the Austrians out of Piedmont, thus enabling the Kingdom of Italy to come into being under Victor Emmanuel.

Appendix C 193

1860
January   Free Trade treaty with Great Britain.
24 March   Treaty of Turin. Nice and Savoy to be ceded to France after a
                 plebiscite, the price agreed by Napoleon III and Victor
                 Emmanuel for French participation in the unification of
                 Italy.

1861–1867
                 Mexican adventure.

1869
8 May   A plebiscite asking voters to approve the reforms whereby
                 the legislative chamber obtains more control over govern-
                 ment action gives Napoleon III a vote of 7,336,000 against
                 1,560,000, with 15 per cent of the electorate abstaining.

1870
19 July   France declares war on Prussia. A series of rapid and
                 disastrous defeats leads to the collapse of the Second Empire
                 and the proclamation on 4 September of the Republic.
                 Napoleon III leaves for England, where he dies at Chisle-
                 hurst on 9 January 1873.

Appendix D Selected Events in the Life and Times of Philippe Pétain

1856

24 April — Birth at Cauchy-à-la-Tour, Pas-de-Calais, of Henri Philippe Benoni Omer Pétain, fourth child but eldest son of Omer-Venant Pétain, farmer.

1859

7 April — After the death of his first wife, Clotilde, closely following the birth of her fifth child in six years, Omer-Venant marries Marie-Reine Vincent, by whom he will have three more children.

Philippe is brought up by his mother's uncle, Philippe-Michel Lefebvre (1771–1866) and by his maternal uncle, Jean-Baptiste Legrand (1818–1899). In an article published in *Le Centenaire du Maréchal Pétain, Le Livre d'Or*, 1956, Louis Dominique Girard points out that Pétain was also much influenced by his maternal grandmother. She told him not only about the miseries of the Seven Years War (1756–1763), of which she had vivid recollections, but also about her own grandmother's memories of the War of the Spanish Succession (1701–1713) and of the invasion of the North of France in 1708 . . .

1875

July — After studies at the local school of Saint-Bertin, Pétain comes 403rd out of 412 candidates in the competitive examination for entry into Saint-Cyr. In 1878, he is classed 229 out of 386, and commissioned in the infantry.

1888

1 November — Enters *L'Ecole de Guerre* (Staff College), having reached the rank of Lieutenant by seniority. After two years' study, promoted Captain. Subsequently Major on 12 July 1900, aged 44 years. Slow promotion explained by his admirers by his refusal to flatter and insistence on accurate rifle fire when the received doctrine was blanket coverage preceding mass attacks.

1895–1899

On the staff of the military governor of Paris.

Appendix D   195

1901–1910

Combines post of lecturer at Saint-Cyr (*professeur adjoint* 1901; *professeur titulaire* 1908) with regimental duties.

1910
31 December Colonel and Commander-in-Chief of the 33rd Infantry Regiment at Arras. De Gaulle, in *Les Mémoires de Guerre*, writes: 'Mon premier colonel, Pétain, me montra ce que valent l'art et le don de commander' (My first colonel, Pétain, showed me how valuable were the art and gift of command).

1914
2 August Germany declares war on France. Pétain – within two years of retirement at the outbreak of war – is promoted General.

1915
21 June Placed in command of the French Second Army.

1916
26 February Given command at Verdun.

1917
15 May After the failure of the Nivelle offensive, made Commander-in-Chief of French armies. Suppresses mutinies, restores morale.

1918
18 November Made *Maréchal de France*. Takes part in victory parade, but with Foch, whose aggressive tactics in 1918 are seen by the French as having won the war. De Gaulle writes: 'La gloire militaire lui avait, jadis, prodigué ses caresses amères. Mais elle ne l'avait pas comblé, faute de l'avoir aimé seul' (Military glory had, in former days, lavished on him its bitter caresses. But it had not satisfied him, for it had not loved him alone).

1920
23 January *Vice-président du Conseil Supérieur de la Guerre et Généralissime Désigné* (Deputy Chairman of the Joint Chiefs of Staff and Commander-in-Chief elect).
14 September Marries Alphonsine Berthe Eugénie, née Hardon, divorced from François Dehérain in 1914. She had been his mistress for some time. The couple had no children.

1925
August–
November Serves in Morocco.

196 French Caesarism

1929

22 January — Elected member of the *Académie Française*.

1931

9 February — Replaced by Weygand as *Généralissime Suprême*. (Weygand is 13 years Pétain's junior.)

1934

9 February– — Minister of War in Gaston Doumergue's government. Re-
8 November — mains member of the *Conseil Supérieur de la Défense Nationale*, with particular responsibility for the defence of France against air attacks.

1939

24 March — Appointed French Ambassador in Madrid.

24 August — Signature of non-aggression pact between Germany and Russia.

1 September — German invasion of Poland. Beginning of Second World War.

1940

10 May — German attack on Low Countries, followed by invasion of France.

18 May — Paul Reynaud summons Pétain to Paris. Appoints him Deputy Prime Minister.

12–13 June — Pétain supports Weygand's plea to the French government to request an armistice.

17 June — Becomes Prime Minister (*Président du Conseil*), orders French troops to cease fighting and asks for an armistice. 'Je fais à la France le don de ma personne pour atténuer son malheur ... C'est le cœur serré que je vous dis qu'il faut cesser le combat.'

22–23 June — Signature of the armistice at Rethondes, in the same railway carriage used to accept the German surrender in 1918.

10 July — Vote by 569 votes to 80 by the *Assemblée Nationale* to give Pétain all powers to establish a government which will guarantee 'les droits du Travail, de la Famille et de la Patrie'. Beginning of Vichy régime. Pétain made Head of State, with the right to appoint his successor, initially Pierre Laval.

13 August — Freemasonry made illegal.

3 October — Law excluding Jews from most professions. Beginning of the persecution which will culminate in the 'grande rafle des Juifs' (great rounding-up of the Jews) on 16 July 1942.

24 October — Meeting with Hitler at Montoire. The photograph of the two men shaking hands is widely reproduced in the French press. Pétain calls on the French to collaborate.

13 December — Pétain dismisses Laval, who has been Prime Minister since 12 July, and replaces him with Edouard Flandin.

15 December — The ashes of 'L'Aiglon' (= the Little Eagle = le Roi de

Appendix D 197

Rome = son of Napoleon I, who had died of tuberculosis in Austria on 22 July 1822) are brought back to Paris.

1941

27 January Senior civil servants and army officers required to take an oath of loyalty to Pétain.

9 February Flandin resigns, to be replaced by Admiral Darlan.

6 May Agreement between Darlan and General Vogl on the use of French aerodromes in Syria by the German air force.

21 June German invasion of Russia.

5 November Pétain sends message of encouragement to the 'Légion des volontaires français contre le bolchévisme', Frenchmen who have volunteered to serve in the German army in Russia – most of whom find the training methods used in the German army rather rough.

1942

19 February Opening at Riom of the trial of French soldiers and politicians (Daladier, Blum, Jules Moch, General Gamelin) held responsible for the French defeat of 1940. This trial is adjourned *sine die* on 14 April, partly because of its inherent ambiguity (if the collapse of the Third Republic and its replacement by the Vichy régime was a Good Thing, then those responsible for what Charles Maurras called 'la divine surprise' ought to be praised, not blamed); partly because the accused showed such skill in defending themselves; and partly because the Germans wanted to make the French declare themselves responsible for the outbreak of the Second World War – which the French judges at Riom refused to do.

18 April In response to German pressure, Laval reinstated as Head of Government.

16 July *Grande rafle des Juifs* in Paris.

8 November Anglo-American landing in French North Africa. Pétain initially orders French forces to resist; but connives, on 13 November, in the secret telegram sent by Admiral Auphan to Darlan, ordering them to cease fire.

11 November The German army occupies the whole of France, putting an end to the fiction of the independent existence of *L'Etat Français*.

18 November Pétain gives Laval authority to promulgate laws in his name.

1943

30 January Establishment of the *milice* (French special police force trained to fight the resistance movement) under Joseph Darnand.

16 February Establishment of the *Service du Travail Obligatoire*, and the sending of French workers to Germany. Generally regarded as the best recruitment agency the resistance movement ever had.

198 French Caesarism

| 13 November | Prevented by the Germans from broadcasting the message whereby his authority would go, on his death, not to Pierre Laval but to the National Assembly. |

1944

10 January	Joseph Darnand placed in charge of public order. From 18 January, members of the resistance to be judged by court-martial.
26 April	Pétain visits Paris, where he receives a triumphant reception.
6 June	Allied landings in Normandy. After chairing his last cabinet meeting in Vichy on 12 July, Pétain is compelled by the Germans to leave Vichy, first for Belfort and then, in September, to Sigmaringen. On 28 August, Admiral Auphan, acting in Pétain's name, tries to make contact with de Gaulle in order to hand over French sovereignty to him. De Gaulle refuses to meet Auphan.

1945

| 26 April | Pétain leaves Switzerland, where the Germans had allowed him to take refuge, and presents himself, to de Gaulle's acute embarrassment, at the French frontier. Between 23 July and 15 August he is tried in Paris for high treason. After making an initial statement in which he argues that he had been entrusted with his authority by the National Assembly, and that he owed an account of his actions only to the French people, whom the Court did not represent, he is sentenced to death on 15 August. The sentence is immediately commuted to that of life imprisonment. |

1951

| 23 July | Death of Pétain on the Ile d'Yeu, just off the Brittany coast, where he is buried. |

1966

| 29 May | De Gaulle makes a speech at Douaumont, where the bones of the soldiers killed at Verdun are buried, in which he declares that there can be no calling into question of the glory acquired by Pétain at Verdun; but refuses to allow his remains to be transported there. |

Appendix E Selected Events in the Life and Times of Charles de Gaulle

1890
22 November   Birth in Lille of Charles André Marie Joseph de Gaulle, second son of Henri de Gaulle and Jeanne Maillot-Delannoy.

1894
October   Alfred Dreyfus accused of selling military secrets to the Germans. Found guilty by court-martial and sent in December to Devil's Island.

1898
14 January   Zola publishes *J'accuse*, a public letter denouncing the irregularities of Dreyfus' court-martial. His trial, at which he is found guilty of slandering the army, divides France into two violently opposed camps: the opponents of Dreyfus, who prefer injustice to disorder; and his supporters, who argue that justice has to be done, whatever the political cost. In 1906 Dreyfus is eventually found not guilty and allowed to rejoin the army, serving with distinction in the First World War.

1905
9 December   Separation of Church and State. France becomes a secular republic. De Gaulle writes a story in which, in 1935, he is himself the general who saves France in a war against Germany.

1909
10 October   Fulfils regulations governing recruitment of officers by enlisting for a year's service as private soldier in the 33rd Infantry Regiment.

1910
     Enters Saint-Cyr, 119th out of 220.

1912
     Graduates 13th out of 211. Commissioned, at his request, in the 33rd Infantry Regiment, then commanded by Colonel Philippe Pétain.

200 French Caesarism

1914

August
First World War. Severely wounded in the leg. Seven months in hospital.

1915

10 March
Wounded again. Left hand so badly damaged that later, when married, always wears wedding ring on right hand.

1916

February
Serves under Pétain at Verdun.

2 March
Missing at Douaumont assumed dead. In fact, badly wounded. Spends rest of war as prisoner, making five attempts to escape. After war, awarded *Légion d'Honneur* for Douaumont action.

1919

April
Joins Joseph Haller's Polish army to fight against Bolsheviks. In July, takes part under Weygand in the battle of the Vistula, at which General Pilsudski defeats the Russians. Awarded the *Virtuti Militari*, the highest Polish military decoration. Returns to France as lecturer in military history at Saint-Cyr.

1921

6 April
Marries Yvonne Vendroux, daughter of a biscuit manufacturer from Calais.

28 December
First son Philippe, later an Admiral in the French navy, born.

1922

November
Enters the *Ecole Supérieure de Guerre* (Staff College).

1924

Shows some obstinacy in refusing, in a field exercise at which he is entrusted with the command of an army corps, to reply to a question about the location of his supply services. Tells Colonel Moyrand, the instructor, that 'De minimis non curat praetor'. Only Pétain's intervention secures him a high enough mark to justify continued promotion. Even then, he is posted to Mainz, in the occupied Rhineland; in charge of supplies (*pain, riz, sel*).

March
Publication of *La Discorde chez l'Ennemi*, which sells fewer than 1,000 copies.

15 May
Birth of Elizabeth de Gaulle.

1927

27 April
As a result of Pétain's influence, appointed lecturer at the *Ecole Supérieure de Guerre*; gives first lecture, on the rôle of

Appendix E

the leader, which is subsequently published in *Le Fil de l'Epée* in 1922, dedicated to Marshal Pétain. Promoted Major; and posted, in December, to command a Battalion of Alpine Chasseurs in Germany.

1928
1 January   Birth of Anne de Gaulle.

1929
     Posted to Beirut. Serves in the Levant.
29 December   *Chambre des Députés* votes money to build Maginot line.

1931
     Returns to Paris. Until 1937, serves on the *Secrétariat de la Défense Nationale*.

1933
30 March   Hitler becomes Chancellor in Germany.
May   Publication in *La Revue Politique et Parlementaire* of an article 'Vers l'Armée de Métier', expanded in May 1934 into a book of the same title. Beginning of close relationship with Paul Reynaud, who tries to have de Gaulle's ideas on the need for a mobile striking force adopted.

1936
7 March   German forces occupy the Rhineland.
May   Popular Front government in power in France.
18 July   Military rebellion, led by Franco, against Spanish republican government. Beginning of Spanish Civil War which Franco, helped by the Germans and Italians, will win, while France and Great Britain follow the policy of non-intervention.
October   Meeting between de Gaulle and Léon Blum, Prime Minister of the Popular Front government.

1937
September   In command of the 507th Armoured Regiment at Metz.
24 December   Promoted Colonel.

1938
12 March   *Anschluss*. In defiance of the 1919 Treaty of Versailles, German troops enter Austria and annex it to Germany.
10 April   99.75 per cent [sic] of the Austrians approve the *Anschluss* in a plebiscite.
30 September   The Munich agreements, disapproved of by de Gaulle, hand the German-speaking Sudetenland territories of Czechoslovakia over to Germany. Publication of *La France et son Armée*.

202 *French Caesarism*

1939

15 March German forces occupy the whole of Czechoslovakia.

24 August Non-aggression pact between Germany and Russia. 'The enemy at last was plain in view, huge and hateful, all disguise cast off. It was the modern age in arms' (Evelyn Waugh, *Men at Arms*).

1940

January De Gaulle sends round a memorandum, entitled 'L'avène-ment de la force mécanique', in which he criticises the unreadiness of the French army for modern warfare.

10 May German armies attack the Low Countries, invade France. By 16 May the battle of France is lost. De Gaulle decides to continue the struggle. His tanks carry out a successful counter-attack at Montcornet near Laon.

27 May He counter-attacks again; near Abbeville, but has to break off the engagement for lack of air support and supplies. He is promoted General; temporary, not substantive rank.

5 June Appointed Under-Secretary for War by Paul Reynaud.

10 June Italy declares war; French government leaves Paris for Bordeaux; de Gaulle supports idea of carrying on the war from a fortified enclave in Brittany.

18 June First broadcast from London, calling on the French to continue the war.

19 June Yvonne de Gaulle arrives in London with the children.

22 June Armistice signed by General Huntziger.

28 June British government recognises de Gaulle as the leader of the Free French.

3 July Attack by British squadron on French fleet anchored at Mers el Kebir.

4 July De Gaulle sentenced to death by French court-martial.

14 July First military parade of Free French, with 300 sailors and soldiers. First appearance of slogan 'La France a perdu une bataille, elle n'a pas perdu la guerre.'

30 August After the French Congo, Chad and the Cameroons have announced their support for him, de Gaulle attempts to land at Dakar; and is repulsed.

1941

March De Gaulle goes to Cairo in order to follow more closely what he hopes will be the peaceful takeover by troops loyal to him of Syria and Lebanon. French troops loyal to the Vichy government resist. Damascus not taken until 21 June, the date at which Germany attacks Russia. De Gaulle much absorbed by quarrels with Churchill about the respective rôles of France and Great Britain in the Middle East.

26 September The USSR establishes contact with de Gaulle. The French Communist Party, which had earlier adopted an attitude of benevolent neutrality towards the German occupation of France, begins to support the resistance movement.

Appendix E   203

7 December	Japanese attack on Pearl Harbor. Germany declares war on United States.
24 December	Admiral Muselier takes over the islands of Saint-Pierre et Miquelon in the name of the Free French, thereby considerably annoying the Americans.

1942

January	Jean Moulin, representing de Gaulle, is parachuted into France to unify the resistance movement.
June	De Gaulle, annoyed with the British for having invaded and liberated Madagascar without consulting him, considers the possibility of moving to Moscow.
10 June	French victory at Bir Hakeim.
8 November	Anglo-American forces land in Algeria. De Gaulle supports the invasion, about which he had not been consulted. Admiral Darlan recognised by Americans as head of French forces in Algeria. Assassinated on 24 December.
11 November	German invasion of the 'Free Zone' officially governed by Vichy. French fleet scuttled at Toulon on 27 November.
December	The resistance movement in France announces its support for de Gaulle.

1943

27 May	First meeting, in Paris, of the *Conseil National de la Résistance*, under the chairmanship of de Gaulle's personal representative, Jean Moulin.
30 May	De Gaulle arrives in Algeria, where he establishes a duumvirate with Giraud over the *Conseil National de la Résistance*. He then gradually excludes Giraud from power.
25 November	French army from North Africa, under command of General Juin, lands in Naples.
28 November	At Teheran, Stalin, Roosevelt and Churchill decide without consulting de Gaulle to land in France the following Spring.

1944

January	Brazzaville conference, at which de Gaulle proclaims the future independence of African countries then under European control.
3 June	The *Conseil National de la Résistance* officially declares itself the *Gouvernement Provisoire de la République Française*.
6 June	Allied landings in Normandy. De Gaulle, although excluded from all discussion and planning, nevertheless calls on the French resistance to join its efforts to those of the allied armies.
14 June	De Gaulle arrives at Bayeux.
6–10 July	Visits the United States and Canada.
13 July	The GPRF is recognised by the Americans as qualified to administer France.
25 August	De Gaulle arrives in Paris, where he goes directly to the War

204 French Caesarism

	Ministry, in the rue Saint-Dominique. Nothing in the offices has changed since he left in June 1940.
23 October	The GPRF recognised by Americans as legal government of France.

1945

February	The Yalta conference, from which France is excluded, nevertheless gives France control over one of the occupied zones into which Germany is to be divided, as well as a seat in the Security Council of the United Nations.
7 May	Capitulation of German forces at Reims.
8 May	End of Second World War. A victory parade in Sétif, Algeria, leads to rioting in which 103 Europeans are murdered. According to Algerian nationalist sources, 45,000 Muslims are then killed by the French army.
13 November	De Gaulle unanimously elected Head of Government. Forms a tripartite administration with the Catholic *Mouvement Répubicain Populaire*, the socialist *Section Française de L'Internationale Ouvrière* and the *Parti Communiste Français*.

1946

20 January	De Gaulle resigns as Head of Government, arguing the impossibility of working with so many divergent political parties in a Constitution which deprives the executive of the necessary authority.
16 June	Speech at Bayeux setting out the basic ideas of what later becomes the Fifth Republic.
13 October	In spite of de Gaulle's opposition, the Constitution of the Fourth Republic, which turns out in practice to be very like that of the Third, is adopted at a referendum in which just over nine million vote in favour; 7.79 million against; and 7.77 million abstain.
23 November	The French fleet bombards Haiphong; beginning of Indochinese war.

1947

7 April	In a speech at Strasbourg, de Gaulle announces the establishment of the *Rassemblement du Peuple Français*. In October, it wins 40 per cent of the votes cast in local government elections.

1948

6 February	Death of Anne de Gaulle.

1951

17 June	The RPF wins only 121 seats in the *Assemblée Nationale*.

Appendix E   205

1953
6 May   De Gaulle dissolves the RPF.

1954
7 May   Fall of Dien Bien Phu leads to Geneva conference of August 1954 at which Mendès France negotiates the French withdrawal from Indochina and the division of the country into a Communist north and a 'democratic' south.
October   Publication of the *Mémoires de Guerre*. 100,000 copies are sold in five weeks.
1 November   Beginning of Algerian war.

1956
January   The 'républicains sociaux', the remnants of the RPF, win only 4 per cent of the votes at a general election marked principally by the unexpected success of Pierre Poujade.
October,   Failure of Anglo-French attempt to overthrow Nasser.
November   Hungarian uprising put down by Russian troops.

1957
25 March   Signing of the Treaty of Rome.

1958
8 February   French planes bomb Sakhiet; Robert Murphy appointed to use his 'good offices' to reconcile France and Tunisia.
13 May   Establishment under General Massu of a Committee of Public Safety in Algiers.
15 May   De Gaulle announces that he is 'ready to assume the powers of the Republic'. Repeats this on 19 May.
27 May   Issues statement that he has begun the regular process (*entamé le processus régulier*) to form a government.
29 May   Asked by President Coty to form a government.
1 June   By 329 votes to 224, and with 32 abstentions, he is appointed Head of Government by the *Assemblée Nationale*; with power to elaborate a new constitution.
4 June   Algiers: 'Je vous ai compris'.
August   Travels to French West Africa, offering independence to French colonial territories in accordance with the Brazzaville declaration of 1944.
28 September   The Constitution of the Fifth Republic approved by a majority of 80 per cent of those voting.
28 November   Krushchev announces that a Peace Treaty between Russia and East Germany, to be signed on 28 May 1959, will mean the transfer of responsibility for access to West Berlin from the USSR to the German Democratic Republic.
21 December   De Gaulle elected Head of State by 78.5 per cent of the votes cast by an electoral college of 80,000 *notables*.

206 French Caesarism

1959

8 January	Officially becomes President of the Fifth Republic.
17 March	States that the manufacture of the French atomic bomb is an absolute priority.
August	Visits Algeria.
16 September	Presents three possible solutions to the Algerian problem: secession; total integration with France; association. In spite of his own obvious preference for the third, this speech marks the beginning of the end of *L'Algérie Française* by accepting the principle of self-determination.

1960

18 January	Publication of an interview in which General Massu criticises de Gaulle's Algerian policy.
24 January	General strike by Europeans in Algeria; *la semaine des barricades*; fighting between the European rebels and the police with at least 24 deaths, 200 wounded. Algiers remains in open rebellion until de Gaulle's speech of 29 January; on 31 January the rebellion collapses.
16 May	Krushchev, in Paris for summit meeting, refuses to meet Eisenhower until an apology is offered for the violation of Soviet airspace by the U2 spy plane; de Gaulle's refusal to be unduly disturbed justified by Krushchev's subsequent abstention from signing the threatened peace treaty with East Germany.
10 June	Secret meeting at the Elysée between de Gaulle and the FLN leaders of Wilaya IV (Algiers).
20 June	Failure of the discussions at Melun between the French government and the *Gouvernement Provisoire de la République Algérienne*.
4 November	De Gaulle speaks on television in favour of a negotiated peace in Algeria, implicitly recognising the possibility of independence. His visit to Algeria later the same month convinces him that the FLN does represent the Algerian people.

1961

8 January	Referendum on the question: 'Do you approve the Bill submitted to the French people by the President of the Republic concerning the self-determination of the Algerian populations and the organisation of the public powers in Algeria after self-determination?' 75 per cent of those voting say 'yes'.
21 April	Attempt at coup d'état in Algiers by Challe, Zeller, Jouhaud and Salan. De Gaulle takes emergency powers and orders the army to obey him.
26 April	The 'quarteron de généraux en retraite' surrender.
20 May	Evian negotiations between France and the GPRA.
13 August	Construction of the Berlin wall begun.

Appendix E   207

5 September	De Gaulle accepts the GPRA claim to the Sahara.

1962

March	Over a hundred terrorist incidents claimed by the OAS in Algeria. Negotiations continue.
8 April	90 per cent of those voting in a referendum approve the granting of independence to Algeria.
3 July	Algeria officially becomes independent. Some one million Europeans leave Algeria and are welcomed in France as 'des rapatriés'.
22 August	De Gaulle narrowly escapes being killed by the OAS at Le Petit-Clamart.
20 September	De Gaulle announces that a referendum is to be held on the election of the President by universal suffrage.
28 October	De Gaulle obtains a majority vote of 66.25 per cent of votes cast in favour of the election of the President of the Republic by universal suffrage.
22–29 October	In order to provide himself with a side-arm persuader in future negotiations over Berlin, Krushchev installs medium-range rockets in Cuba, and withdraws them when Kennedy blockades the island. De Gaulle gives full support to the United States.

1963

14 January	De Gaulle declares in a press conference that Great Britain is not ready to join the European Economic Community.
22 January	Signing of a Franco-German treaty of alliance and co-operation.
21 June	French fleet withdrawn from NATO command.

1964

27 January	France officially recognises Communist China.
October	De Gaulle visits South America.

1965

30 June	Faced with the Hallstein proposal to enlarge the powers of the European Commission, France adopts the policy of the 'empty chair', refusing to take part in further discussion on the future of the European Community. In May 1966 the Luxembourg Compromise marks the triumph of the Gaullist Concept of 'L'Europe des Patries' over the federal ideal of a fully united Europe.
5 December	In the first round of the Presidential election, de Gaulle fails to win an outright majority, receiving only 44 per cent of the votes cast against 32 per cent for François Mitterrand and 16 per cent for Jean Lecanuet. At the second ballot, on 19 December, he wins with 54.6 per cent against Mitterrand's 45.4 per cent; thus becoming the first – and only – Caesar to win an election against official opposition.

208 French Caesarism

1966

7 March — De Gaulle tells President Lyndon Johnson that French forces will no longer be part of the NATO military command structure. France remains a political member of the alliance.

1 September — At a speech at Pnom Penh, in Cambodia, de Gaulle criticises American intervention in Vietnam.

1967

22 May — Egypt blockades the Gulf of Aqaba. De Gaulle advises the Israeli foreign minister, Abba Eban, not to start hostilities, and suspends shipments of French arms to the Middle East.

5 June — Israel launches and wins the Six Day War.

24 July — Gives speech from the balcony of the town hall in Montreal including the phrase 'Vive le Québec libre!'

27 October — Rejects second British application, put forward by Harold Wilson, to join the Common Market, remarking as he does so that 'une transformation radicale de la Grande Bretagne s'impose'.

27 November — De Gaulle describes 'the Jewish people' as being 'un peuple d'élite, dominateur et sûr de lui-même', which, if not an unambiguous compliment, is a remarkable piece of self-description.

1968

22 March — Beginning of student rebellion in Paris. De Gaulle seems to lose his nerve, and on 29 May leaves Paris to consult General Massu at Baden-Baden.

30 May — Mass demonstration in support of de Gaulle marches from the Place de la Concorde to L'Etoile. De Gaulle dissolves the National Assembly, enabling Georges Pompidou to transform the very narrow majority he had won in 1967 into a majority of 358 out of 485. He is nevertheless dismissed by de Gaulle and replaced by Maurice Couve de Murville.

1969

27 April — Referendum on regionalisation and the reform of the Senate: 53 per cent vote against. De Gaulle resigns.

15 June — Georges Pompidou elected President of the Republic.

1970

23 October — Publication of volume I of *Mémoires d'Espoir*.

9 November — Death of de Gaulle. Buried on 12 November at the cemetery at Colombey-les-deux-Eglises by the side of his daughter, Anne.

Appendix E

ALL GALL

This old man, he played one,
He played nick-nack at Verdun.
Cognac, Armagnac, Burgundy and Beaune,
This old man came rolling home.

This old man, World War Two,
He told Churchill what to do.
Free French General, Crosses of Lorraine,
He came rolling home again.

This old man, he played trois,
'Vive la France, la France c'est moi!
Gimcrack governments, call me if you please –
Colombey-les-Deux-Eglises.'

This old man, he played four.
'Choose De Gaulle or civil war!'
'Come back President, govern by decree.'
Referendum: oui, oui, oui.

This old man, he played five.
'France is safe – I'm still alive.'
Plastique, Pompidou, sing the Marseillaise.
Algérie n'est pas française.

This old man, he played six.
'France and England they won't mix.
Eyetie, Benelux, Germany and me –
That's my Market recipe.'

This old man, sept et huit,
'NATO, give me back my fleet!'
Kiss-kiss, Adenauer, ratified in Bonn.
One old man goes on and on.

This old man, nine and ten,
He'll play Nick 'til God knows when.
Cognac, Armagnac, Burgundy and Beaune –
This old man thinks he's St Joan!

– Donald Swann from *At the Drop of a Hat.* Reproduced by permission of the publishers, Chappell Music Ltd.

Further Reading

In 1850 an ex-*préfet* called François-Auguste Romieu published a book entitled *L'Ere des Césars*. In it he denounced the excesses which he saw as bound to arise as a consequence of the freedoms proclaimed by the Second Republic and called for a Caesar to present himself as the saviour of society in order that 'the sword might defeat the idea'. In 1852 he published a second warning, this time about the red peril. It was entitled *Le Spectre Rouge de 1852*, and the ideas it expressed were enthusiastically endorsed by the Catholic writer Louis Veuillot.

L'Ere des Césars is not currently in print. The views it expresses do not command the instant assent of the average late-twentieth-century reader. It is nevertheless salutary to reflect that the presuppositions running through *French Caesarism from Napoleon I to Charles de Gaulle* may seem as quaint to the reader of 2150 as M. Romieu's do to us today. The only serious right-wing thinker in contemporary Britain, Roger Scruton, does not even include Caesarism in his *A Dictionary of Modern Political Thought* (London: Macmillan, 1982). He mentions only Caesaropapalism, the doctrine that the sovereign secular power should have authority over the Church.

Most of the books I have used in the preparation of this essay are mentioned in the Notes. The most recent general history of France since 1787 is the eighteen-volume *Nouvelle Histoire de la France Contemporaine*, published by the Editions du Seuil. Each period is dealt with by a separate scholar, and each volume contains an extensive bibliography. Basic facts about French history are most easily checked in Alain Decaux and André Castelot, *Dictionnaire d'Histoire de France* (Paris: Perrin, 1981), which has the additional advantage of being magnificently illustrated. René Rémond's *Les Droites en France* (originally published 1955; latest edition, Paris: Aubier, Montaigne, 1982) enables the phenomenon of Caesarism to be seen against a wider background. There is an English version, *The Right Wing in France from 1815 to de Gaulle*, translated by James M. Laux (University of Pennsylvania Press, 1969). John Stewart Ambler's *The French Army in Politics* (Ohio State University Press, 1966) is an excellent study.

In 1961 a new and detailed edition of the Comte de Las Cases' *Mémorial de Sainte-Hélène* was published by the Editions Garnier in Paris. This account of the conversations which one of Napoleon's most fervent admirers had with him between 29 June 1815 and 11 November 1816 was the bedside book of Stendhal's Julien Sorel in *Le Rouge et le Noir*. It remains immensely readable. In Paris, the rue Las Cases, in the VIe *arrondissement*, forms an appropriate right angle with the rue de Solferino (Napoleon III's victory of 24 June 1859 over the Austrians) where the Institut Charles de Gaulle is housed. From 1947 onwards, this was the Paris headquarters of the *Rassemblement du Peuple Français*. I am most grateful to Olivier Delorme, curator of the Institut Charles de Gaulle, for allowing me access to its magnificent collections.

Peter Geyl's *Napoleon. For and Against* (London: Cape, 1949) translated

210

Further Reading 211

from the Dutch by Olive Renier remains one of the best antidotes to the enthusiasm with which the Comte de Las Cases recalls how Napoleon evoked his career. M. J. Sydenham's *The First French Republic* (London: Batsford, 1974) is an excellent account of the political experiment which enabled Bonaparte to seize power. *French Society and the Revolution*, edited by Douglas Johnson (Cambridge University Press, 1976), collects a number of major articles from *Past and Present* which present, for the reader brought up in the French tradition, a somewhat revisionist view. The volume includes William Doyle's *Aristocratic Reaction in Pre-Revolutionary France*, an article casting considerable doubt on whether or not such an event took place. The second volume of Régine Pernoud's *Histoire de la Bourgeoisie en France* (Paris: Editions du Seuil, 1962) is most illuminating both about Napoleon I's use of war as an instrument of pillage and the use that he made of the French professional middle class to administer France itself and the First French Empire.

Stuart L. Campbell's *The Second Empire Revisited* (New Brunswick: Rutgers University Press, 1978) offers a very useful summary of what historians have said about Napoleon III. For reasons connected more with Louis Napoleon than with Professor Campbell, it is a less envigorating read than Peter Geyl's book on 'Napoléon le Grand'. Like most other books, it does not mention the *préfet* Romieu, whose case for Caesarism appeared under the imprint of the house of Ledoyen. Theodore Zeldin's *The Political System of Napoleon III* (London: Macmillan, 1978) remains the best account of the subject based on previously unpublished sources. Howard C. Payne's *The Police State of Napoleon III, 1851–1860* (University of Washington Press, 1966) makes you realise how amateurish the nineteenth century was in such matters compared to Hitler's Germany and post-revolutionary Russia. Adrien Dansette's *Louis-Napoléon à la conquête du pouvoir* (Paris: Hachette, 1961) is a brisk and highly readable account of France's least attractive go-getter.

Pierre Viansson-Ponté's two-volume *Histoire de la République Gaullienne* (Paris: Fayard, 1971) remains one of the best introductions to the subject. It presents the referendum of 28 October 1962 on the election of the President by universal suffrage as introducing a decisive change in the constitutional history of the Republic. The same author's *Les Gaullistes, Rituel et Annuaire* (Paris: Seuil, 1963) is highly entertaining and informative. Jean Charlot's *The Gaullist Phenomenon*, translated by Monique Charlot and Marianne Neighbour (London: Allen and Unwin, 1971) is also very good. The French themselves recognise the value of Stanley Hoffman's *Decline or Renewal? France Since the 1930s* (New York: The Viking Press, 1974). The best academic analysis of the Fifth Republic is Jean-Louis Quemonne's *Le Gouvernement de la France sous la Ve République* (Paris: Dalloz, 1980). It points out that all three Presidents and all Prime Ministers to hold office between 1965 and 1981 were, or had been, if not actually civil servants, salaried employees of the state: de Gaulle, 1959–1969, who was a regular soldier from 1911 to 1940; Georges Pompidou, 1969–1974, who before becoming a *Conseiller d'Etat* in 1946 had from his entry into the *Ecole Normale Supérieure* in 1931 been a teacher, and therefore a civil servant through his membership of the *Corps de l'Education Nationale*; Valéry

212 *French Caesarism*

Giscard d'Estaing, 1974–1981, who before his election to the *Assemblée Nationale* in 1952 had been a member of what is hierarchically the third of the *Grands Corps de l'Etat*, L'Inspection Générale des Finances.

Michel Debré, Prime Minister from 1959 to 1962, was a member of the first of the *Grands Corps*, *Le Conseil d'Etat*; Pompidou succeeded him as Prime Minister from 1962 to 1968; he was succeeded from 1968 to 1969 by Maurice Couve de Murville, who before becoming a professional diplomat had been an *Inspecteur des Finances*.

On his election as President in 1969, Pompidou appointed as Prime Minister Jacques Chaban-Delmas, who had been at the *Inspection Générale des Finances* in 1943 and 1945. In 1972, Chaban-Delmas was replaced by Pierre Messmer, who before 1939 had been a colonial administrator, having graduated from the *Ecole Nationale de la France et d'Outre-Mer* in 1938. On his election to the Presidency in 1974, Giscard d'Estaing appointed Jacques Chirac, a member of the second of the *Grands Corps de l'Etat*, *La Cour des Comptes*; in August 1976, Chirac was replaced by Raymond Barre, who since 1950 had been a university teacher and thus a member of *L'Education Nationale*.

François Mitterrand, who is an *avocat* (lawyer) is thus the only President not to have spent some time as a salaried employee of the state; and his first Prime Minister, Pierre Mauroy, has the same distinction. Laurent Fabius, who replaced Mauroy in 1983, is a member of the *Conseil d'Etat*; Michel Rocard, appointed Prime Minister in 1988, of the *Inspection Générale des Finances*. It should be noted that French civil servants do not have to resign before standing for elective office. They can obtain leave of absence (*se faire mettre en disponibilité, obtenir un détachement*) in order to lead a political career. If this political career proves disappointing, they can *ré-intégrer leur corps d'origine sans perte d'ancienneté*, go back to their original *corps* without losing seniority. The rule of the French civil service, amusingly evoked in Jacques Mandrin's *L'Enarchie, ou les Mandarins de la Société Bourgeoise* (Paris: La Table Ronde de Combat, 1968) remains a less dramatic but perhaps more important feature of French society than the now abandoned habit of calling in a soldier.

Index

Abbeville, 116
Action Française, 7, 72, 110, 137
Adenauer, Konrad, 13, 142
Algeria, 8, 13, 15, 40, 126–39, 147
Allied Military Government
  Occupied Territories, 12
Alsace Lorraine, 63, 68
Alternance, 106–7
Amiens, Peace of, 43
Amouroux, Henri, 7, 168
Antisemitism, French, 86–9, 168,
  169, 196
Arc, Joan of, 121, 143
Argentina, 13, 55
Army, French:
  accepts civilian jurisdiction, 71
  alliance with Church, 58–9
  always gets it wrong, 14–15
  bad at winning wars, 61–3, 129,
    151
  enthusiasm for in Third Republic,
    67–8, 72
  keeps out of politics, 51–2, 68,
    165; *but see* 136–9
Aron, Raymond, 5, 130, 161, 173
Assignats, 29
Augereau, Pierre, General, 23
Auriol, Vincent, 105
Austerlitz, battle of, 11, 64, 186
Australia, 11, 46; *see also*
  Afterthoughts
Austria, 2, 11, 40, 41, 55, 60
Azéma, Jean-Pierre, 153
Aymé, Marcel, 86

Bagehot, Walter, appreciation of
  constitution of Second Empire,
  151
Bangladesh, 45
Bankers, rôle of, 25, 59, 140–1
Barras, Paul, Vicomte de, 20, 23, 24,
  25, 184
Barre, Raymond, 212
Barrès, Maurice, 59

Baudin, Alphonse, 53
Bazaine, François Achille, 56, 62–3
Bazin, René, 86
Beauharnais, Joséphine de, 21, 35
  infertile with Napoleon I, 41, 45
  Napoleon III's grandmother, 50,
    62, 184
Beaumarchais, 27
Bernadotte, Jean-Baptiste,
  subsequently King of Sweden, 24,
  188; *see also* Afterthoughts
Bernstein, Henri, playwright, denies
  existence of indigenous French
  antisemitism, 88
Bichelonne, Jean, forecasts
  inevitable German victory in 1940,
  162
Bismarck, Otto, 55, 60, 102, 171
Blanning, T. C. W., 160
Blum, Léon, 72, 77–8, 92, 103, 154,
  197, 201
Bonapartism:
  de Gaulle accused of, 140
  distinguished from Caesarism, 15,
    65–6
  popularity in provinces, 49
Bonnemain, Marguerite de:
  Boulanger spends night of election
    with, 69
  Boulanger's suicide on grave of,
    69
Boulanger, General Georges, 68–9,
  80, 123, 167
Bugeaud, General Thomas Robert,
  127

Caesar, Augustus, 46, 65, 156
Caesar, Julius, 12, 14, 17, 22
Caesarian:
  adjective used by English
    historians, 161–2
  French of naturally Caesarian
    temperament, 70
  gynaecological parallel, 12, 40

213

214 French Caesarism

Caesarism:
consequence of breakdown in normal politics, 45, 97
defined, 11, 15, 32, 76
distinguished from Bonapartism, 15, 65–6
element of illegality, 12–13, 48, 114, 117
homme providentiel, 162
nation incarnated in one man, 31–2
not altogether a bad thing, 147, 150; *also passim and* Afterthoughts
possible causes in France, 123, 145, 156, 167
triumphant end of, 159

Caesars, French:
attitudes to education, 59, 152
bad at foreign policy and winning wars, 56–7, 153–5
better at home policy, 64–5
cannot come to power except through crises, 8, 80–1, 122–3, 155
direct line to people, 26, 111–12, 134, 140, 171
good for business, 141
govern through civilians, 14, 23–4, 73–4, 154
helped to power by civilians, 24, 37, 71, 73, 78, 81, 152; as well as by poor quality of French civilian politicians, 14, 77, 125
hostility to English, 42, 109
seek to change constitution, 69
succeeded by civilians, 150
unifiers, 89, 121
use of plebiscites and referenda, 2, 4, 5, 9, 12, 131, 134, 138, 140, 148, 161, 192–3, 208

Calvet, Henri, 31
Cambacérès, Jean-Jacques, 2
Camus, Albert, 10, 13, 84, 127
Carlyle, Thomas, 21
quoted, 163, 169
Catechism, Imperial, 35, 94, 152
Catholic Church:
attitude to Vichy, 65–6

conflicts with Revolution, 27, 33–4, 175–6, 178
protects Jews, 87–8
Cavaignac, Gen., 4, 14, 49, 66, 191
Cazmajou (joke: *casse-ma-joue*, break my cheek), 51
Chaban-Delmas, Jacques, 131, 212
Chambord, Comte de, 59
decisive role in failure to restore monarchy, 66
Changarnier, Nicolas, 69
describes Napoleon III as melancholy parrot, 165
Charlemagne, 46
Charles I and II of England, 155
Charles V of Spain, 60
Charles X of France, compared to James II of England, 3, 51, 66
Chauvineau, General Narcisse, 81, 100
Chirac, Jacques, 107, 212
Chislehurst, 5, 12, 193
Churchill, Winston, 13, 76, 92, 115, 118–19, 124, 154
quoted, 170, 203
tells de Gaulle of British preference for *le grand large*, 42
Civil Service, importance of in France, 14–15, 36–8, 211–12
Clemenceau, Georges, 13, 114, 136, 154
Cleopatra, 156
Cobhan, Alfred, 26, 29
Cohabitation, 104, 105, 106, 113
Comédie Française, 19
Common Market, 42, 141, 182, 207, 208
Commune, la, 43, 60, 66, 84, 158
Communism, decline of, 147–8
Concordat, 35, 36, 46, 181
Conseil d'Etat, 37–8, 180, 212
Constitution civile du clergé, 33, 175
Continental System, 22, 42–3, 44, 187, 188
Coty, President René, 48, 105, 130
Coups d'état:
conditions favourable for, 23–4, 129
relatively bloodless in France, 154–5

Index

215

Coups d'état:
du 18 Brumaire, 2, 4, 24, 48, 131,
140, 180, 185
du 18 Fructidor, 23–4, 179, 185
du 2 décembre 1851, 4–5, 49–53
Cour des Comptes, 37–8, 212
Crimean War, 54, 129, 141, 192
Cromwell, Oliver, 13, 23, 32, 33,
118, 167
Cuba, de Gaulle's attitude to 1962
crisis, 144, 207

Daladier, Edouard, 78, 82, 96, 197
Darlan, Admiral François, 77, 98,
109, 124–5
Churchill and de Gaulle on, 172,
197, 203
Darnand, Joseph, 91, 197, 198
Daudet, Léon, 88
Daumier, Honoré, 51
Debré, Michel, 59, 106, 133, 212
Déclaration des droits de l'homme et
du citoyen, 1–2, 20, 23
central ambition realised by
Napoleonic Code, 2, 38, 159
Delbecque, Léon, 9, 131
Denmark, treatment of Jews in, 87
Déroulède, Paul, 69, 71
Diderot, Denis, 20, 67
Dien Bien Phu, French defeat at,
122, 129, 205
Directoire, 14, 146, 147, 152, 178–9
Douaumont, 89, 99, 198
Doumergue, Gaston, 79, 80, 114
Doyle, William, 21, 160, 164
Dreyfus case, 15, 70–1
discredits army, 88
de Gaulle's father on, 109
Ducos, Roger, 24, 25
Dunkirk, 77, 126

Ecole Nationale d'Administration, 15
Education:
achievements of Third Republic,
67–8
different attitudes of French
Caesars to, 58–9
Imperial University, 35; monopoly
broken, 58, 152, 181–2

la laïcité, 83
monopole de diplômes, 152
Egypt, 22, 40
Eisenhower, Dwight D., 11, 102,
124, 206
Empire, First, 14, 46, 53, 181–2
Empire, Second, 192–3
achievements, 5, 46, 64–5
fall, 59
forerunner of modern
totalitarianisms, 116
social inequalities in, 57–8
Ems telegram, 60
Estaing, Valéry Giscard de, 107,
109, 211
Etat Français, 7, 83
Evian agreements, 138, 159

Fabre-Luce, Alfred, 92
Falloux, Frédéric, disagreements
with Napoleon III, 58–9
loi Falloux, 58, 182, 191
Finer, S. E., 11, 23, 76, 114, 150
First, Ruth, 10
Fisher, H. A. L., 17
Fleurus, battle of, 41; see also
Afterthoughts
Foch, Marshal Ferdinand, 7, 114,
195
Fouché, Joseph, 24, 36, 151
France:
double crisis in, 147
weakness of political life in, 153
divisions in political life explained
by past, 157–8
Franco, Francisco, 9, 33, 78–9, 133,
201; see also Afterthoughts
French, the:
judged by de Gaulle and
Napoleon I, 156–7, 173
natural leaning for Caesarism, 70
not suited to democratic
government (?), 15–16, 70, 153,
167
Freud, Sigmund, 41
Fronde, 30
failure of, 32

Galtieri, General, 13

216 *French Caesarism*

Gamelin, General Maurice, 197
Gaudin, Maurice, 36
Gaulle, Anne de, 123–4, 201, 204, 208
Gaulle, Charles de, 100–49, 199–208
  acts illegally in 1940, 117–18
  advantages of nuclear defence policy, 148; *see also* Afterthoughts
  Anglo-Saxon views on, 172
  assessment of Pétain, 91–2, 94, 99, 195
  behaviour in 1968, 144–5
  cavalier attitude to Prime Ministers, 145
  changes constitution of Fifth Republic, 9
  concepts of deterrence, 102–3, 116, 142
  conflict with army, 132–4
  de minimis non curat praetor, 200
  emphasises importance of regular organs of state, 120
  essentially a politician, 116–17, 120
  Europe des Patries, 207
  family man, 123
  first Caesar to come to terms with democracy, 109, 112
  gives women vote, 39
  hard to take seriously at times, 101, 112, 143, 146
  helped by Pétain, 99, 200–1
  impeccably hawkish on central Cold War issues, 142
  importance of civil over military authority, 10, 108
  indifference to money, 52, 123–4
  keeps Britain out of Common Market, 141, 207, 208
  launches RPF, 113, 121, 158, 204
  like Napoleon, a second son, 41, 110
  most successful of French Caesars, 99, 100–2, 106–7, 113–14, 120, 133, 139, 158–9
  opposes US policy in Vietnam, 142, 208

parallel with Continental system of Napoleon I, 42
performance in rôle of de Gaulle, 143
prevents Communist coup d'état in 1944 (?), 120–1
primacy to constitutional matters, 100
removes French forces from NATO command, 141
reported dead, 115, 200
return to power in 1958, 12–13, 130–2, 205
seeks authority for action in 1940, 117–18
seen by *The Times* as right-wing in 1940, 108–9, 121; wrongly, 138
sense of humour, 135
sensitive to criticism, 112
sentenced to death, 202
song, 'All Gall', 209
strong views on politicians, 108
success of *Mémoires de Guerre*, 123
value (?) of mobile striking force, 116, 120
views on aerial warfare, 81–2, 116, 171
visit to Quebec, 55, 143, 208; and to South America, 55
Gaulle, Henri de, 110–11
Gaulle, Yvonne de, 123, 200, 202
George III of England, views on French Revolution, 28
Germany, 11, 17, 63, 148
Gide, André, 10, 83
Giraud, General Henri, 8, 116, 124, 125
Goethe, 62, 177
Gouges, Olympe de, 176
Greece, 9, 120
Greer, Donald, 163
Gresham's Law, 29
Grévy, Jules, 67, 68
Guérard, Albert, 166
Guillemin, Louis, 58, 166
Guillotin, Dr Joseph, 27; *see also* Afterthoughts
Guillotine, use of, 27, 176, 177

Index

Hamlet, as many interpretations possible as of French history, 16–17
Napoleon III likened to eponymous hero, 167
Haussmann, Baron Georges, political implications of rebuilding Paris, 59–60, 141, 166
Hegel, 15
Hervé, Gustave, 8, 79
Hitler, Adolf, 11, 15, 40, 97, 166; *see also* Afterthoughts
Ho Chi Minh, 120
Holland, 77, 87, 179; *see also* Afterthoughts
Horne, Alistair, 168, 169, 171
Howard, Elizabeth, 52, 191
high wages of sin, 165
Hugo, Victor, 53, 190
Hunt, Lynne, 26

Imperial Catechism, 35–6, 94, 181
India, 147
Indochina, 122–3, 147
Italy, 2, 11, 22, 33, 55, 145, 147

Jacobins, Napoleon seen as one, 152
James II of England, 3, 156
Jaruzelski, General, 9
Jecker, Jean-Baptiste, 56
Jena, battle of, 73
Joffre, Joseph, Marshal, 7
Johnson, Lyndon B., asks what de Gaulle really wants, 172, 208
Johnson, Paul, 81
Joubert, Barthélemy, General, 14, 24
Jourdan, Jean-Baptiste, Marshal, 19
Juarez, Benito, 56–7
Jurien de la Gravière, Admiral, 56

Keitel, Wilhelm, Field Marshal, 126
Kennedy, Jackie, 143
Krushchev, Nikita, 142, 205, 206, 207

Lacouture, Jean, 140, 171, 173
Laïc, Laïcité, 6, 110, 157
Lamartine, Alphonse de, 5, 48–9

Lasserie, André, 93
Laval, Pierre, 74, 81, 196
Lebrun, President Albert, 94, 101, 118
Lebrun, Charles-François, 2, 180
Le Chapelier, loi, 39, 54
Ledru-Rollin, Alexandre, 4
Lefebvre, Philippe-Michel, 79
Leipzig, battle of, 44, 189
Lenin, Vladimir, 157
Lévy, A.-L., 45–6
Liddell-Hart, B. H., 116
Lottman, Herbert, 90, 168, 169
Louis XIII, 93
Louis XIV, 13, 27, 86–7, 114
Louis XVI, 3, 20, 34, 176, 177, 178
Louis XVIII, 3, 31, 44, 182, 189
Louis-Philippe, 3, 178, 191
Louisiana purchase, 43, 64, 186

Mac-Mahon, Edmé, Marshal, 66, 105
Maginot line, 15, 82, 102, 132, 201
Magnan, Bernard, Marshal, 51, 69
Maistre, Joseph de, 15, 110
Malraux, André, 133, 141
Mandel, Georges, 76
Mao Tse Tung, 120
Marengo, battle of, 43, 186
Marie-Antoinette, 41, 178
Marie-Louise of Austria, 41, 188
Mark Antony, 156
Marrane, Georges, 105
Marseillaise, 67, 177, 209
Martin, Kingsley, 27
Marx, Karl, 4, 15, 58, 153
Marxist analysis:
of Caesarism, 16–17, 57–8, 59
of first French Revolution, 160
Massu, General Jacques, 129, 130, 133, 143, 206, 208
Mauriac, François, 94
Mauroy, Pierre, 212
Maurras, Charles, 15, 72, 88:
sees defeat of 1940 as a 'divine surprise', 197
Maximilian, Emperor of Mexico, 57, 184
Mayer, Daniel, 119, 172

218 *French Caesarism*

Mayer, René, 121
Mendès France, Pierre, 106, 111, 121, 129, 139, 144, 154, 205
Mers el Kebir, 125, 135, 202
Mitterrand, François, 104, 105, 106, 113, 144, 152, 154, 207, 212
Mollet, Guy, 106, 129
Moltke, Helmuth von, 61
Monck, General George, 156, 167
Monnerville, Gaston, 140
Monnet, Jean, 50, 90
Montijo, Empress Eugénie de, 57, 62
Moreau, General Jean, 14, 24
Mornet, André, 89
Morny, Duc de, 53, 56, 59
Moscow, 19, 44
Moulin, Jean, 121, 203
Mouvement Républicain Populaire, 157–8, 204
Mussolini, Benito, 11, 33, 154, 166

Nantes, Revocation of Edict of, 27; consequences of, 87
Napoleon I, 18–47, 183–9; *see also* 2, 4, 7, 112, 131, 132, 145:
ability to inspire loyalty, 19
a good thing? yes, 146; no, 163
attitude to religion, 34
changes name, 26; joke about Buona Parte, 21
compares himself to Julius Caesar, 42
contribution to German unification, 64
crowns himself Emperor, 35, 43, 181
debate about after 1815, 184
death of, 17, 189
did not shine on 9 November 1799, 25
eating habits compared to those of de Gaulle, 19
eclectic in choice of servants, 36–7
governs through civilians, 36
interest in money for France, 21, 43, 52, 163, 185, 211; and self, 52

jacobin sympathies, 20, 152, 184
judged by de Gaulle, 2, 160
leaves France with dangerous myth, 121
Mediterranean attitude to family, 184; and women, 39
middle-class figure (?), 46
military campaigns and tactics, 19, 22–3, 168
ni bonnet rouge ni talon rouge, 25
reasons for failure, 41–2; *see also* Afterthoughts
sells France's American Empire, 43
several mistresses, 123
unifier, 29, 89, 121
Napoleon II (for Bonapartists), duc de Reichstadt, roi de Rome, 4, 35, 41, 188, 190
ashes brought to Paris in 1940, 196–7
Napoleon III, 48–65, 190–3; *see also* 4, 5, 7, 12, 14, 127, 141
accepts military advice from wife, 62
belief in state intervention, 50
compared to Hamlet, 167
contributes to German unification, 64
death of, 5, 17, 193
financial problems, 52, 165
liked by Queen Victoria, 151
man of the right, 137; except on colonial policy, 127
Metternich on, 166
Mexican adventure, 55–7
not a genuine military man, 14, 150
not physically attractive, 165
politically inept, 60–1
re-eligible for election, 5, 160
Saint-Simon on horseback, 50, 137
sexually promiscuous, 123
somewhat second-rate, 148
special constable in London, 50, 191
Swiss vulture to imitate eagle, 50
unfavourably judged by *TLS*, 166

Index

219

Napoleonic code, 2, 37–8, 46, 47
  achieves central ambition of
    Revolution, 39
  poor position of women in, 39
  possible effects on birth rate, 95,
    106, 180, 181
Nasser, Gamal Abdel, 45, 129, 205
Nelson, Admiral Horatio, 22, 185
New Zealand, 11, 64
Nobility, French, rôle of under
  ancien régime, 30–1
  fiscal privileges before 1789, 30,
    160 (?), 164
Nordlinger, Eric, 12
Norway, 11

Ollivier, Emile, 14, 60
Orange, William of, 3, 156

Paris, rebuilding of by Haussmann, 5
  contribution of Malraux and
    Pompidou, 141
  political implications of, 6, 166
Parti Communiste Français,
  collaborates with Germans in
    1940, 148, 158
  supports resistance after 22 June
    1941, 169–70, 204
Pascal, Blaise, 156
Paxton, Robert, 14, 168, 169
Perlmutter, Amos, 153
Pétain, Marshal Philippe, 75–99,
    194–8; *see also* 6, 7, 10, 11, 12,
    21, 40, 48:
  acceptable to USA and USSR, 92
  age and education, 79, 194
  death of, 17, 198
  de Gaulle on, 90, 91, 94, 99, 195
  encourages French to fight
    Bolshevism, 197
  legality of power, 13, 115, 118
  marriage, 195
  model constitution, 89, 169
  not antisemitic but, 88–9
  not involved in plots against Third
    Republic, 168
  on air power, 81
  rebel against establishment before
    1914, 80, 184

  sentenced to death, 17, 198
  song about, quoted, 93
  somewhat second-rate, 148
  tells French to stop fighting, 7, 96,
    167, 196
  trial, 75–6, 168, 198
  triumphant reception in Paris in
    April 1944, 93, 198
  very interested in money, 52, 71,
    165
  views on politics, 170
  vision of France, 153
Piaf, Edith, song sung by Foreign
  Legion, 137
Pinay, Antoine, might have been
  preferred by *notables* to de
  Gaulle, 122
Pius VII, Pope, 35, 188
Pius IX, Pope, 54
Pflimlin, Pierre, 135, 136
Plebiscites, use of by French
  Caesars, 2, 4, 5, 12, 53
  listed, 161, 192–3
Poincaré, Raymond, 13, 180
Pol Pot, 15
Pompidou, Georges, 109, 141, 144,
  145, 211
Popular Front, 6, 7, 83
  reforms continued by de Gaulle,
    111
Portes, Hélène de, influence on Paul
  Reynaud, 78
Préfet, foreshadowed by *Intendants*,
  31
  rôle of, 38, 180
Protestantism, possible role in
  fostering democracy, 17, 32–3
  elements of in de Gaulle, 118
Proust, Marcel, 10, 83, 166
Prussia, 2, 13, 14, 33, 64, 68, 73, 193

Québec, de Gaulle visits, 55, 143
Queuille, Henri, outmanœuvres de
  Gaulle in 1951, 121–2, 140

Racine, Jean, 136
Ramolino, Laetizia, mother of
  Napoleon I, quoted, 41

220 French Caesarism

Rassemblement du Peuple Français, 107, 113, 121–2, 126
Ratapoil (slang: *aura-ta-poil*, have your skin=guts for garters), 51
Reichstadt, duc de, *see* Napoleon II
Referenda, 9, 12:
de Gaulle leaves after defeat in 1969, 208
de Gaulle's use of, 131, 134, 138, 140, 144, 206
listed, 161
Rémond, René, 41, 139
Renan, Ernest, 9
Republic, First (1792–1804; or 1808), 3–4, 48–9
Republic, Second (1848–1852), 3, 48–9, 131–2, 139, 191–2
Republic, Third (1870–1940):
achievements, 6, 65–7
colonial policy, 127
constitutional defects, 48, 96–7
criticised by de Gaulle, 101–3
falls, 60, 106, 155
Republic, Fourth (1946–1958):
successes after 1946, 10, 40, 60, 106
defects of political system, 106, 122, 129–30
more voters against than for, 112, 113
rebuilds France after 1946, 10, 40, 60, 106
Republic, Fifth (1958—):
born of Caesarian, 12, 40
electoral system, 106–7
state planning, 50
Révolte nobiliaire, 30–1
existence doubted, 211
Revolution, French:
main events in, 174–180; *also* 19–21, 26–35, 45, 146–7
middle-class or not? and other debates, 160, 164, 211
Revel, Jean-François, doubts on democratic nature of France, 15
remarks about de Gaulle, 115, 162
Reynaud, Paul, 6, 76, 77, 96, 117, 124, 143, 154, 201, 202

Richelieu, Cardinal Armand Duplessis de, 13
better at foreign policy than any French Caesar, 63
Ritchie-Hook, Brigadier Ben, similarity to Napoleon I and de Gaulle, 168
Riom, trial, 82, 87, 197
Robespierre, Auguste, 20
Robespierre, Maximilien, 15, 20, 25, 40, 146, 176, 178
Rocard, Michel, 212
Rochebouet, General, 67
Roosevelt, Franklin D., 13, 92:
hostility to de Gaulle, 19
views on France, 203
Rothschild, bank of, 59
Rouher, Eugène, 55
Rousseau, Jean-Jacques, 67, 118
Rubicon, 12, 22, 51, 114, 117, 118, 192
Russia, 148, 188

Sacré Cœur, vœu au, 84–5
Sadowa, battle of, 61, 103
Saint-Just, Antoine de, 20, 179
Sainte-Beuve, Charles, 50
Sakhiet, 119
Salan, Raoul, 9, 130, 135, 138, 150, 206
Salazar, Antonio de, 99, 154; *see also* Afterthoughts
Sartre, Jean-Paul, 84, 87, 130
comparison with de Gaulle, 158–9
Section Française de l'Internationale Ouvrière, 157, 204
Sedan, battle of, 5, 62, 65
Separation of Church and State, 6, 71, 83, 199
Sétif, massacre at, 128, 204
Shakespeare, 14, 17, 113
Sieyès, Emmanuel Joseph, 2, 24, 25, 31, 180
Soboul, Albert, 160
Solferino, battle of, 55, 61
appropriately angled street, 210
creation of Red Cross, 192
Sophocles, 113
Soustelle, Jacques, 131

Index 221

Spain, 32, 44, 145
Staël, Germaine de, 39
Stalin, 15, 27, 40, 203
Stavisky, Serge, 60, 72
Stendhal, 14, 37
Sweden, 11; *see also* Afterthoughts

Talleyrand, Charles Maurice, 24, 28–9, 30, 36, 151, 175, 186
Tennyson, Alfred Lord, 3
Terror of 1793–4, statistics and political function, 27, 164, 178–9
Thiers, Adolphe, 6, 13, 62:
responsibility for repression of *Commune*, 62, 127, 153
terror at being arrested, 166
Times, The, smack of firm government, 10
correspondence about treatment of Napoleon I after 1815, 164
sees de Gaulle as right-wing in 1940, 108, 121
Tilsit, Treaty of, 44, 73
Times Literary Supplement, 166
Tito, 120
Tocqueville, Alexis de, 9, 10, 150
Tournoux, J.-R., 12, 40, 108, 142, 160
Trafalgar, battle of, 42, 64:
Darlan obsessed with, 125, 186
Tricolour, origins of, 174

Union pour la Démocratie Française, 107
Union pour la Nouvelle République, 107
Universal Declaration of Human Rights, 2

Valéry, Paul, 93
Valmy, battle of, 41, 62, 177; *see also* Afterthoughts
Verdun, battle of, 74, 76, 79, 83, 94, 114, 195, 198
Versailles, 27:
social rôle of, 30–1
Veuillot, Louis, 58, 210
Vichy régime, 13, 14, 17, 73, 77, 99, 137, 162
attitude to Church, 83–4
ideology, 84–5
legality, 13
reality, 98–9
Victoria, Queen, liking for Napoleon III, 151
reaction forecast by Gladstone, 61
Voltaire, 9, 67

Wagram, battle of, 44:
Napoleon I's comment on casualties, 188
Wallon, Henri, 65
Waterloo, 44
Waugh, Evelyn, 168:
quoted, 202
Weal, Ernest, 166–7
Weidlé, Wladimir, 26
Wellington, Duke of, 11, 161
Weygand, General Maxime, 14, 72–3, 77, 82, 86, 117, 154, 196
Wittgenstein, Ludwig, 16
Wordsworth, William, 6

Yalta, treaty of, 6

Zeldin, Theodore, 90
Zola, Emile, 9, 58, 70, 199

Afterthoughts

Just as nightfall, according to Hegel, inspires the owl of Minerva to take flight, so the reading of printer's proofs induces Afterthoughts. This is especially the case if one has been privileged to give lectures on the topic of Caesarism to audiences in the universities of Australia, and to clarify one's views by answering the questions put by students and colleagues.

Page 11, line 3
I am grateful to the anonymous questioner in Canberra who drew my attention to the fact that Australia did on one occasion experience a military take-over. It was on 8 January 1808, when Captain William Bligh was overthrown as Governor of New South Wales by a group of officers headed by Lieutenant George Johnston. The band played *The British Grenadiers* as an accompaniment. The government of the Colony was nevertheless taken over again in 1812 by Lachlan Macquarie – who was a soldier himself, of course; a Lieutenant General – who returned power to civilian hands. Johnston was court-martialled and dismissed the service.

I am also grateful to the American questioner who drew my attention to the 1978 book by William Manchester entitled *Douglas MacArthur. American Caesar*. The point that his question enabled me to emphasise was that MacArthur failed in his bid for power, and was dismissed from office by President Truman. It is an incident which supports the contention that ultimate power in the United States has always been in the hands of civilians. Washington was indeed a general. But when, like Eisenhower, he was twice elected to the Presidency, it was as a civilian politician.

Page 11, line 22
I do not think of Hitler as a Caesar. He did not come to power as a result of the prestige he had previously obtained by his own or somebody else's military achievements. He also played a major personal part in overthrowing the state. He did not merely profit from its collapse. Like the two Napoleons, he did lose power because of a military defeat (*et comment!*); but unlike Napoleon I and Charles de Gaulle, he left no positive achievement behind him.

Franco falls more easily into my definition of Caesarism; except for

224 *French Caesarism*

the fact that he overthrew the Spanish Republic by force of arms. Like Hitler, he did not merely take advantage of a collapse which had already taken place. But like Napoleon III and Pétain, he remains an essentially controversial figure, in the sense that few historians can agree on whether there is more to be said for his contribution to his country's history than against it.

He did perform the immense service of keeping Spain out of the Second World War. When Hitler went to see him at Hendaye, in October 1940, to request permission for German troops to pass through Spain in order to attack Gibraltar, Franco insisted on so many preconditions and so many unilateral advantages for Spain that Hitler is said to have remarked afterwards that he would, next time he wanted a difficult interview, visit his dentist. A Spain under a left-wing Republican government would not have been able to show the same obstinacy. One in which a Communist government was in power might, in the high noon of the Nazi–Soviet pact, have agreed to any request which Stalin might have made on Hitler's behalf to allow German soldiers to pass through.

But there can be no agreement on such hypothetical issues, just as there can be no agreement as to whether France would have industrialised successfully if Napoleon III had not established the Second Empire. Similarly, there can be no agreement as to whether Pétain did more harm than good in 1940. Although Franco showed an even greater tenacity than de Gaulle in clinging on to power when he was no longer needed, he did leave behind him, in 1975, a Spain which made as easy a transition to classic parliamentary democracy as France did after 1870 or even after 1944. In Spain, Greece and Portugal – as in France – it proved relatively easy to replace a dictatorial or authoritarian régime based on one man, or on a group of men, by a workable democratic system. It certainly proved easier than in countries dominated by an impersonal ideology and ruled over by a single party.

It has never been difficult to 'de-Napoleonise', to 'de-Pétainise' or even to 'de-de Gaullise' France; any more than it was hard to 'de-Francoise' Spain or to 'de-Salazarise' Portugal. To de-Stalinise Russia, on the other hand, has proved so difficult that the very term has now been abandoned.

France, on the whole, has benefited from its four Caesars who took power. There is no doubt about this in the case of Napoleon I and de Gaulle. It is even arguable for Napoleon III and Pétain. This is the principal thesis of this book; a thesis whose existence I clearly recognised only after lecturing on the topic – and reading the proofs.

Afterthoughts

Page 27, line 9

Some of the experiments on animals which were held to test the reliability of the guillotine took place on the first storey of a house at the top of the *rue de l'ancienne comédie*, just opposite the statue of Danton, one of the most famous revolutionary leaders, which stands in front of the Odéon cinema. Danton was sent to the guillotine by Robespierre, on twin charges of corruption and moderation. The first was certainly justified, the latter less so. Danton would undoubtedly have given Bonaparte a run for his money, as would Robespierre. But both had fallen victim to the ingenious invention of Dr Louis.

Dr Guillotin, who had presented the case for the guillotine to the National Assembly, insisted that he did not want the machine to be named after him. He died, in his bed, in 1814, at the age of 76. Repulsive though the idea – and the reality – of the guillotine undoubtedly is, there is a case for seeing it as a humanitarian measure. When, in 1757, the servant Robert Damiens tried to stab Louis XVI with a penknife in order to remind him of his duties, he was sentenced to have his right hand burned off, boiling pitch poured into his wounds and to be torn apart by horses. He commented, to the horrified admiration of Diderot: 'La journée sera rude' ('It's going to be a hard day'). On the morning when the sentence was carried out, all the windows with anything like a reasonable view had been hired several months in advance by spectators, many of them from the aristocracy. Madame Lafarge had some illustrious predecessors.

Had Damiens been a nobleman, he would have enjoyed the privilege of decapitation, extended by the Revolution to all sorts and conditions of men (and women).

Pages 41–2

Historians more favourably disposed than I am to Napoleon's foreign policy argue that the wars which led to his downfall were forced upon him by a combination of historical and geographical circumstances which neither he nor anyone else could ever have overcome. The germ of Waterloo, they maintain, was already there in the victory of the revolutionary armies at Valmy on 20 September 1792. This victory made it possible for the Revolution to fulfil the age-old ambition of the monarchy to establish the 'natural frontiers' of France by extending them up to the left bank of the Rhine and encompassing what is now Belgium. But to do this, France had to treat the Low Countries as a satellite state. This, in turn, led to conflict with the English, who would never have allowed a power as traditionally hostile to British interests as France to dominate the

226 *French Caesarism*

Channel ports. Since the mid-nineteenth century, British foreign policy had always involved paying continental allies to do its land fighting for it. England was thus led, inevitably, to ally itself with Austria. France itself could not, therefore, avoid war with Austria; and thus with the rest of what is now Germany.

At the same time, France could defeat England itself only by ruining its overseas trade. An invasion had never really been a practical possibility. It became even less so after the overwhelming victory of the English at the battle of Trafalgar in 1805. But the attempt to use the 'Continental System' to ruin England financially by forbidding the entry of British goods into the Continent meant that France not only had to dominate the ports of the Low Countries, Germany and the Baltic; it also had to prevent British imports from entering Spain, Portugal and Russia. The Spanish adventure of 1808, like the invasion of Russia in 1812, were thus necessary and inevitable consequences of the Continental System; and it was Napoleon's failure to conquer Spain and Russia, each of which offered a type of warfare to which his armies were not accustomed, which led to his downfall. Had he, by some miracle, been able to decline the inheritance of the Revolution, and proclaim that France was no longer interested in permanently securing her 'natural frontiers', all would have been well. France would have been able to go back to the size she was in 1789. Napoleon would have been able to avoid the incessant warfare which bled France white and alienated the rest of Europe. He would thus have ended his days as the peaceful and successful ruler of an efficient and prosperous France. But a voluntary limitation of legitimate national territorial ambitions which had existed for centuries was impossible. This was especially so for a régime whose new and vulnerable nature could not allow it to pursue anything but a successful foreign policy, and which was also faced by an implacable enemy across the Channel.

This way of looking at Napoleon's conquests and eventual defeat has a certain appeal. It brings together two people not frequently found in each other's company: Admiral Darlan and the Greek historian Thucydides. It takes from the former the vision of an England inspired by an unremitting hostility to legitimate French national interest. It shares with the latter a concept of history in which the external behaviour of nation states is decided by geographical, political and psychological forces over which they ultimately have no control. Running through the analysis of Athenian imperialism set out in *The Peloponnesian War* is the view that the Athenians

Afterthoughts

cannot choose but rule. Once an empire reaches a particular size, any failure to grow leads to inevitable decline and eventual collapse. Under the capitalist system, a company which does not increase its size and profit margins every year is ripe either for bankruptcy or a take-over bid. So, in international affairs, no powerful country can stand still. Any group of people resting on their laurels will rapidly find these crowns of glory withering into wreaths of mourning.

Neither Admiral Darlan nor Thucydides can be totally refuted. Until the creation of the European Community, British foreign policy did always aim at cutting down the tall European poppy. It generally succeeded. Spain, France and Germany were all seen as potential enemies from the moment that each of them threatened to dominate the continent of Europe. The Athenian empire collapsed because the Athenians could not bring themselves to accept the possibility of a compromise peace which was available after the victory of Pylos. Had they shown more moderation, they might have spared themselves the spectacle of the Spartan soldiers parading triumphantly round the walls of Athens to the sound of flutes. Philip II of Spain, Louis XIV, Napoleon, Wilhelm II and Hitler all failed to moderate their ambition to dominate Europe. And each was defeated by a continental alliance inspired and financed by England.

But while it would indeed have been difficult for Napoleon to tell the French, after he had seized power in 1799 and especially after he had become Emperor in 1804, that they really must learn to curb their desires, cut their losses, and go back to where the monarchy had left them, there is little evidence that he ever thought of doing so.

Page 93, line 11
I was mistaken. André Lassery only sang the song, 'Maréchal nous voilà!'. It was composed by Charles Courtioux and André Montagard. Like Maurice Chevalier, who also offered support to the reconstruction programme undertaken by the Vichy régime by a vigorous interpretation of 'La Chanson du Maçon' in 1941, André Lassery resumed his career as a singer of other kinds of song after France had been liberated.

Pages 126–39
In my admiration for de Gaulle, I have given what his less enthusiastic supporters would see as far too favourable an impression of his Algerian policy. I have, in other words, suggested that he went straight for what now seems to have been the only possible solution –

228 *French Caesarism*

complete independence for the whole country – and took four years to achieve this conscious and well-considered ambition only because of the opposition he encountered from the army, the European settlers and right-wing elements in metropolitan France.

This desire to present de Gaulle in as favourable a light as possible stems partly from a feeling of guilt at having been wrong in 1958. Like many other young people at the time – and some older ones – I was strongly opposed to de Gaulle's return to power. I even went to the extent of trying to join in the street protests which accompanied his presentation to the people of Paris, on 4 September 1958, of the Constitution of the Fifth Republic. The fact that the French police dispersed the demonstrators with even more brutality than usual confirmed my view that France was heading for a Franco-type régime in which de Gaulle would become a military-style dictator whose policy was aimed simultaneously at keeping Algeria French and at making France itself a less democratic country. The two aims were, at the time, seen as inseparable; just as it was widely assumed on the left that the triumph of the FLN would lead to a more democratic régime in France as well as in Algeria itself.

This was by no means an unusual view at the time. A few days later, I attended a protest meeting in the Latin Quarter addressed by Claude Bourdet and Jean-Paul Sartre. Bourdet expressed strong hostility to every aspect of de Gaulle's personality and supposed policies. Sartre spoke vigorously against the use of torture by the French army in Algeria. 'Je ne crois pas que de Gaulle approuve personnellement la torture', he said, 'Il doit trouver ça vulgaire.'

But although, as events showed, de Gaulle's opponents on the left totally misread his intentions, this does not mean that he set out from the very beginning to do what Bourdet and Sartre wanted, to give Algeria total independence. The summer and early autumn of 1960 were taken up by official and unofficial negotiations on two points about which de Gaulle, like the French themselves, felt very strongly: the future of the European population in Algeria; and the right to develop the oil resources of the Sahara. Consistent efforts were made to provide a special status for the Europeans. At one time, it was argued that they should be given dual nationality. At others, it was suggested that the country should be partitioned, with the Europeans being given a separate state in the coastal areas and in the larger towns. The French also wanted to retain the right to market the oil from the Sahara, and to have privileged access to it. Had de Gaulle accepted, from the moment he returned to power in 1958, that

Afterthoughts

Algeria would become independent, he might well have ended the war by 1960. He did not, it is argued, need to wait for an opportune moment to win the struggle against the army and the settlers. Popular support for a settlement in Algeria at almost any price was powerful enough from the late 1950s onwards for him to have acted much more quickly than he did.

This is the case against him on the left. It is certainly a useful correction to the hagiographic tone which comes out in my account of his achievement. On the right, he is accused of giving up when the war was virtually won. He is also blamed for shamefully neglecting the rights of the European settlers and for making no attempt to protect the lives of the *harkis*, the soldiers and policemen of non-European origin who had taken the side of the French in the Algerian war. These men, together with their wives and children, were treated with great cruelty and brutality by the FLN after 1962, and there is no gainsaying the fact that the ending of the Algerian war was a messy business. The question that de Gaulle's critics nevertheless have to answer is not only whether anybody else could have done any better, but whether anyone else could have done it at all.

This same view of politics as the art of imposing the lesser of two evils also recurs in the defence which I now find myself prepared to advance, at the age of 60, for the behaviour of the French police who so terrified me when I was 30. A country like France, in which there have until very recently always been enough extremists of the right as well as of the left to make it seem quite possible to bring down the government by force, has always had great difficulty in developing the more civilised approach to street demonstrations which used to characterise English society. The lack of ambiguity in the police response to the street riots of February 1934, of September 1958 and of May 1968, may in the long as well as in the short run have saved lives. Nobody was killed by the police in 1958, and there is definite proof of only one death in 1968. It may well be that even the French police will modify their behaviour when the consensus established by de Gaulle leads to a situation in which genuinely peaceful demonstrations are the norm. If they did so, it would be an interesting example of civil de-escalation. At the same time, it would support the view that all violence is, of necessity, a form of counter-violence.

Pages 142-3

De Gaulle's critics on the left also argue that his insistence on the possession of a genuinely independent nuclear deterrent was as

230 *French Caesarism*

empty a gesture as his offer (see page 55) to replace American help to South America by aid from France. As Philip Cerny points out in his *The Politics of Grandeur* (Cambridge University Press, 1980), the French Mirage IV bombers were in the 1960s dependent upon American-supplied KC-135 jet tankers for refuelling in mid-flight. Otherwise, they would not have been able to reach their targets in the Soviet Union. Dr Cerny nevertheless does also quote Henry Kissinger's 'trip wire' theory to the effect that any use of its atomic weapons by France would compel the United States to come to the help of a Western ally rather than see it obliterated. Had an American president been tempted to abandon West Berlin to the Russians, de Gaulle would have still been in a strong position to make him change his mind.

Where de Gaulle's foreign policy is open to criticism is in the defect identified by Raymond Aron when he said that de Gaulle had 'appris aux Français à se tromper d'ennemi' – taught them to identify the wrong country as enemy. At a time when the Soviet Union was pursuing a highly aggressive foreign policy, de Gaulle encouraged the French in their view that the real enemy was the United States.

It could also be argued that although de Gaulle was critical in the 1960s of American policy in Vietnam, he was in power when the Indochinese war began in 1945 and did nothing between 1946 and 1954 to encourage the French to give up the attempt to retain their empire in Indochina. This is fair comment. Had de Gaulle been in power throughout the Indochinese war, he might well have made as much of a mess of things as the civilian politicians of the Fourth Republic. On the other hand, he would certainly have agreed with Mendès France's view that France had to choose between two clear, defined policies: abandoning Indochina completely, or making an all-out effort to win the war by sending conscripts and no longer relying on a relatively small, professional army.

Page 188, line 35
The case for seeing Bernadotte as a Caesar is not a strong one. Admittedly, he succeeded to the Swedish throne in 1818 because of the prestige he had won in rising in Napoleon's army from non-commissioned officer to Marshal. The initiative to make him King came from a Swedish army officer, Lieutenant Mörner, after a military coup had deposed Gustavus IV. But Bernadotte had been unanimously elected Crown Prince at a regularly convened meeting of the Riksdag in August 1810. There was no military threat, no major crisis and no illegality.

I realise that my insistence on the specific qualities which constitute and define French Caesarism may seem like the enthusiasm of a botanist at having identified a new specimen. I do not claim to have been the first to spot the phenomenon. I do think that I am the first to have isolated and described its defining characteristics.

French Department,
The University of Western Australia   *July–September 1988*

Printed in Great Britain
by Amazon